Games programming

ERIC SOLOMON

GAMES PROGRAMMING

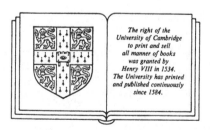

The right of the
University of Cambridge
to print and sell
all manner of books
was granted by
Henry VIII in 1534.
The University has printed
and published continuously
since 1584.

CAMBRIDGE UNIVERSITY PRESS
Cambridge
London New York New Rochelle
Melbourne Sydney

CAMBRIDGE UNIVERSITY PRESS
Cambridge, New York, Melbourne, Madrid, Cape Town, Singapore, São Paulo

Cambridge University Press
The Edinburgh Building, Cambridge CB2 2RU, UK

Published in the United States of America by Cambridge University Press, New York

www.cambridge.org
Information on this title: www.cambridge.org/9780521271103

© Cambridge University Press 1984

First published 1984

A catalogue record for this publication is available from the British Library

Library of Congress Catalogue Card Number: 83-26292

ISBN-13 978-0-521-27110-3 paperback
ISBN-10 0-521-27110-X paperback

Transferred to digital printing 2005

Contents

page

1 Introduction 1
    The value of play 1
    A short history of computer gaming 2
    Published software 4
    This book 5
    What you need to know 7

2 Computer participation in games 9
2.1 Introduction 9
    What is a game? 9
2.2 Game classification 10
    Game theory 11
    Knowledge diagrams 12
2.3 The computer as opponent 15
2.4 The computer as second 18
2.5 The computer as moderator 19
    Adventure games 19
    War games 21
    Management games 23
    Kriegspiel 23
    Black Box 24
    Automata and Life 25
2.6 The computer as lawgiver 26
    Eleusis 27
    Self-modifying games 28
2.7 The computer as research tool 30
    Ranking tournament players 30
    A coaching aid 32

3 Program design and implementation 33
3.1 Introduction 33
3.2 Preliminary program design 35
    TOP-DOWN DESIGN 36

	OTHER DESIGN PROCEDURES	39
	FLOWCHARTS	41
	System flowcharts	41
	Program flowcharts	44
	SUMMARY	47
3.3	Detailed design	48
	Names and identifiers	48
	Subprograms	50
	Types of variable	51
	Arrays	52
	How modules exchange data	53
	Stepwise refinement	55
3.4	Language coding	56
	Which language?	57
	BASIC	58
	PASCAL	59
	FORTRAN	60
	ASSEMBLY LANGUAGES	61
	Efficient coding	63
3.5	Language processing	66
	Interpretation	66
	Compilation and link-editing	67
	P-code processing	71
3.6	Program testing	71
	Debuggers	72
4	**Programming techniques for games**	74
4.1	Introduction	74
	Notation	75
	Game independence	75
4.2	Reading items of data	76
	CHARACTERS	77
	Character input–output	77
	DATA ITEMS	80
	The item input subprogram READIT	82
	Symbol-state tables	83
	READIT PHASE 1	84
	READIT PHASE 2	87
4.3	Reading game commands	90
	SYNTAX DIAGRAMS	90
	INTERNAL REPRESENTATION OF SYNTAX	96
	Use of the command control list	98
4.4	Structured data – a general view	101
	Graphs and digraphs	102
	Representing graphs in computer memory	103
4.5	Storage and retrieval of text	107
	Method 1 – linear storage and search	108
	Method 2 – hashing	109

Contents vii

	Method 3 – partitioned linear storage and search	114
4.6	Flags and bit-masks	116
	Testing a bit	117
	Setting or unsetting a bit	117

5	**Mathematical techniques for games**	118
5.1	Introduction	118
5.2	Elements of probability	118
	Mutually exclusive events	119
	Complementary events	119
	Independent events	120
5.3	Random numbers and their use	120
	PSEUDO-RANDOM NUMBERS	121
	Range and type conversions	121
	DISTRIBUTION OF A RANDOM VARIABLE	123
	Mean and variance	124
	Standard deviation	126
	The normal distribution	126
	Sampling from a random normal distribution	127
5.4	Random walks on a square grid	129
	Biassed random walks	131
5.5	Distance approximations	131
	Error	133
	Toleration of error	134
	Extension to three dimensions	134
5.6	Simulation of motion	135
	COORDINATES	136
	MOVEMENT	138
	Directions and destinations	139
	Unit time stepping	142
	Unit distance stepping	143
	GRID MOVEMENT ALGORITHM	146
	Avoiding obstacles	147
	Shortest-route algorithms	148
5.7	Sorting small lists	149
	Three elementary methods	150
	Tournament sort (FORTRAN code)	152
5.8	Functions and interpolation	154
	Linear interpolation	156
	Quadratic interpolation	156
	Polynomial interpolation	157

6	**Simulation games**	158
6.1	Introduction	158
	The role of the computer	159
	Continuous and discrete simulation	160
	Simulation languages	161
6.2	Time control	162

viii   *Contents*

	TIME ADVANCE METHODS	162
	Typical time variables	164
	Residual time	169
6.3	War games	171
	SIMULATION ACTIVITIES	171
	OBJECTIVES	172
	UNITS AND UNIT TYPES	172
	Attenuation of parameters	174
	FATIGUE	175
	OBSERVATION	176
	Acuity and visibility	177
	The observation probability function	177
	Observation over extended periods	179
	Attenuation of observations	179
	Implementation notes	180
	LINE OF SIGHT CALCULATIONS	180
	MODELLING COMBAT	182
	Determining combat efficiency coefficients	184
	Small units	185
6.4	Management games	186
	SIMULATION ACTIVITIES	187
	Decisions phase	187
	Query phase	188
	Open reports phase	188
	Trends computation phase	188
	Processing phase	188
	A GENERAL VIEW	188
	TIME SERIES	189
	Generation of time series	192
	CONCLUSION	193
6.5	Sports simulations – a warning	193
7	**Terrain models**	195
7.1	Introduction	195
	Use of a DTM	196
7.2	Structure of a DTM	197
	DTM DEFINITION DATA	200
	BLOCK FORMAT	200
	Block paging	201
7.3	DTM input and editing	202
7.4	Generating a DTM	203
	BASIC OPERATIONS	204
	Spotting	204
	Random walking	205
	GENERATING GROUND LEVELS	205
	Smoothing	206
	Levels equalisation	206
	GENERATING TERRAIN COVER	207
	CONCLUSION	209

Contents

7.5	A DTM for microcomputer games	210
	Levels	210
	Terrain cover	211
	Block elements	212
	DTM definition data	212
7.6	DTM output	213
	Partitioned maps	217
	Use of maps	218
7.7	Interpolation for ground levels	218
	Three points known	221
	Two points known	221
	One point known	222
8	**Abstract games**	223
8.1	Introduction	223
	Algorithms and heuristics	224
8.2	Merit values and game trees	224
	MERIT FUNCTIONS AND VALUES	224
	A simple heuristic method	225
	GAME TREES	226
	An example – the game of Kono	226
	Storage of tree data	229
	Tree search and backtrack	229
	Conclusion	231
8.3	The α–β algorithm	231
	MINIMAX SEARCH	231
	Search economisation	233
	α–β PRUNING	234
	Cutoff implementation	235
	Improving performance	236
8.4	Programming the α–β algorithm	237
	GAME-DEPENDENT SUBPROGRAMS	237
	VARIABLES	238
	ALPHAB FLOWCHART	239
8.5	A simple merit function	239
	THE GAME OF BILLABONG	241
	Merit function for Billabong	243
8.6	Learning programs	243
	Univariate search	244
	The Spendley simplex search method	245
8.7	Games of imperfect information	247
	Probabilistic merit functions	248
	Bayes' theorem	249
9	**The future**	250
	References	253
	Index	255

Solomon *Games Programming*
ISBN 0 521 27110 X
Erratum (1984 printing)

p.22, line 6, *should read as*:

games through the use of concealed off-board pieces though often at enorm-

Preface

Countless articles in countless computer magazines have presented game listings, and proffered advice on how to implement programs for specific games. With few exceptions, and quite understandably, these are small scale and fairly trivial exercises in BASIC programming. The time is ripe for owners of home computers to raise their sights.

This is a book for those who enjoy programming and playing computer games, but who yearn to do more than shoot down VDU 'sprites' and flee through mazes pursued by alien blobs or whatever. The accent is on games with some intellectual content rather than games which exhaust memory with program and data for displaying pretty pictures – though it is readily admitted that good graphics enhance any game.

Assuming a rudimentary knowledge of BASIC, the reader is introduced to the fundamental concepts of the more powerful languages now available for microcomputers, and which are essential for the full utilisation of the machine. Though the main objective is the production of recreational games, it is hoped that the book will serve to equip the reader with a clear understanding of the processes involved in writing programs in other areas of application.

The author is indebted to Neil Peppé and Gerald Newman who, like him, have fallen prey to the computer 'conspiracy', for their suggestions and encouragement. In particular, he is grateful to Barry Moulds who read the entire manuscript.

] Introduction

The presenter of a BBC series on microcomputers, referring to 'silly games', stated that it seemed 'somehow degrading to use computers for playing games'. Those who recognise in games the most powerful of all educational aids would strongly disagree. They might view the use of computers as mere labour-saving devices as equally degrading. A less shortsighted view is that neither labour-saving applications nor the use of computers in recreation are to be scorned. We should exploit the machines in every way which improves the quality of life, and not least in those creative directions which are so vital for the balanced development of the young.

Just as entertainment has dominated broadcasting since its earliest days, so games playing has emerged as the predominant mode of use for the home computer. For every program which carries out the household book-keeping there are ten for playing games. The young games programmer of today is the computer technologist of tomorrow. This book aims to help him on his way by showing him how to write good programs for good games and, hopefully, how to have a good time doing it.

The value of play

It was Marshall McLuhan who first remarked on the analogy between manual tools, which act as an extension of the hands, and electromagnetic communications, which extend the human nervous system. Just as play is essential for the development of manual skills so it can serve to familiarise us with the new tools of the electronic era. In particular, 'computer play' is of value in training for tasks where practical experience at the novice level is impossible, or impossibly expensive.

Aeronautical and space-flight simulators provide the most obvious examples of such play systems within which the operator may err without any concomitant catastrophe. These, and systems which simulate decision processes in other areas, enable the player to exercise his judgment in new ways and in unfamiliar roles.

Extending the idea further some simulators represent environments so bizarre and hostile that no one ever has been nor, one hopes, ever will be required to cope with them in real life. The Adventure games introduced in Chapter 2 fall into this category. They are, perhaps, pure play and none the less estimable for it.

Games, as idealised decision processes, are an important element in the study of artificial intelligence and pattern recognition – subjects which may hold the key to our electronic future. Here the more abstract games, notably Chess, occupy centre stage. One of the more startling developments has been the ability of certain computer Chess programs to play the game to a high standard. The most powerful of these run on large machines with special hardware. However, there are several microcomputer programs available on the software market which are capable of taxing the good club player. Such programs achieve their success by the remorseless application of those abilities characteristic of the computer – namely speed and accuracy of data recall. The incorporation of human-like pattern handling capabilities is an area of lively interest and advances will influence progress in almost every field of inquiry from Robotics to Medicine.

A short history of computer gaming

Whilst entertainment took over radio almost from its inception, recreational computing has been somewhat tardy. Those who entered computing in the late 1950s, when commercial machines first became available in universities and large companies, are aware of a sort of cycle – of history repeating itself so to speak. In those early days the programmer, the program coder, and the operator were usually one and the same person. As the valves glowed, and the relays clicked, he sat at the console prestidigitising on banks of handswitches. The machine was his to control. Manual interruption of a program for the purposes of testing and guidance was common-place.

Although machines of this period were slow, and consequently very fully occupied with 'serious' matters, their immediacy made it possible for the adventurous to program the odd game. These were necessarily rudimentary. Reaction testing games and musical composition on the hooter could be programmed quickly, and run without undue interference from the department head.

But as computing became big business the operator was born, and with him the batch-processing procedure. The programmer found his access to the machine barred by a high counter, air-conditioning doors, and personnel in white coats. He became a mere customer, delivering his program as he might deliver his linen to the laundry! These were the 'dark ages' for computer gaming, though some inventors used the machines for generating probability tables and other aids for board games.

In the mid 1960s interactive computing returned with the introduction of timesharing services. Terminals were hired out to clients who communicated with a central mainframe computer. If anyone had the notion that they might try some games programming it was soon dispelled by the arrival of the first invoice from the computer centre or, for that matter, by the telephone bill. The machines were very slow, with execution rates of around ten BASIC-like statements a second being regarded as quite normal. This approach to computation did not realise the hopes of its backers and batch-processing continued to dominate for a further decade.

With the introduction of the 16-bit minicomputer, then of the 8-bit microcomputer, interactive computing made a vigorous comeback. But it was not until the Commodore Pet was launched as a personal computer for the domestic market that the user could indulge in some recreational computing without the need to look over his shoulder.

It has always been the case that software development lags behind that of hardware and when home computers became available there were, initially, few marketed programs of real interest. Even the essential operating systems and language processors left much to be desired. These have now, to a large extent, caught up. Unfortunately, this cannot be said of applications software, nor of recreational software in particular. To those who read the advertisements in the many computer magazines the vacuum may appear to have been filled – but with what?

The opportunists, seeing a market, asked themselves: 'How can we most rapidly provide what home computer owners think they need?' The answer was to commission programs for existing board and card games including, in some instances, modern proprietary games for which, in most cases, no permission was sought of those who held the copyright. Speed was of the essence and everything else, including quality, went by the board. Many games were produced and marketed by people who had not previously given a moment's thought to the balance and ergonomics of any game, let alone to what makes a game interesting and exciting. The attractive graphics facilities of many of the machines burgeoned a rich crop of 'arcade' games nearly all of which could be summarised as 'shoot down moving object'! Progress in this field seemed mainly to consist of renaming the various elements of the game with ever more terrifying titles.

But worse was to come. Some individuals and organisations who had taken the trouble to design, program, test, and distribute worthwhile games software, soon found that they were competing with look-alikes. The pirates had arrived.

There are two types of pirate. First, there is the person with a home computer who, having purchased software, allows others to take copies of the cassette or disc. Although this form of piracy is to be expected – friends can be very persuasive – it does constitute a deterrent to anyone wishing to market software. Some companies have estimated that they lose around 30% of their potential market from this altruistic activity. The second form of piracy is more overtly criminal. Some companies, with the aid of disassemblers, special copying facilities, and considerable industry, are capable of analysing marketed software to the point where they can produce a look-alike product which is, at the same time, sufficiently different from the original to make litigation expensive and its outcome uncertain.

It is not the purpose of this book to discuss piracy, nor how to combat it, at any length. However, the subject deserves mention because it is one cause of the dearth of good recreational software. Efforts are being made to tighten the law in respect of software copyright but, for the present, programmers who wish to market their work will have to live with the problem.

Published software
Apart from games software marketed on tape cassettes or discs there are other sources. Many magazines for the home computer user publish listings of games as a regular feature. Some of these games are good, and a few are exceptional, but limitations of space and proof-reading time dictate that they are small and very prone to contain bugs (errors). Usually the bugs are quickly

reported by readers and corrections are published in due course. (Keep taking the magazine and all will be well!) Nevertheless, because of size limitations, and because they are almost invariably written in BASIC, they are unable to realise the full potential of a computer game.

Another source of programs is the user group library for the particular make of computer concerned. Some of these are quite international in character and frequently contain a large amount of material. Whilst some of the programs may be quite sophisticated these too are prone to be bug-ridden. Vetting effort is always scarce and programs are accepted onto the library with virtually no checking. Indeed the term 'public domain software' is sometimes stated to be a euphemism for 'rubbish'! However such library material is cheap, and searching it can be quite enjoyable. One disadvantage of this source of software is that the programs are generally short of documentation. Contacting the author of a library program, possibly at a range of several thousand miles, can be very frustrating.

In view of these various factors growing numbers of owners are resolving to write their own software. Of course, a significant proportion had every intention of doing this from the start. For many, there is more enjoyment in writing one's own program than in using a program written by someone else. However, for the newcomer to computing, there is more to this than reading, and understanding, the language manual. Some have been misled by reports that programming is easy or that, to paraphrase one widespread advertisement for a program generator: 'No one needs to write programs any more'!

The newcomer frequently overlooks several points. First, most of the work associated with programming a computer has little to do with writing statements in the language to be used for the final coding. A program must be designed before it can be coded. Second, it is a feature of games software that the problems to be solved are more akin to those which occur in scientific programming and operations research than to those which occur in the much more widely reported field of commercial data processing. Hence the task may require a little mathematical knowledge.

This book

The home computer programmer needs guidance, and that is what this book sets out to provide. Primarily, it has been written for the non-specialist majority who have decided to gain programming experience and enjoyment by writing games software for themselves, their families, and friends. Hopefully, it will also assist the professional programmer who has, perhaps, never given the subject of games design any particular attention. Equally, it may extend the horizons of the games inventor who is new to computing.

At a time when new machines for home use are arriving on the market almost monthly, when 64K-byte memories are becoming commonplace, and when the prices of sophisticated peripheral devices such as graphics printers are falling, it would seem unnecessarily restrictive to specify any hardware limitations for the material included here. However, it is recognised that some readers will have bought small machines with no great capacity for expansion. Users of every type of machine will find useful information, and it should be remembered that the principles of programming have evolved to be relevant for all machines which call themselves computers. Because the market is so fluid, references to particular products have been kept to a minimum.

The book is divided, informally, into three parts. The first part, comprising Chapters 2–5 inclusive, deals with those general aspects of computers which are involved in game playing, programming methodology, and some generally useful programming and mathematical techniques. The second part, Chapters 6 and 7, is concerned with the extensive topic of simulation games with particular reference to the modelling of the terrain over which so many are played. The third part, consisting of Chapter 8 only, discusses the implementation of abstract games in which the machine acts as the opponent. An important part of this chapter presents the 'α–β algorithm', by far the most effective method for this purpose.

A short word about terminology and notation would not go amiss at this point.

Words or phrases in italics are technical terms defined in the sentence which includes them, about to be defined, or which are defined at some specified place in the book. Normally such words are italicised once only, on their first occurrence. Single quotes are used for emphasis, and sometimes to enclose a technical term which should be noted but for which an immediate definition is not essential.

It is hardly surprising that the word *programmer* recurs with some persistence. We use the term in its original sense to mean the person who designs, writes, and tests a computer program. Some years ago it became fashionable to split these functions between systems analysts, programmers, coders, software engineers, program validators, or whatever. In the context of home computing such titles are irrelevant.

What you need to know

This introduction would be incomplete without stating what is assumed of the reader. As remarked above, the book is intended to be of assistance to the non-professional programmer who has recently purchased his machine. However, it is not proposed to teach details relating to any particular computer language. In other words, it is assumed that the reader has already digested his language manual, probably for BASIC, and understands the fundamental idea of serial processing. He will be encouraged to regard computer languages as a means to an end, rather than to accept that if he knows BASIC he will be equipped for all eventualities. Unfortunately the presentation of languages to the home computer user is such as to suggest that a change of language is a major step. This is not always the case. The similarities between different languages often outweigh the differences, and the programmer should choose that best suited to his application.

Games programming inevitably calls for some elementary mathematics. One could hardly expect, for example, to simulate motion without recourse to some trigonometry. Similarly, anyone wishing to program a card game would make little progress without some appreciation of the concept of probability.

It is sometimes hard for those in mathematical occupations to understand the difficulties of the non-mathematician. In many cases the main obstacle is an inability to associate symbols with things, especially when the 'things' are operations rather than concrete objects. One educationalist has observed that the problem may have little to do with the formal rules for manipulating the symbols, but arises as soon as the argument states: 'Let X denote . . . .!' In this respect some experience of computer programming can be of great assistance because of the close parallels between named variables and symbolic quantities, between named subprograms and symbolic operations, and familiarity with array calculations can resolve the 'mystery' of the subscripted symbols used throughout mathematics.

We assume a knowledge of mathematics roughly equivalent to that possessed by a student starting his A-level studies. To give one example, we shall not pause to define the sine and cosine functions, but on the rare occasions when less familiar functions, such as sinh (the hyperbolic sine) and cosh (the hyperbolic cosine), occur they will be introduced.

2

Computer participation in games

2.1 Introduction

The objective of this chapter is, briefly, to point out various ways in which the computer may be directly involved in playing a game. We shall refer to many examples of traditional board games, card games, modern boxed games, and so on, but it is emphasised that the computerisation of existing games is not the sole aim of this book. As many readers will appreciate, the machines make it possible to create new games which could not be realised in wood and cardboard nor even, in some cases, within our own spacetime. If it is your ambition to extend these frontiers an understanding of game structure is indispensable. Such awareness is certainly no hindrance if the intention is to program some favourite game hitherto played 'across the table'. With this in view we develop a simple pictorial representation of some of the principal features of any game. These figures, which we call 'knowledge diagrams', will furnish a framework within which to discuss the role of the computer.

What is a game?

It is customary for books about games to attempt a formal definition of what constitutes a game. Such definitions either fail to include every type of game, or they encompass other human activities such as economic competition and warfare. It is a notoriously difficult problem. Educational psychologists in particular, who find considerable use for games, seem to delight in failing to define the term. Those of us who know what a game is can, perhaps, derive some amusement from reading about 'overt competition in ongoing goal-directed decision processes'.

Whilst we avoid the definition trap, it is useful to have some idea about the distinguishing characteristics of different types of game. Some writers, such as Bowen [1], have developed quite complex schemes of classification with an appropriate notation to act as a shorthand when specific games or their characteristics are to be discussed. Bowen's is an algebraic notation applied primarily to games used in operational research for industrial and military purposes whilst our pictorial notation is somewhat less rigorous and is intended to embrace the very wide range of games played for fun.

Other writers have devised methods for classifying games but one sometimes suspects that the matter has been introduced largely to satisfy a thirst for problems. It can be quite challenging to fit an unusual game into a scheme, yet the task may have little to do with any primary objective. In the case of the pictorial scheme used here I hope to persuade you that it is a real aid to understanding, and even a catalyst to invention. It is certainly well suited to identifying roles for the computer. If it is occasionally a puzzle also, please regard that as a bonus!

2.2   Game classification

Anything can be classified either by function, or by form. The function of a game corresponds to the use to which it is put. It may be used in education for teaching skills and imparting information, it may be used in research to investigate a process which, for reasons of cost or accessibility, cannot be observed directly, or it may be used recreationally, for fun. We assume here that what the home computer user wants is fun. It is fun to play computer games, and it is fun to write games programs. Unfortunately, a program is a program whatever its function, and a games program will call for the same clear thinking and attention to detail demanded by any other programming task of equivalent complexity. This may come as a shock to a few who have been beguiled by magazine articles into thinking that they can tackle games programming with the same jolly abandon with which they hope to play the result! Initially, then, we must concentrate on the matter of form. Fun and function will come later.

Beyond the commonsense, but broad, classification of games as *simulations* in which the interest lies in the way the game reflects reality, as *abstract games* in which the interest centres on the game itself, and as *sports* in which physical skill plays a predominant part, there are other important parameters. It is hard to escape noticing, for example, how many players are involved.

A majority of the classical board games are two-person games. Multi-person games are by no means infrequent amongst the card playing fraternity, and most marketed family games require four or more players. It is customary to regard a puzzle as a one-person, or solitaire, game though sometimes it is classified as a two-person game in which one of the players is an absent problem-setter. Alternatively, and depending on its source, a puzzle may be regarded as a 'game against nature'. If this sounds contrived, how about the zero-person game?

In a zero-person game there are no players, only observers. Undoubtedly, the most popular game in this category is Conway's game of Life [2], and we shall refer to it again as an example of an *automaton*. Some would argue that since a zero-person game lacks any element of competition it should not be classified as a game at all. Nevertheless, most writers do acknowledge that puzzles and automata such as Life should be regarded as games because they are used recreationally. From the point of view of the games theorist it would seem unwise to exclude them simply because they involve fewer than two players. After all, what is so special about the number two?

Game theory

Game theory is the branch of applied mathematics founded by John von Neumann and Oscar Morgenstern [3] to describe and predict the behaviour of systems in economics. The elements of such a system compete for various resources and it is not difficult to see the parallel with a game as we understand it. Certain very simple games can be completely analysed by the methods of game theory, but its success in the field of 'real' games has been modest. The principal benefit to come from the subject has been a consistent and widely accepted terminology, and a little of this must inevitably find its way into our discussion.

As an example, the theory develops the notion of information as it applies to a game. A game of *perfect information* is one in which the players know all the rules of the game, the current game position, and how it was arrived at. However, a player does not know what his opponent's next move will be. Obviously, Chess and Go are games of perfect information. while many card games are not. Card games such as Bridge and Poker are games of *imperfect information* because a player does not in general know what cards are held by his opponents. The hands of cards are part of the current game position, or *game state*. What the players 'know' about a game is the key to our pictorial classification.

Knowledge diagrams

Consider the fundamental constituents of any game.

There is the visible part of the game which might show a playing area and the disposition of various material items such as pieces. Associated with this are elements of the game which, though not visible to the players, would be seen by an independent observer. Such elements might be cards held by the players, or hidden pieces. A complete specification of these would uniquely define the *game state* at some moment in time.

It is sometimes useful to distinguish between the static and dynamic aspects of the game state. The static features include such things as the arrangement of squares on a board, the types of pieces involved and, in a war game simulation, the historical period and location of the action. The term *scenario* is applied to the set of static features. The dynamic features are governed by the *rules* which specify how pieces are to move, how cards are to be played, and so on.

The *objective* of the game specifies under what conditions a player has won or lost. In most games the objective is fixed and can properly be regarded as part of the scenario. However, it is common practice to include it with the rules.

At some point in his turn a player makes a *decision* which will affect the state of the game, hopefully in his favour. Until he moves a piece or takes some other action his opponent will be in ignorance of the decision unless, as frequently happens in Chess and Draughts, the decision is *forced*. Normally a player will select his decision from a set of possible decisions – a *decision set*. A forced move implies simply that the decision set has only one member. For the purposes of this classification the decision set is immaterial. We shall assume that a player has already selected his preferred decision and is about to reveal it by executing his move. When we come to discuss games playing algorithms, in Chapter 8, the form of the decision set will become very important, but for the present we deal only in single decisions.

For economy let us employ the following notation:

G_0 – the initial game state.
G – the current game state.
R – the set of rules.
D – a decision about to be revealed.

Occasionally we shall need to refer to decisions which are made at different times, or by different players. To distinguish these in our diagrams we shall employ the symbols:

D_0 – the first decision of the game.
D' – a decision different from decision D.

The ways in which G_0, G, R and D influence each other in any game can be represented as a sort of mathematical snapshot as shown in Figure 2.1. In the diagram the rules R, the initial game state G_0, and the current game state G are enclosed in irregular boundaries to denote that they are sets containing a number of elements. For example, R may comprise 20 rules, and G might represent 30 pieces on a board of 100 points. The arrows denote *influence*. The bolder the arrow the more definite is the influence. Thus the player who makes decision D must follow the rules at all times so the arrow from R to D is bold. Similarly the arrow from D to G is bold because it is only through decisions such as D that the game state can be changed. On the other hand a player is not compelled to take full account of the game state in arriving at his decision. Of course, he will play rather badly if he totally disregards it, though in some situations he can safely ignore some aspects of the position he sees before him. The arrow from G to D is therefore of intermediate boldness. The initial game state G_0 will affect the game to a decreasing extent as play proceeds so the arrow from G_0 to G is slender.

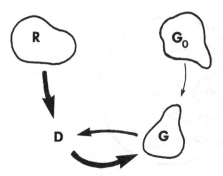

Fig. 2.1. Snapshot of a game.

The human and machine participants must now be introduced into the diagram. These are not invariably contestants as we shall see. Let us represent humans as large circles and computers as large squares. The area inside each shape is used to display the knowledge possessed by the entity concerned. For example, a human referee would be denoted by a circle containing at least the whole of set R. A referee who did not know the rules would be something of a liability. In most games a blind referee would be equally ineffective, so we would expect at least part of G to lie within his circle.

In general certain knowledge will be common property, so to avoid repeating R, G, etc. we overlap the shapes denoting the participants to some extent. We can now transfer R, G_0, G, and D into the appropriate areas to produce the next stage of the knowledge diagram. Figure 2.2 shows two humans playing a two-person game of perfect information, such as Chess. As both players make moves affecting the game both circles are assigned a decision symbol, but one is primed to indicate that it is a different decision from D. In most games the decisions are made sequentially, at different times. We take this as implicit in a knowledge diagram. In certain war games and business simulations the decisions are made simultaneously by all the players in an attempt to model reality more closely. In manual games these are, in any case, announced and put into effect sequentially. As can be imagined, this leads to difficulties associated with unpredicted conflicts in the execution of the decisions. The computer can overcome these difficulties to some extent by breaking down execution into smaller steps than would be tolerable in a manual game. The end result justifies the assumption that decisions are never strictly simultaneous.

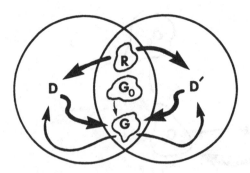

Fig. 2.2. Two-person game of perfect information.

Two small adjustments complete the evolution of the knowledge diagram. First, notice that the influence arrows never vary. (The decreasing influence of G_0 on G as the game proceeds does not affect the argument.) They may therefore be omitted. This enables us to use arrows for a different purpose. Henceforth they will denote the *drift*, or gradual movement, of a set (R or G) from one area into another. Second, and as a result of this change of use for arrows, we may omit G_0 which develops into G as the game progresses. Provided G_0 and G always lie in the same area no arrow will be required.

We are now equipped to investigate the role of the computer in game playing.

2.3 The computer as opponent

The machine opponent is possibly the most familiar role for the game playing computer. In Figure 2.3 the computer (square box) is playing a game of perfect information against a human (circle). The rules R and the game state G are fully known to both adversaries. A decision D affecting the game G is followed by a decision D' made by the machine. Figure 2.3 is in fact equivalent to Figure 2.2 except that one of the human players has been replaced by a computer.

From the programmer's point of view the main problem is how to persuade the computer to make sensible decisions D'. A great deal of valuable work has been done in this field and one particular algorithm (a precisely formulated method) has been specially effective. This, the α–β algorithm, will be described in detail in Chapter 8.

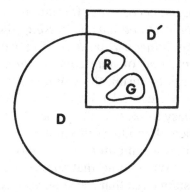

Fig. 2.3. A machine opponent (perfect information).

There are many marketed programs and preprogrammed machines for playing two-person games. The Chess playing machines are undoubtedly the most popular, and many will beat the average club player. How can they achieve this?

Once, the ability to play a strong game of Chess was regarded as a sure sign of a keen intellect. Now, people are not quite so certain. But one thing is certain – they are not going to admit that the machine which they bought this morning, and which beat them at Chess this afternoon, is more intelligent than they are! For the present they are right, but soon – who knows? As has been said many times already – it all depends what you mean by intelligence.

The human Chess-master wins because he is capable of examining the consequences of a given move to a considerable depth. He will have built up a fund of knowledge about the potential of various types of position, and because of this he will be able to reject certain moves as weak without having to devote time to their analysis.

The computer wins because it is particularly accurate in its short term calculations. It can generate and assess all possible positions which could occur over the next three or four moves. (We count a move as a turn taken by a single player here.) The α–β algorithm enables the program to extend this look-ahead by mimicking the human player's ability to reject unpromising moves. It does this not by drawing on past experience of previous games, but by spotting quickly those lines of development which would be refuted by an opponent with its own powers of computation.

The 'great problem' is this. How does the human brain organise its knowledge of past experience so that relevant details can be recalled so rapidly. It certainly does not have to search its files in the same way as we would program a computer for data retrieval. The secret may lie in a combination of *parallel processing* (the use of many computers working simultaneously on different parts of a problem) and a very clever method of *data condensation* (the exploitation of repeated patterns to shrink the volume of stored data). This problem is one of the central issues in the study of artificial intelligence, and it is easy to see why the game of Chess is regarded as such a valuable research model in this field.

Let us now briefly consider how a computer could compete in a game of imperfect information. We assume that the rules R are fully understood by both contestants, but that each knows only part

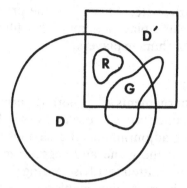

Fig. 2.4. A machine opponent (imperfect information).

of the game state G. Figure 2.4 shows the knowledge diagram for this situation. Card games afford the most familiar examples of this type of game. A player knows what cards he holds but does not, initially, know what cards are held by his opponent. As the game proceeds he may glean some information about the opponent's hand from the way the latter plays cards or bids. Thus the game tends to become one of perfect, or nearly perfect, information – at which point most card games become mechanical. It is the lack of information that makes the game interesting. One could say that the real objective of the game is to shift the set G into one's own area of the knowledge diagram. Until this is achieved a human plays by experience and intuition, and to a lesser extent on the basis of probabilities. The computer must rely entirely on probability calculations which, needless to say, it can perform more accurately than its human adversary. The basic concepts and calculations of probability are central to games programming and these are introduced in Chapter 5.

Before leaving the topic of computer opponents we should mention multi-person games. The theory of games involving mutual competition between three or more players, though voluminous, is not well understood. It is of particular interest to those attempting to produce models of international economics but has little relevance for most games players. The difficulty is that the players will, from time to time, collaborate. The opportunity for collusion is indeed one of the most attractive features of multi-person games but it makes life very difficult for the mathematician. Fortunately for the programmer there seems to be no great appeal in inviting the computer to participate. After all, if the principal interest is to see how the machine plays a game, why dilute its effectiveness by involving further human players?

2.4   The computer as second

Competitors in Chess tournaments are generally permitted to employ seconds principally, one suspects, because it would be impractical to ban them. During adjournments the seconds assist in analysing the current state of the game and suggest lines of development, but they are not permitted to advise during sessions of play. As yet, no computer has been engaged in this role but there seems to be no reason why a suitably modified Chess program should not serve as a useful tool – as a second's second perhaps! Obviously the machine would not recognise that: 'Goldstein reached this position against Silverstein in 1910, and resigned two moves later.' The human second would remain essential for strategic considerations based on experience, but the machine could conduct a particularly thorough analysis of the next few moves, pointing out significant threats without fear of oversight. The knowledge diagram for this cooperative role is shown in Figure 2.5. The diagram is similar to those representing a machine opponent except that there is a single decision arrived at jointly. Any game program capable of acting as an opponent can be modified to act as a second. All that is required is the addition of facilities

(a) For setting up an initial game state which corresponds to the current state of the actual game.

(b) For allowing the machine to play against itself for a predeter-

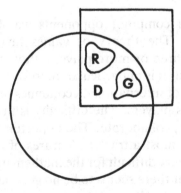

Fig. 2.5. The computer as a second.

mined number of moves, or until some important event, such as a capture, occurs.

(c) For producing reports relating to a specified set of eventualities.

In a less sophisticated role computers have been used to assist players of simulation games. A player might, for instance, wish to find out how far a cross-country vehicle can move in a given time. The nature of the route might make estimation difficult, and the computer operates merely as a calculator. Such a mode is unambitious but is the first step towards the full computer moderation of a game.

2.5 The computer as moderator

A computer moderated game is one in which the machine provides the environment for the game. Information is displayed to the human participants as it is requested, or when it becomes available. Such information relates to the game state, to the rules, or both. Information of the type which constitutes advice, such as that provided by a second, is normally excluded.

Whilst there will undoubtedly be advances in the programming of computers to act as opponents, it is in the field of computer moderation that the most exciting developments will occur. In playing purely manual games one is constrained by the labour of handling large sets of pieces, and one's capacity for assimilating rules is already severely tested by certain marketed simulation games. The greater the realism the greater is the profusion of game elements. Let us look at some examples of the liberation afforded by the computer.

Adventure games

Many owners of home computers will have met with computer moderated games in the form of the so-called Adventure games which are obtainable on the software market under a variety of more or less Gothic titles. The general idea is that the program generates an internal map representing an 'exploration area' inhabited by various hazards such as man-traps, monsters, time-warps, or whatever. The player enters this area, choosing his own route, with some objective in mind. This may be to recover concealed treasure, reach some specified point, or simply to acquire experience and gain some sort of promotion. To help him in his task he may equip himself with weapons, climbing irons, glass beads for the natives, and so on. In some games these goods are bought with limited funds from a catalogue, to introduce an element of investment. In others they are obtained during the journey as purchases, prizes, or plunder. At each stage the program tells the player what he can see from his current position and reports the outcome of any encounters with hazards. In the true Adventure games (those closest to Will Crowther's original program which was inspired by Gygax's purely manual game Dungeons and Dragons) the player must discover for himself what input commands achieve what results – sometimes a very trying business!

In the Adventure games, then, the computer acts as a referee or as an umpire. We distinguish between them in a way which, although not supported by the dictionary, is useful and not without precedent in the language of games and sports. A referee decides questions of law, whilst an umpire decides matters of fact. In a typical Adventure game the program must be able to reject a player's proposed course of action because it is against the rules. It performs the duties of a referee. The point is that the discovery of the rules, through trial and error, is one of the principal attractions of the game. The mark of a well-designed game of this type is that the rules reveal a consistent style, and are not merely arbitrary.

The knowledge diagram for a game of this type employing a computer referee is shown in Figure 2.6. Both R and G are partly unknown to the player, but as the game proceeds his awareness increases as indicated by the drift arrows.

In some games it does not take long for the relevant rules to become evident, and what remains is to attain the main objective.

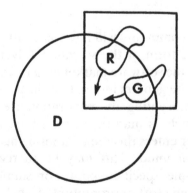

Fig. 2.6. The computer as referee.

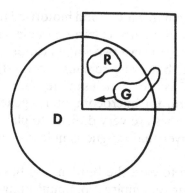

Fig. 2.7. The computer as umpire.

This situation is illustrated by the knowledge diagram of Figure 2.7 in which only facts about the game state are revealed by the machine.

An Adventure game is an example of what a games theorist would call a cooperative game. If there are many players, as is often the case, they function as a team. There may be some rivalry, but that is not the purpose of this type of game. On the other hand there is an important class of competitive games which can benefit greatly from computer moderation.

War games

A large majority of the marketed war games suffer from serious shortcomings. Serious, that is, if the intention is to simulate the logical conditions under which a commander makes his battle-field decisions. In reality he functions in a state (one hesitates to use the term 'game') of very imperfect information, yet most of the packaged products are games of almost perfect information. The player can usually see the entire disposition of the enemy units, and that of his own units also. Neither is a realistic assumption.

A second, and equally unrealistic assumption, is that his orders can be put into immediate effect. Thus, if Napoleon wishes to halt the headlong charge across the board of Marshall Ney's cavalry, he simply issues the order and all is well. In reality Ney would be in no position to receive messages. He would not be able to interpret semaphore signals, nor could a despatch rider catch up with him. His radio, of course, has yet to be invented!

A third simplification is that all units are indefatigable. Foot soldiers march across country all day long with undiminished speed, and cavalry participate in numerous charges without so much as raising a sweat.

The introduction of radio communications and motorised transport means that war games with a modern scenario suffer less from the inaccuracies which result from the last two simplifications. The problem of hidden movement, however, remains acute. There have been attempts to remedy these deficiencies in a few board war games, and in tape cassette form for microcomputers (generally ous cost in complexity. Such games are very difficult to play, and those who try them soon discover that fatigue is indeed a major factor.

Before the computer arrived to ease the burden, the best war games were those employing human umpires communicating with players in separate rooms. Indeed the British Army still employs such methods in officer training because it is felt that an experienced umpire can introduce more relevant contingencies for this purpose than could be programmed for the machine. Some of the more ambitious table-top war gaming societies have also used umpires in this way. Nevertheless, they, and the very considerable body of board war gamers are now looking to the small computer as a means for increasing the accuracy of their simulations and the enjoyment of their hobby. At the very least, a war game moderator can rectify the three main shortcomings described above.

The knowledge diagram for a computer moderated war game is shown in Figure 2.8 in which we have assumed that the rules R are fully known to both human contestants. The game state G, which incorporates unit dispositions, is only partly known to either player but fully known to the machine which, at intervals, tests whether any unit can see any other unit and reports successful observations to the player concerned. This aspect of a war games moderator

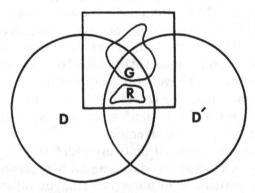

Fig. 2.8. A war games umpire.

involves some fairly tricky logic which will be discussed in some detail in Chapter 6.

Management games
Under this title we group all games having to do with the investment of resources for a return. More particular examples are trading games in which the players buy and sell commodities, business games in which the players invest capital and time in various activities such as the production of goods, research and development, and advertising, and economics games in which, perhaps, taxation levels must be determined. It is a vast field and one of considerable interest to real-life managers and economists. However, management games are also played for fun. For some reason the idea of investment is a sure-fire ingredient where games are concerned.

Management games usually involve a fairly large number of players and the principal role for a computer moderator is to save time in, and guarantee the accuracy of, the computations. In some games the computer serves to conceal the player's decisions until their effects become evident. The knowledge diagram of Figure 2.8 applies equally to management games though there will normally be more than two players.

Kriegspiel
The use of the computer as an umpire, referee, or games-master is by no means confined to simulation games. The game of Kriegspiel is a war game in name only. It is Chess played semi-blind. The two players have their own boards, and are divided by a screen or occupy different rooms. The player taking his turn announces his proposed move to a referee who has his own board showing the fully up-to-date state of the game. The duty of the referee is to pronounce the move legal or illegal. If the move is legal and effects a capture both players are told that a capture has occurred, but the capturing player is not told what kind of piece he has won, and the other player is not told what type of piece his opponent moved. Checks are announced to both players.

There are several variants of Kriegspiel which differ in the amount of information revealed by the referee, and readers who wish to find out more about the game should consult Wetherell, Buckholtz & Booth [4].

The advantage of using a computer as the referee in Kriegspiel is that the machine is not subject to the human errors which can sometimes invalidate the game to the considerable annoyance of the players.

Black Box

The author's game Black Box (Prichard [5]) is suitable for computer moderation for the same reason as Kriegspiel. Indeed it has already appeared in numerous books and articles on computer games, and in tape cassette form for microcomputers (generally without permission). However, there is the difference that the computer not only acts as the umpire but acts as an opponent in the sense that a puzzle-setter is an opponent.

Black Box is played on a square grid of 64 cells. One player secretly positions four (or five) 'atoms' on his private copy of the grid. The other player then attempts to discover where these are hidden by sending notional 'rays' into the grid along any chosen rows or columns. A ray is affected by any atoms it encounters and is either absorbed or emerges along a row or column announced by the player who knows the atomic arrangement. The actual route taken by the ray is not revealed, only its ultimate fate. The rules governing how a ray is absorbed or deflected by an atom are known to both players, so the experimenter's objective is to discover the game state G, and to do this in the most economic way as measured by the number of 'ray markers' he places around his own, initially empty, grid.

The knowledge diagram for a computer implementation of this phase of Black Box is shown on the left of Figure 2.9. The computer

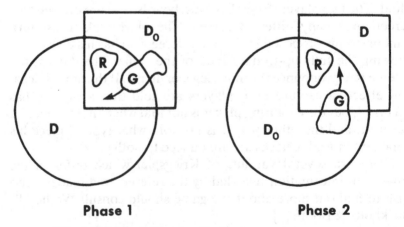

Phase 1   Phase 2

Fig. 2.9. A Black Box moderator.

decision D_0 relates to the initial disposition of the atoms. The human experimenter makes all subsequent decisions D, and the computer's role is that of an umpire.

In the manual version of the game the roles are now reversed so that both players can acquire a score. This phase in the corresponding computer game is shown to the right of Figure 2.9. To the author's knowledge nobody has yet succeeded in writing a program which performs well as the experimenter – a challenge for the reader perhaps!

Automata and Life

If you program your graphics computer to display, for example, a succession of coloured triangles whose vertices are positioned at random within the area of the screen you will get an attractive dynamically changing picture to look at. What you will have done is to create an *automaton*. In the context of a game an automaton is nothing more than a sequence of game states generated by a rule which specifies precisely how each state will be succeeded by another. Beyond setting up the initial state your role is that of an observer. You just fold your arms and watch a zero-person game. The computer is an ideal tool for investigating the behaviour of automata but, as might be expected, specimens like the triangle generator soon become pretty boring. Yet one particular automaton has an enthusiastic following.

John Horton Conway's game of Life was first announced in the columns of Martin Gardner's famous series in *Scientific American* [6] in 1970 and immediately caught the attention of mathematicians and computer scientists worldwide. It is an example of a 'cellular automaton' operating over an infinite square grid. Cells of the grid are either dead (empty) or live (occupied) and Conway gives a set of simple rules governing which dead cells come alive, which live cells die, and which remain unchanged at each successive change of state.

A computer is essential for Life but it is obviously necessary to confine the action to a finite grid. This is usually done by adding a further rule that the peripheral cells (not necessarily represented in memory) are always dead. Life is interesting to watch and new discoveries concerning the propagation of special 'constellations' of live cells are frequently published (Berlekamp, Conway & Guy [2]). Figure 2.10 shows a knowledge diagram for Life or any similar automaton.

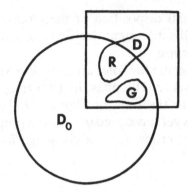

Fig. 2.10. An automaton.

The decision D_0 initialises the automaton. In Life, for example, this comprises the selection of a set of live cells. G is fully visible to the observer but note that the decision D, which is a sole consequence of the rules, has been placed within R. Although the observer knows the rules followed by the automaton it is not practical to foresee the results within a reasonable length of time. Thus the effect is the same as if part of the rules were unknown to the observer, and it is in this portion of R that we place D. However, D is not truly a decision at all; rather it is one of an infinite set of rules representing the *extensive form* of the fundamental rules. That is, we may regard each possible state as having its own rule precisely defining the succeeding state.

2.6   The computer as lawgiver

As a research tool the computer can be of great value to the conscientious games inventor in deriving realistic rules for his simulation game, well-balanced rules for his abstract game, or minimal rules for his arcade game. Many games involve an element of chance, whether dice are involved or not, and 'tuning' the rules will always necessitate probability calculations or the more laborious equivalent Monte Carlo experimentation. In the first case the machine can help, and in the second it is practically essential. However, as stated earlier, what concerns us here is computer participation during the game rather than its 'off-line' use in design and assessment.

A relatively new and interesting class of games has variable rules. That is, modification of the rule set is an integral part of play. We briefly describe the best-known game of this type and conclude with a discussion of self-modifying games in general.

Eleusis

In the mid 1950s the American inventor Bob Abbott first described his card game Eleusis which was, in one respect, a milestone in the history of games design. The complete rules for Eleusis can be found in Abbott [7], and those for an updated version, the New Eleusis, in Gardner [8]. For the present we sketch only the broad features of the original game.

Eleusis can be played by two, but preferably more, players one of whom, called the 'dealer', has special duties. He secretly devises a rule, generally a composite of several simple rules, specifying what constitutes a valid sequence of cards to be played face up by the other players. The latter have the task of discovering the dealer's rule. As each card is placed the dealer announces whether the play is legal or illegal, and an illegal card is returned to the player's hand. The player's function individually, not as a team, but the cards played are visible to all. The earlier a player hits upon the correct rule, the quicker he can get rid of his cards, and the higher his score. The dealer also receives a score at the end of the round, which cleverly reflects the quality of his rule. A good rule is one which is just easy enough to be determined quickly by an astute player, but just too difficult for the rest.

As play proceeds the active players form hypotheses which they test by the play of their cards and, if necessary, reject in favour of better hypotheses. Thus the game simulates the process of scientific research and is often quoted (see for example H. Charles Romesburg [9]) in papers on science education and the philosophy of science.

The knowledge diagram for Eleusis played with a machine dealer, who makes no mistakes in applying his secret rule, is shown in Figure 2.11. Sets R and G have been given partially dotted

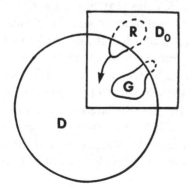

Fig. 2.11. A machine dealer for Eleusis.

boundaries to indicate that the degree to which they are unknown is indefinite. It depends on the particular rule selected by the dealer, which may or may not render a player's hand of cards important. Furthermore, whilst the objective is certainly to move R into a player's knowledge area, it is difficult to say whether he partly understands the dealer's rule or whether he is barking up the wrong tree altogether. His recent success may owe more to flukery than to facility!

Self-modifying games

One of the rules of Eleusis concerns the addition of a new rule. The new rule is, however, enacted only at fixed points in the game – between rounds. During each round the rules of play are constant. There has recently been some interest in games where the rules are modified in a more continuous fashion. The idea is that rule amendment should form a part of every turn, or at least an option. Actually this idea is not all that new. The author recollects playing, some years ago, an elaborate unmarketed game which simulated the Italian parliament. In each turn, bills were voted upon, and some of these concerned procedural aspects of the chamber itself, and hence of the game itself. Such games appeal to the legal mind, and also to those with a passion for the paradoxes of self-reference.

The most complete example of a game of this type is Nomic invented by Peter Suber and described by Douglas Hofstadter [10]. Suber defines a set of 'initial rules' for getting the game started, but before long the rule set can look very different because every rule is a candidate for change. To simulate the hierarchical structure of law Suber divides his initial rules into two categories, one of *immutable rules* and the other of *mutable rules*. The terminology is somewhat misleading. Immutable rules may be changed, but only after they have been moved to the set of mutable rules. Once a rule has been included amongst the 'mutables' it may be repealed or amended. A repealed rule is removed altogether, but an amendment is a new rule, initially mutable, which may itself be repealed or amended. The object of the game is simply to acquire the largest score – or rather, it was! The objective is stated in one of the rules which may, of course, be amended. A player trailing the field could, in principle, enact an amendment specifying that the player with the lowest score was the winner, provided he could persuade the other players to vote for it. Of course, he might first have to amend the voting rule!

The task of keeping track of a constantly changing rule set can be very taxing, and the value of a computer in playing a game such as Nomic will be evident. Essentially the program will be an editor capable of producing up to date listings of the rules, or of selected rules, and able to renumber rules and their references to take account of insertions. The knowledge diagram for a computer assisted self-modifying game is shown in Figure 2.12. The rule set R, as it is a dynamically changing entity, must properly overlap the game state G. Two interesting questions arise. First, can there be a self-modifying game in which the whole of R lies within G. When a set of rules for a game is complete from the point of view of a games player, the answer is yes. From the point of view of a philosopher the answer is no. There always exists an implicit rule external to the set R. For example, what specifies that we must obey the rules in R? If we include a rule in R which reads: 'All rules in R must be obeyed.', what tells us that this particular rule must be obeyed? Hofstadter [11] has discussed this problem with clarity, and in some detail.

The second question is whether a self-modifying game can evolve to the point where R is completely separate from G. Provided a self-modifying game can concentrate the specification of its repeal and amendment powers into a single rule with the power to repeal itself, the answer is obviously that it is capable of 'committing suicide' in this way. Whether this concentration is attainable in every self-modifying game, for example in Nomic, is a more difficult question which we shall not attempt to answer here.

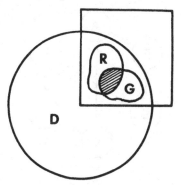

Fig. 2.12. A self-modifying game.

2.7   The computer as research tool

This chapter concludes with a short review of several ways in which the computer is coming to the aid of coaches and managers. We refer, in the main, to people connected with organised sporting activities.

Ranking tournament players

Consider the problem of ranking players who participate in a tournament. Provided that, at some stage, every player competes with every other player, an acceptable method of ranking would be to place the winner of the largest number of games at the top. The rank of every other player similarly reflects the number of wins he has achieved. Sometimes, however, it is necessary to eliminate ties.

If two players have tied on the number of games won we might be able to resolve the matter by comparing the total number of wins achieved by the two sets of losers. This suggests the following iterative method for resolving all ties.

We assign a number called a *grade* to every player. Initially the grade is equal to the number of games won. If there are any ties we replace every grade by the sum of the grades of the beaten players. This gives a new set of grades. If ties persist we repeat the process using these new grades. This is continued until, hopefully, no ties remain. However, it is possible for certain ties to remain permanently, and then it is necessary to consider other factors such as the number of points scored in the various games.

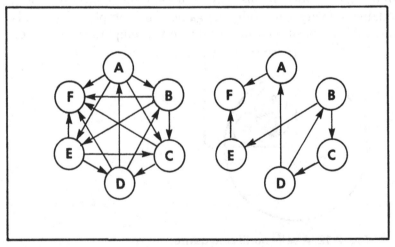

Fig. 2.13. Complete and incomplete tournaments.

The diagram on the left of Figure 2.13 represents, in graphical form, the results of a tournament involving just six players named A, B, C, D, E, and F. The arrows indicate who beat whom. Thus A beat B, who beat C, and so on.

If we grade the players according to their wins in the complete tournament we obtain the sequence shown in the left-hand column of Table 2.1. As B, D, and E tie we calculate the total grade of the players beaten by each participant to obtain the second column. Here, B and E still tie so we repeat the calculation using the grades in the second column. Now A and D tie, but one more iteration yields a tie-less ranking.

This is only one of many possible grading techniques. Whatever the justice of the final result it does have the merit of being based on a complete tournament. What are we to do if the tournament is not completed, as shown in the diagram on the right of Figure 2.13?

If the players have gradings determined from some earlier tournament – or from the deliberations of some committee – it is possible to apply arithmetical rules for adjusting grades as results become available. Many such systems are used for Golf, Tennis, Croquet, Chess, and so on. That adopted for the grading of Chess players is exemplary, and is fully developed and discussed by Elo [25]. The grading increments depend upon the grade of the winning player, the grade of the losing player, and upon the order in which the results are processed. Complexities arise from the need to keep grades within a predetermined range of values – the iterative system illustrated above suffers from inflation of course!

The determination of grades based solely on one incomplete tournament is a particular case of a recurring problem known as the 'statistical missing value problem'. There are two main schools of thought. One attempts to eliminate inconsistencies such as those

Table 2.1. *Grading table*

Iteration no.		0	1	2	3
Player	A	4	8	13	25
	D	3	7	13	21
	E	3	5	10	20
	B	3	5	8	17
	C	2	3	7	13
	F	0	0	0	0

represented by a cycle in the tournament diagram (B, C, D in Figure 2.13, for example). The other accepts such inconsistencies as representing high grade (original) data.

Many solutions have been proposed and practically all demand the use of a computer. These effectively try to complete the tournament diagram, but as the mathematics is quite difficult we shall not continue the discussion here. For readers who wish to pursue this interesting problem further, Broyden [23] discusses its solution in relation to the grading of students who answer different examination questions, and includes a comprehensive set of references.

A coaching aid

Players of fast interactive games – Tennis, Badminton, Squash, etc. – produce a rapid succession of responses to each others play. The definition of a response must include not merely the type of stroke played, but also the player's position on the court and his state of motion. Of course, one has to limit the detail in some respect.

One problem facing the coach is to detect weaknesses in the execution of particular types of response. Another, much more difficult problem, is to recognise sequences of responses which are prone to culminate in failure. The availability of a telerecording, or of some written record of the play, is no guarantee that the coach will identify the critical sequences.

Downey [24] has proposed a system of annotation for Badminton and has suggested that a computer be used to recognise critical patterns of play. The idea is that the record of play should be transcribed (manually) to a sequence of codes which are then scanned by the program. Statistical tables based on subsequences of coded responses would be built up on successive passes, and those followed immediately by failure could be selected for output. The success of such a system would depend upon the degree of detail used for describing responses, and upon the volume of the data necessary to achieve statistical significance.

We might conceive of some future 'expert' system capable, not only of analysing play, but of recommending tactical improvements!

Program design and implementation

3.1 Introduction

Throughout this chapter we shall be concerned less with games and more with computing. The objective is to review programming methods from the first steps in design through to the testing of the finished program. If there is any bias it is towards games programming in that examples are drawn from this area. As we remarked in the first chapter games programs have more in common with those written for scientific and operations research purposes than with those used in the commercial data processing field. Accordingly, little will be said about the techniques for handling large data files. As games programs are generally inter-active, run-time efficiency is a topic of some concern to us. This is reflected in the coverage of several matters not usually included in an introduction to programming.

Many owners of home computers have yet to employ a true *compiler* – something which is essential for most worthwhile games programs. Many will have written small programs in BASIC for execution by an *interpreter*, and others will be about to tackle their first program in any language. For all such this chapter aims to clarify the terminology (including that italicised above) and offer guidance on the steps to be followed in carrying a project through to a successful conclusion.

The matters discussed and the order of presentation might surprise a few more-experienced programmers and computer educationalists. Naturally, they reflect the author's views and experience but equally they derive from the experiences and difficulties of a number of young people who have started to write programs for their own machines. Introductory texts on computing often start at the machine end of things by explaining how a computer represents numbers and coded instructions. Historically this was adopted as the usual mode of presentation partly because of the novelty of the concepts, and partly because such works were intended for a wide readership of potential programmers, engineers, users, and laymen. On the assumption that the reader of this book will have had some exposure to a computer, and that his intention is to write programs, we proceed in chronological order from design to testing, with machine- and language-dependent factors entering at a late stage. Having said this, it must be admitted that a few departures are inevitable. To give one example – the design of a program can be radically affected by the availability of specific ways of representing data in the chosen computer language. Hence variable types are introduced some time before language coding is discussed.

Before embarking on the journey let us briefly consider a broad philosophical aspect of what takes place when we program a computer.

Computing is all about representation or, rather, all of computing is about representation. When we look at the world about us we create a representation of it in the form of neural and chemical activity within the brain. Although little is known about the nature of this process it seems that the representation must be very good in the sense that it enables us to recall, or reconstruct, whatever gave rise to it in the first place. In preparing a computer program every step leads to a representation of what went before. Even the final results of a computation are in reality just a representation of features of the program and of the data supplied to it. Not all these representations are reversible in the way human memory is, but like memory they help us to gain access to information concealed in the real world. Each computer representation is the product of a process such as *coding, compilation, assembly*, and *link-editing*. If some, or all, of these terms are unfamiliar be reassured that they will be described in the course of this chapter.

But why do we need all these representations intermediate between the initial statement of a problem (such as the specification of a game) and its final solution (in the form of a working program to play the game)? Simply because we are fallible. If we bite off more than we can chew we get the wrong answers, or indigestion. In every field of inquiry it is found that the most powerful and reliable means of solving a problem is to decompose it into subproblems, solve these separately, and then assemble the sub-solutions into a solution of the original problem. To mention a familiar example – we multiply two numbers digit by digit then add the results to obtain the final answer.

Now there have been a few calculating freaks capable of multiplying 12-digit numbers without recourse to pencil and paper or any other aid, and who use methods which they cannot describe. Similarly, there are programming freaks who can find short cuts along the way to a finished program, provided it is not too large. In the early days of computing, before high level languages were developed, this facility had some value. Then, a programmer had of necessity to write in the closest possible representation of machine code. Severe limitations on memory size meant that the best programmer was the clever person who could write the most compact code, and to achieve this he might resort to the use of 'program puns' – sections of code which could be made to serve several different purposes after self-modification or relocation. The really clever programmer could ensure that he was practically indispensable, because nobody else could understand his programs! All this is, or should be, in the past. In modern programming practice one of the most desired qualities is transparency. The good program not only runs correctly and efficiently but can be understood and modified by others or, as is often the case, by its original author after he has been involved with other work.

The sequence of representations which has evolved to become the generally accepted methodology not only assists in the production of the program, but also in its maintenance and its portability from one programmer to another, from one computer to another, and even from one computer language to another.

3.2 Preliminary program design

The preliminary stage of program design is perhaps the most difficult to describe because there is no single format for the representation it produces. This might consist of assorted notes, a list of hardware requirements, and some flowcharts or an equivalent way of mapping the overall form of the program. Furthermore there is no clear dividing line between preliminary and detailed design, the latter gradually refines the former until the programmer is able to start coding. Nevertheless it is helpful to introduce a point in the rather lengthy design stage at which it is possible to pause and take stock. This section suggests where this might be placed.

Strange though it may seem, preliminary design is the stage most frequently postponed by the inexperienced programmer. What happens is that he plunges into the detailed design of sections, which he knows to be necessary, which he understands, and in which he can show progress. On just a few occasions this approach can be justified. The success of the whole project may depend critically on the speed of a particular operation or on the ultimate size of an expanding set of data in the machine memory. In such a case it is a good idea to complete the development of the critical part of the program and test it in a simplified environment – a *test bed*. From the test results the programmer can then decide whether it is worth proceeding with the remainder of the program. More usually though, some of the aspects which could or should have formed part of the preliminary design are encountered in the shape of difficulties demanding the repetition of work thought to have been completed. But is this not a characteristic of every design process? Of course it is, but the programmer can minimise the holdups by thinking through the gross features of the program at the earliest opportunity.

TOP–DOWN DESIGN

There have been many attempts to formalise the design process for computer programs, and a large number of possible approaches have been identified and named. Of these, the top–down method is widely accepted as best for producing well-structured programs capable of being read and understood by all. To some degree this is the method implied by our ordering of the sections in this chapter. The idea is to decide the function and inter-connections of the larger features of the program before designing the smaller features. The program is conceived as a set of *modules* at various *levels*. At the 'highest' level there is just one module – the complete program. At the next lower level we might have, for a very straightforward program, a data input module, a calculation module, and a results output module. Note that these modules lie **within** the highest module. Next we decide upon a set of modules for the data input module. These might comprise modules for prompting the user, reading an item of data, verifying that an item of data is syntactically correct and, if it is correct, determining what it represents and where to store it. The same decomposition is performed for the calculation module, and then for the output module. We now move down to the next lower level. Here, for example, we might break down the item input module into modules for reading one character, and modifying simple program switches (integer variables) to indicate the type of character read (letter, decimal digit, symbol, etc). By proceeding in this 'disciplined' way we shall eventually obtain a program planned in sufficient detail for coding to start.

The vital characteristic of a program designed top–down is that the higher level modules determine exactly what information will be passed down to, and up from, modules at a lower level. Of course, at the preliminary stage we do not know the precise mode of storage for this data, but we must at least define what it is, or what it means. It will be sufficient, for example, to make a note that one module A passes down to another module B a list of feasible directions in which a particular piece of a game may move. And that B returns to A the same list of directions but sorted into an order of preference.

We have just considered a very uncomplicated program easily decomposed into input, calculation, and output modules. What happens if we wish to program a game in which the players are in constant communication with the program? Here, it would seem that data input is inextricably intertwined with the other functions. From the point of view of someone stationed inside the computer this may be true, but it does not follow that the logic of the design must be similarly tangled. The key to orderly top–down design is to decide what controls, or *drives*, what. We must ensure that driving modules contain driven modules, and not vice-versa. In our game program the player's input commands determine what calculations are to be performed and what outputs are to be produced. We must therefore expect to recognise the input module at a high level, though not necessarily at the highest level because something must decide when input is due.

Figure 3.1 illustrates a preliminary stage in the top–down design of a game in which the machine provides one of the contestants. The level of each module is indicated by its degree of inset and by an enclosing box. The program as a whole comprises three modules at the first level for, respectively, initialisation, play, and termination. (Note that if level-numbers are used or implied a high level module has a low level-number. The complete program module is considered to be at level zero.)

As we have specified no particular game we obviously cannot say a great deal about the virtues of this particular modularisation. It has been assumed that the game initialisation module is simple and

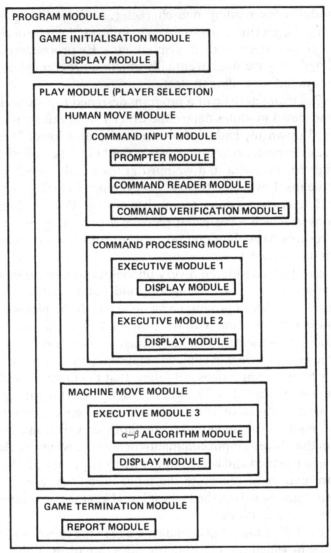

Fig. 3.1. Preliminary top–down design for a game.

includes only one other module whose function is to display the starting position. Similarly the termination module has little to do but report the result of the game. Let us discuss the play module in a little more detail.

The function of the play module is to select the next player, human or machine, and call the appropriate module at level 2. If the human player has the move the command input and command processing modules are executed one after the other. The input module has three main tasks. The first of these is merely to indicate that a command is due by outputting a prompt symbol to the display device. This is so simple that no further modularisation would be required here. The second task is to read the actual command. For many games this might be a fairly complex operation requiring many further levels of modularisation. The third task is to check that what has been read constitutes a valid command for the game. The verification module will probably need to be broken down into modules for displaying error messages and re-entering the command input if there has in fact been an error on the part of the player.

We have assumed that the command processing module can call one of two executive modules depending on what command has been read. As each will alter the state of the game it will always be necessary to display the game when they have executed the command. Thus each contains a display module. It is important to realise that this can physically comprise a single piece of program code although it is regarded as a constituent of more than one module at the design stage. Where the design diagram shows a module the final code may contain nothing more than a call statement.

We emphasise again that the diagram shows only an early stage of the design. Remember that high level modules are identified before low level modules, and that no detailed design is carried out beyond deciding what data is to be transferred between the modules. On this basis, the next stage will identify modules within the command reader module.

One advantage of top–down design is that work on modules can be farmed out to the members of a programming team who need know nothing about the form of the program as a whole. It is unlikely that the owner of a home computer will be able to press his family into service for this purpose, nor would he wish to if he seeks job satisfaction!

OTHER DESIGN PROCEDURES

In *bottom–up* design the programmer starts with the lowest level modules trusting, through experience or intuition, that they will in fact be needed. Obviously the low level modules determine the nature of the information to be received from, and returned to, the high level modules. Quite frequently there exists a library of potentially useful low level modules whose inclusion will save time and effort provided they are relevant to the program in hand. Before dismissing this approach as ridiculous consider that this is how Darwinian evolution works. Small mutations become established, or disappear, according as they confer advantages to the organism concerned. Unless you are a confirmed Creationist you would probably accept that we have been designed bottom–up! The point is that this process has taken millions of years. Evolutionary dead-ends could similarly delay the completion of your program.

A variety of design procedures which are intermediate between top–down and bottom–up have been devised. Some have been invented by writers merely to support arguments in favour of the top–down approach, and these will not be described here. However, several of the *inside–out* methods deserve consideration, not least because they are practical.

The so-called *systems analysis* method concentrates on the sequence of computer operations. As each part of the program is executed we imagine the point of attention moving through the program along a *control line*, and we speak of the *flow of control*. Along this notional line the programmer identifies the main modules. These may transfer control to submodules on side branches of the main control line. In general the modules identified by this process will be different from those defined by top–down design. This is hardly surprising as they are disjoint, whereas those of the top–down method are nested one within another. For very large and complex programs the systems analysis method is reputed to produce more efficient final code than top–down design, though it is certainly less well structured and less comprehensible to a newcomer. For reasons to be discussed later, the latter may be more a result of incomplete *flowcharts* (described below) than of any intrinsic shortcomings of the method.

Once a program has been designed, by whatever means, and is fully operational, it is usually not too difficult to see how it could have been structured in a top–down manner. Those who write on such matters are often academic computer scientists who tend to base their deliberations on existing programs rather than on direct experience of program design in industry or commerce. It is natural that they should unreservedly advocate top–down design. There is, however, no ultimate truth which states that the most hygienic method of design will invariably produce the most comprehensible or most efficient end result. Sometimes it is difficult to identify high level modules without some detailed understanding of processes at a lower level, and many programmers who fully recognise the merits of top–down design are occasionally forced to adopt other strategies.

It has been said that there are three levels of understanding – that resulting from study, that necessary to teach, and that needed to write a computer program. Perhaps we should add a fourth – that necessary to employ top–down design with absolute rigour. Despite this we recommend the adoption of the top–down philosophy in the preliminary design stages, and that this should be continued throughout later stages if it seems natural and leads to no impasses. If difficulties do arise the programmer should feel no guilt in temporarily adopting the systems analysis approach with its concomitant flowcharts. If he can identify critical processes at a low level he should design, write, and test these as early as possible. However, he must resist the temptation to continue with bottom–up design once it has served this purpose. Thus, other design techniques should be regarded as interruptions to the main top–down procedure which should be re-established at the earliest opportunity. Perhaps the most important thing to know is which design method is being employed at any particular time.

FLOWCHARTS
Several times we have referred to flowcharts and these are now described with examples. There are two main types – one showing the flow of data, and the other showing the sequence of program operations (the flow of control).

System flowcharts
Whatever strategy is adopted for program design it is useful to draw up a system flowchart at the very start of the project. This will show all peripheral devices such as keyboards, visual display units (VDUs), printers, and so on. Arrows indicate the transfer of information between the devices, usually via the computer. General comments are placed in square brackets.

A system flowchart (some writers call them *block-charts*) contains little information relating to the sequence of data transfers. For that, it is necessary to look at a program flowchart (described later).

All types of flowchart employ symbols but, unlike those used in program flowcharts, those used in system flowcharts are far from standardised. There has been, perhaps, less pressure for standardisation because system flowcharts are normally quite compact and the symbols are often accompanied by descriptive text.

For most computer games the system flowchart will be very simple. A Chess playing program, for example, might require no more than a representation of the terminal (VDU plus keyboard), the computer, and possibly a *backing store* device such as a cassette tape drive or a disc drive from which the program is loaded into the machine. The flow of data during play would be shown as two arrows, one labelled 'PLAYER MOVES IN' and the other 'MACHINE MOVES PLUS BOARD DISPLAY OUT'. To illustrate system flowcharts we have chosen a slightly more complex example which includes the rerouting of some data.

Figure 3.2 shows the system flowchart for a computer moderated game between two players named BLUE and RED. Some liberties have been taken. For example, at the top of the chart is shown a representation of the three disc files used, but we have omitted a symbol to represent the actual disc drive. If it was essential for the files to be loaded in parallel we should have to indicate separate disc drives.

At the start of the game the program is loaded then followed by data specifying the scenario (see Chapter 2). Play proceeds in cycles with the players issuing commands via the keyboard and then receiving various reports on the state of the game before issuing further commands. As there is only one VDU, reports which are confidential to a particular player must somehow be hidden from the other player. This is achieved through the use of a password system operated entirely by the program – there is no special security hardware. Each player sets his own private password which is stored within the program. To gain access to his confidential reports he must type in his password at the keyboard. Once he has digested their content he can clear the screen and hand over to his opponent. In the flowchart this procedure is indicated by the use of password gates, the triangles containing the letter P. Similarly, each player's commands are input at the keyboard only after he has gained access through the use of his password. This prevents one player from issuing 'silly' commands on behalf of the other.

Certain reports are 'open' and may be seen by both players. The flowchart indicates that these are directed to a printer in this example.

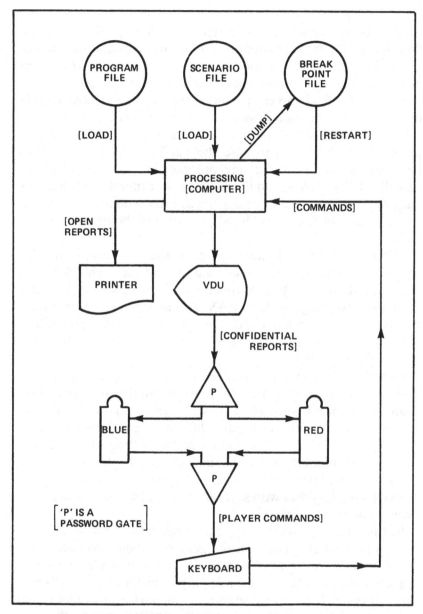

Fig. 3.2. System flowchart for a computer moderated game.

The game is a long one to be played over a whole weekend. It is therefore necessary to take a break from time to time. By jointly issuing a special 'dump' command the players can preserve the state of the game on a break-point file. When the game is to be restarted all three files must be loaded.

Program flowcharts

At one time, but for a relatively short period, program flowcharts were regarded as an essential part of program documentation. However, programmers found it very difficult to keep them up to date during program development, and most looked upon the drafting of the final 'fair copy' flowcharts as a chore. Consequently these tended to be merely spaced-out rewrites of the final *source code* – the language statements. Some automatic flowcharting programs were written to ease the burden. These accepted as input the source code for any program in a specific language (usually FORTRAN) and produced a printed flowchart as output. As might have been expected, their renderings provided no more insight than was already on offer in the original source code!

Where top–down program design is used the proper use for program flowcharts is as a visual aid in the final, highly detailed, stage just before coding commences. Even here, the use of a structured language such as PASCAL may render them superfluous. If, on the other hand, the systems analysis approach to design is employed then program flowcharts are essential throughout the design stages.

Flowcharts have uses outside the design of a specific program. They can be of great assistance in understanding someone else's source code, or for getting to grips with a tricky algorithm. To give one instance, it would seem quite difficult to gain familiarity with the program operations associated with the α–β algorithm without the aid of a flowchart such as that included in Chapter 8.

Figure 3.3 illustrates the standard symbols used in program flowcharting, together with several additional symbols which have been found to be helpful.

In this diagram, what the programmer writes has been hand-written as it would appear in the genuine article. Printed text is annotation. In a program flowchart the arrows indicate all possible sequences of operation, not the physical transfer of data. All entry and exit points for the section of program portrayed are indicated by sausages containing the words ENTER, EXIT, or STOP.

If all the control lines were drawn in full many flowcharts would resemble a bird's nest, so breaks are introduced with the use of connectors. These are matched up by the labels they contain. If your flowcharting template does not contain the broad arrow off-page connector use the circle symbol but incorporate the page

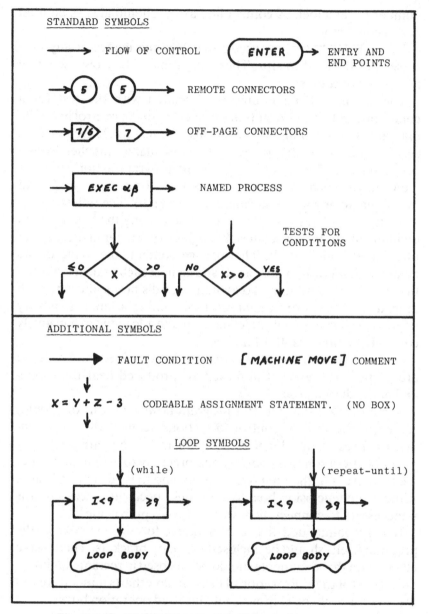

Fig. 3.3. Symbols for program flowcharts.

number in the label. A control line arrow should always be used near a connector.

Rectangular boxes are used to enclose the names of any processes not detailed in situ. These might have their own separate flowcharts of course.

The lozenge shape is always associated with the test for a condition, and always results in a branching of the control line. The diagram shows two alternative forms of a test for X greater than zero. Quite often it is necessary to show many branches from a condition test. For example, different program actions may be required for each of the conditions I=1, I=2, I=3, I=4, and for I equal to any value outside the range (1,4). The tidiest way to show this is to have a single control line leaving the lozenge then dividing into branches set at right angles to it, rather in the manner of the teeth on a comb. The lozenge contains the name of the quantity under test, in this case I, and against each branch is written the associated condition. To avoid the bird's nest syndrome each branch terminates on a connector containing a label. It is very important to check that the exits from a test lozenge exhaustively cover all possible results of the test.

The non-standard symbols are now described. Several of these are particularly relevant in flowcharts produced near the coding end of the design process.

Some of the branches of a program flowchart will, or should, represent the flow of control to sections dealing with fault conditions. These can be highlighted by the use of solid arrows.

Many operations may correspond precisely to assignment statements present in the final source code, and these can be indicated without any enclosing box. Where these occur in succession it is unnecessary to connect them with a visible control line.

It is recommended that commentary, forming no part of the program itself, should be enclosed in square brackets. There was a convention that comments should be enclosed in rectangular boxes positioned at the side of control lines. In flowcharts under development these could be confused with inserted operation boxes.

We now come to the somewhat contentious matter of representing program loops – sections of program to be repeated until some condition is satisfied. The standard symbols offer no single representation of language-supported loops such as the BASIC for-loop, the FORTRAN do-loop, and the PASCAL while-loop. Thus, there is no formal way of distinguishing between 'open-coded' loops and those generated by a loop statement. For the purposes of publication this is a serious shortcoming. The loop symbols shown at the bottom of Figure 3.3 rectify this.

Both comprise a rectangular box divided by a heavy vertical line. The left-hand compartment is associated with the continuance of the loop, and the right-hand one with its termination. There are two fundamental types of loop as follows:

(a) *The while-loop*. In a while-loop every traversal of the body of the loop, including the first, is 'preceded' by a test for continuance of the loop. If the test indicates that termination is due before the first transversal, the body of the loop will not be executed at all. To indicate that the test is performed before the loop body is entered the initial entry control line, entering from above the symbol, is drawn so that it does NOT directly meet the heavy dividing line.

(b) *The repeat–until loop*. In a repeat–until loop the test 'follows' the execution of the loop body. Hence the body will always be executed at least once. To indicate this the initial entry control line is drawn to meet the heavy dividing line to convey the idea that it 'passes through' the test.

There are no strict rules about what may be written inside the two compartments – it is left up to the programmer. Note that the symbol does not imply any initialisation or advancing of a *loop controller* such as is used in a BASIC for-loop and a FORTRAN do-loop. Such operations must be explicitly included in the flow-chart. However, for programmers in these languages we would remark that the BASIC for-loop is akin to the while-loop, and that the FORTRAN do-loop is of the repeat–until type.

SUMMARY

If you follow the course recommended you will reach a point at which you have the following documents:

(a) A system flowchart showing all hardware devices and the nature of the information transferred between them.

(b) A top–down program plan showing the first few levels of modularisation.

(c) A set of notes describing the data to be transferred between the modules shown in the program plan.

But isn't there an extraordinary omission from the above list? If you were handing the project over to someone else a program specification detailing the function of the program, and the form of all inputs and outputs, would be essential. However, programmers working on their own behalf rarely prepare a written specification, though some say they should. To sound a somewhat cynical note, perhaps they realise that the firmer the specification the more certainly it will need to be changed! Where the programmer is also the person who conceived the program in the first place it is probable that he will have a reasonably complete mental picture of what the program is to do. In this respect, what is cost effective in a professional environment where a program specification must be agreed by a number of different people, such as clients and software managers, is not always desirable in a private project. To some extent the specification is embodied in the system flowchart, and this should be omitted by no self-respecting programmer.

Where then do we draw the line between the preliminary and detailed stages of the program design? Our answer is – at the point where it becomes necessary to assign specific names to parts of the program and to the items of data processed within the program. In other words – when it becomes necessary to name modules and program variables.

3.3   Detailed design

That the names for program modules and variables are decided at some point after the start of the project but before coding commences should be evident. At the start the programmer is concerned only with the overall plan for the program in the form of a system flowchart and a module chart. At this stage it is unwise to be too specific because named entities tend to persist in the mind and act as a brake on free thought. However, at a later stage this same characteristic becomes a virtue. As each new level is mapped out it becomes necessary to keep track of a rapidly expanding collection of modules and a similarly growing volume of information to be transferred between them. Thus it soon becomes far too cumbersome to rely on description as the only means of identification. At the point when the programmer decides to conduct affairs with named entities we take it that detailed design has started.

Names and identifiers

If you examine the formal specification of a computer language you will find that different terms expressing the idea of a name are used in different contexts. Furthermore these terms vary from one language to another. In one case, for example, programs have 'titles', I–O (input–output) devices have 'identifiers', and everything else has a 'name'. In another language everything has an 'identifier'. Working programmers in any language, as distinct from language theorists, usually get by with the term 'name' and if there is any danger of confusion qualify it as 'program-name', 'file-name', 'variable-name', and so on. However there is one thing to watch out for. Nowhere is the term 'name' applicable to anything starting with a decimal digit. Usually a name is understood to start with a letter, though it may contain digits in character positions other than the first. In some languages, on the other hand, the term 'identifier' includes decimal numbers assigned to specify particular I–O devices.

Although we have remarked that program documents, such as module charts and flowcharts, should be language independent it is obviously sensible to choose names which accord with those allowed in the language most likely to be adopted for the source code. Thus, if you decided to write in a microcomputer version of FORTRAN you would limit the length of your names to six characters. PASCAL allows names of practically unlimited length, but in such a case it is a good idea to impose your own limit. Overlong names are tedious to write, prone to error, and actually degrade the performance of the compiler or interpreter (see Section 3.5) to some extent. If you have chosen to write in one of the dialects of BASIC which permit only names comprising a single letter optionally followed by a decimal integer all we can do is offer our condolences!

As to the actual names chosen, these should bear some relation to what they identify. A program module for decoding a data item (whatever that may mean) is far more memorable as ITDCDR than as JK46A7. Short but pronounceable mnemonic names can often be derived by omitting most of the vowels and reducing runs of the same consonant to a single letter, somewhat after the manner of Dalton's Weekly which cmprs. prprty. advrts. in this way. A friend of the author has described this technique as 'reductio ad not quite absurdum'!

At this point, although we have not yet reached the coding stage, we must briefly review the different types of program module which occur in almost every computer language. We shall then go on to describe the different types of variable, and how information is exchanged between modules. Some knowledge of these matters is practically essential for the continued refinement of the program design up to the point where coding starts.

Subprograms

Most, ideally all, of the modules identified in the pre-liminary design will become named modules of the source code. We call such modules *subprograms* to distinguish them from those which arise at a late stage of the design, which are small, and which will not need names in the source code. Depending on the language chosen these subprograms will be *procedures, subroutines, bricks,* etc.

There are two principal kinds of subprogram. Ordinary sub-programs (referred to simply as subprograms) are named sections of program which are explicitly called by a statement within another subprogram – a *calling subprogram*. Called subprograms may themselves be calling subprograms and, whilst there is always a limit to the depth of such nested calls it will not be reached by any realistic program. Some languages, such as PASCAL, allow a subprogram to call itself! This recursive re-entry capability makes possible some elegant solutions to certain programming problems. However, it is always possible to get by without using recursion and the subtleties of re-entrant programming are best left until the programmer has acquired some experience in 'bread and butter' programming.

When a subprogram has completed its task it transfers control to the statement immediately following the call statement within the calling subprogram. A few languages, it is true, permit sub-programs to have multiple entry points and multiple return points. That is, a particular subprogram may be called under a number of 'aliases' which cause entry at different points in the body of the subprogram, and it can be arranged to return to the calling subprogram at places other than the statement following the call. Using such options is a prescription for disaster unless, possibly, you are a very experienced programmer writing in an assembler language (Section 3.4) for the purpose of attaining the ultimate in run-time efficiency.

The second type of subprogram is the *function subprogram*. A function subprogram (referred to simply as a function) is never called explicitly in the way an ordinary subprogram is called. Instead, it is called implicitly wherever its name occurs in a place which could otherwise be occupied by a variable-name or by an expression involving variable-names. A function-name is associated not only with a program module but also with a data variable having the same name. As an example, consider a program which must evaluate the distance between two points located by their Cartesian coordinates in the plane. By writing a function for this purpose the programmer can save memory space, reduce coding effort, and enhance comprehensibility at the expense of a small increase in execution time. Where he might otherwise write a source code statement such as:

$$D=SQR((X1-X2)*(X1-X2)+(Y1-Y2)*(Y1-Y2))$$

he can now write:

$$D=DIST(X1,Y1,X2,Y2)$$

where DIST is the chosen name for the function and the coordinates X1,Y1,X2,Y2 are provided as *parameters* in the function call. We shall say more about parameters shortly.

That function calls may be nested should be evident when it is realised that SQR is also a function – but one provided by the supporting software of the language, not by the programmer. Every language has a library of such functions for common operations such as calculating a square root.

Types of variable

The memory of many computers, especially microcomputers, is divided into units of 8 binary digits called bytes. Each of these is addressed by a simple location number in the range 0 (zero) upwards to the limit of the available memory. The name of a variable in a high level language, such as BASIC, PASCAL, FORTRAN, etc., is essentially the name of a small set of locations where a specific item of data is stored. These locations are contiguous and contain just enough space to hold the type of data concerned. By using these names the programmer completely avoids the necessity of having to deal with numerical memory addresses, just as by using subprogram names he avoids having to discover where sections of his program are stored.

It is advisable to determine the type of each variable as it is introduced during the design stage because certain operations are forbidden for certain types of variable. Most languages on microcomputers offer some or all of the types listed in Table 3.1 below. Each type is separated from the next by a horizontal line and where there are several entries in a compartment they are synonymous. Refer to your programming language manual for information on which of these are available in the language you have selected.

Table 3.1. *Common types of variable*

Type of variable	No. of bytes	Range of values
Logical Boolean	1	Two values only interpreted as 'TRUE' and 'FALSE'
Character Char Byte Integer*1	1	(−128, +127) or (0,255) depending on use. Often interpreted as a character code (e.g. in ASCII)
Integer Int Integer*2	2	(−32768, +32767) or (0,65535) depending on use
Real	Usually 4 Sometimes 5 or 8	Number is stored in floating point format and range depends on storage allocated to the exponent part

The integer related types are undoubtedly the ones most frequently needed by programmers in every field, yet they are not available in many of the BASIC interpreters, which press real variables into every kind of service. Subject to requirements of range and accuracy the shorter types are preferable to the longer as they save memory space and operations with them are faster. On microcomputers the type REAL should be avoided where possible because the necessary floating point operations are normally carried out by library software, and are therefore slow in comparison to hardware operations. Even when floating point hardware is available it is advisable to check if it can in fact be used by the particular language chosen. In Section 3.4 we shall continue the discussion of factors relating to the choice of variable types.

Arrays

It is often necessary to refer to an entire group of variables by a single name. Such groups, which are called arrays, are catered for by all high level languages. One-dimensional arrays are simple linear lists holding a succession of variables, all of the same type, and each identified by the name of the array augmented by an index number. Thus the fifth element of an array named LADDER would be LADDER(5). Two-dimensional arrays correspond to rectangular tables of elements each requiring two indices (notionally a row and column number). Again, all the elements must be of the same type.

What makes arrays so useful is that the indices may be held in integer variables. The same piece of program can operate on the whole array merely by changing the contents of the indexing variables and re-entering the appropriate section of the program some specified number of times.

Games programs frequently require integer arrays in which the elements hold information associated with board positions. As an example, an element identified by BOARD(ROW,COL) might correspond to a chessboard square in the row whose index is held in the integer variable ROW, and whose column index is held in the integer variable COL. The value of the element could be set equal to a small integer identifying the piece located in that square, or zero if the square is vacant. The piece numbers themselves might be used as indices for a one-dimensional array containing textual piece-names or, more likely, as one of the indices for a two-dimensional array holding the text. The programmer's decisions on these storage allocation matters are properly part of the detailed design stage. They should not be left until coding starts.

How modules exchange data

Those who have done a little programming in BASIC, but in no other language, may be inclined to ask why this topic needs any discussion. In BASIC all variables are *global variables*. That is, any part of the program may refer to and alter any variable. This means that a BASIC module (a subroutine) requires no special interface with the rest of the program. It also means that the programmer must ensure that it receives data already set in the variables expected by the subroutine. Furthermore, conflicts must be avoided. For example, if a subroutine is called from within a loop, the programmer must ensure that it does not change the loop controller. Any loops in the subroutine must use different loop controllers.

Other languages have rules governing the *scope* of each variable. The scope is the area of the program in which the variable may be recognised and used, and this depends upon where the variable was *declared*. That is, where its name was assigned and its type identified. In contrast to global variables we say that such a variable is *local* to its scope.

This is not the place to discuss the scope rules for any particular language. However, we would remark that it is always possible to declare a variable so that its scope covers the whole program. Such a variable can then be regarded as global and the ex-BASIC programmer might therefore be tempted to declare all his variables in this way. He could then transfer data between subprograms in his customary way, but he would lose the advantages of having local variables which are:

(a) That subprograms can perform their operations with data held in different places.

(b) That subprograms have clearly defined interfaces with the rest of the program.

(c) That variable-names are reuseable without the risk of conflict.

If subprograms are not to exchange data by using global variables another mechanism is required to provide the interface. This is called a *parameter list*.

The parameter list is a list of variable-names written in brackets and placed immediately after the subprogram-name. The individual elements of the list are usually separated by commas. In the subprogram itself elements of the parameter list are variables which are local to the subprogram and which are called *formal parameters*, or sometimes *dummy parameters*. In the program statement which calls the subprogram the parameters are *actual parameters*. The language compiler (Section 3.5) which processes the source code must match up the actual parameters with the formal parameters so that the subprogram operates with the correct data. As the idea is very important we picture in Figure 3.4 a subprogram and several calls from different places in a program. What the subprogram actually does is immaterial in this example but we have assumed that it receives some data in the first two parameters, and leaves the results of its work in the last two parameters. Of course, if the subprogram produces only a single numerical, or logical, result it could have been written as a function with the subprogram-name acting like a variable-name as described earlier.

In this example we have used a FORTRAN style of programming because it requires somewhat less explanation than others. The subprogram named SUB is called from two places in the program. In the first case the first two actual parameters are literal

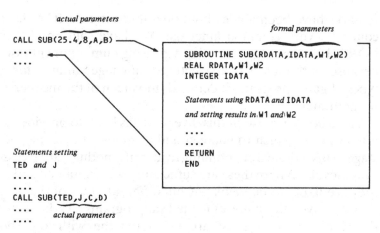

Fig. 3.4. Actual and formal parameters.

constants. These are matched up with the first two formal parameters RDATA and IDATA which are, respectively, real and integer
variables as can be seen from the declarations within SUB. The
subroutine SUB performs its task and writes the results into the
formal parameters W1 and W2 which match up with A and B in the
call statement. SUB finally returns to the statement situated
immediately after the call. The dots merely signify program statements of no interest to us here.

In the second call to SUB the first two actual parameters are
variables TED and J. These must of course have been set before
the call is executed. They are matched up with RDATA and
IDATA so they must be of the same types – TED is a real variable
and J an integer variable. Subroutine SUB is entered and sets W1
and W2 as before but this time they match up with the actual
parameters C and D.

Stepwise refinement
We have just concluded a somewhat lengthy diversion
which described features which some might regard as more relevant to the coding stage. The topics discussed were the two principal
types of subprogram, the common types of variable, and the two
methods by which subprograms exchange data. On the whole the
discussion has been kept reasonably language independent. What
has been said applies equally to all the commonly used languages
with the exception of BASIC and FORTH. A number of specific

remarks have been made about operations in BASIC which is, of course, a very common language. We have said nothing about FORTH – a language attracting a growing number of enthusiasts – because, although it is a structured language suitable for many types of game program, it demands too much of the inexperienced programmer.

The whole purpose of this diversion has been to provide us with a notation in which to conduct and complete the detailed design stage. This is done by continuing to identify modules at successively lower levels. Where these are sufficiently self-contained and where they are likely to be invoked from different areas of the program they are given the status of named subprograms. At the same time their formal parameter lists are set out, together with notes specifying the type of each parameter and its meaning in the context of the application, which is presumably a game.

This process of stepwise refinement continues until the design has reached levels at which all modules are simple enough for direct coding to begin.

3.4   Language coding

Language coding, or just coding, is the manual conversion of the various design documents into a form which can be processed by another program able to produce a representation more nearly resembling the final object code to be executed by the machine. The result of coding is called source code and the program which processes it is a compiler, an assembler, or an interpreter, depending on the particular language used and on the precise nature of what it generates. In this section we discuss only the writing of source code, and the work carried out by the language processor is described in the next section. That is, we are concerned here with the 'pencil and paper' job of writing a string of characters to represent the program.

The greater bulk of the literature which reaches the newcomer is concerned with describing language features and conveys the misleading impression that coding is the most vital activity involved in the creation of a program. Because the source code is the most compact and self-contained representation which can be read by the programmer it is natural that it should attract considerable attention. Thus the average home computer comes with a slim volume dealing with the *operating system*, the control program needed when using the machine for any purpose, and a relatively fat programming manual for some computer language, usually BASIC.

In fact, the greater part of the time and effort of a programming project (remember we use the term 'programming' in its widest sense) is expended in the design stages. If the design is complete and well structured the task of coding should be very straightforward. It should demand little or no creative effort, though it does demand concentration, attention to detail, and accuracy. Because language processors require strict observance of the grammatical rules, or syntax, it is in the coding that most errors are made. Fortunately, the majority of such errors are quickly detected by the compiler, assembler, or in some cases by the interpreter. The worst errors are those which misrepresent the program design with syntactically correct source code. Techniques for locating these are discussed in Section 3.6.

Which language?

Any well-designed program is capable of implementation in almost every computer language which has ever existed. Depending on the nature of the program it may be marginally easier to code it in one language than in another. Source code in one language may lead to more compact or faster running object code than would be generated by another. A program in one language may be more comprehensible and easier to modify than in another. The choice of language depends upon a 'trade off' of these various considerations because no language is ideal from every point of view. It is quite difficult to make an objective assessment of these factors in most cases, and this is where the beginner needs advice.

Naturally such advice will always reflect the experience of the person giving it. No one has written significant programs in every language, and very few have written programs of widely differing types in any one language. Indeed, to judge from some magazine articles, much of the advice comes from people who have written no programs, significant or otherwise, in any language!

The first thing to consider is language availability. Obviously one should not plunge into the task of coding in GARBLE if no GARBLE compiler has been written for one's own computer. However, a large range of languages has now been implemented for microcomputers.

One very important point should be noted. Apart from BASIC

very few language processors have been written to operate on one specific make of computer. To widen the market, the majority are designed to run under the control of one of the machine-independent operating systems such as CP/M (Digital Research) or UNIX (Bell Laboratories). If you have a Super Whizzo computer your BASIC will probably run under the Super Whizzo operating system. But, should you decide to write in FORTRAN you will almost certainly have to buy not only a FORTRAN compiler but an operating system also. The costs are comparable but it is in any case advantageous to switch to one of the commonly used operating systems. Such a move makes available to you a very wide range of marketed software, enables you to exchange experience with many other computer owners through one of the user groups, and increases the market potential of your own programs should you decide to sell them. Apart from these considerations the universal operating systems are in general very much superior to those provided by manufacturers for their own machines.

We now conduct a necessarily very brief review of the programming languages which are commonly available for microcomputers.

BASIC

It is ironic that BASIC which was devised by Kemeny and Verty at Dartmouth College in the USA for the purpose of teaching programming has, in the opinion of the author, become the greatest impediment to this end. The language does little or nothing to encourage modular programming and has other shortcomings which we shall not detail here. However, recognising that it is an easy language to learn, nearly all manufacturers provide BASIC interpreters for their products. Recognising also that the language had shortcomings they augment their versions with numerous extra facilities. The result has been to render programs in BASIC the least portable of all. That is, a BASIC program for one computer cannot in general be transferred to another without modification.

Most BASIC's run in an interpretive mode (Section 3.5) which makes execution very slow in comparison with an equivalent compiled program. A few BASIC compilers have been produced but the language was not specified with this in mind, and the resulting object code does not run particularly fast.

On the positive side BASIC is a useful language in which to

develop and test isolated modules before inclusion in a larger program. In particular, tricky mathematical algorithms can be written and debugged rapidly because editing is carried out interactively without the need to reload source code. Of course, after such an exercise it is necessary to translate back into the language to be used for the final program.

For some time after microcomputers became widely available to the public BASIC was the only language on the market. Many firms and private individuals who quickly took up the machines had no alternative but to develop programs in BASIC. Consequently there is now a lively trade in program conversion services.

PASCAL

PASCAL is the very antithesis of BASIC. It is a highly structured language specified by Wirth in Zurich about 1971. It is strongly based upon ALGOL (the 'algorithmic language') which found its principal use as a vehicle for publishing programs. ALGOL has not caught on as a language for the implementation of large programs though it was for a time quite popular in the east European countries. PASCAL, on the other hand, has been enthusiastically adopted in many areas. The University of California (San Diego) developed a means of interfacng PASCAL with a wide range of computers, and assumed the role of a coordinating body for the language. They published a standard language specification, slightly more restricted than Wirth's, known as UCSD PASCAL.

One objective of the language is machine independence. This has been the aim of many languages but seems never fully attainable. The UCSD approach is to process the source code into an intermediate language (another representation!) called P-code. The P stands for 'pseudo'. Provided a computer has a P-code interpreter or assembler it can run any PASCAL program. There is, however, a trend towards the production of direct compilers for PASCAL. One hopes that it will not lead to too many different dialects, which would defeat the aim of machine independence.

From the programmer's point of view the main feature of PASCAL is that it carries the top–down design philosophy through to the coding stage. Statements are nested within compound statements which may themselves be nested within larger compound statements. Indeed the whole program may be regarded as a compound statement just as we regarded the program as a single module in Section 3.2. ALGOL had practically the same structure but amendments to the source code necessitated recompilation of the whole program. This drawback has been overcome in PASCAL though further development is needed before it rivals FORTRAN in this respect.

It is inevitable that coding in a highly structured language such as PASCAL should be somewhat slow compared to coding in less formal languages like BASIC and FORTRAN. Like ALGOL before it, PASCAL is replete with punctuation – colons and semi-colons abound. At the same time, though, the resulting source code is far less error prone and subsequent testing is completed more rapidly.

Many owners of home computers use PASCAL but it must be admitted that some people have expressed doubts about its suitability for large projects. Odd though it may seem, some regard it as too modular! They suspect that too much execution time is spent in handling the mechanics of module linkage. In other words, the programs run rather slowly in comparison with equivalent programs in other languages.

For the games programmer who enjoys programming for its own sake, and who takes a pride in producing elegantly structured bug-free programs PASCAL may be the answer.

FORTRAN

FORTRAN is an old language and for that reason is discounted by certain fashion-conscious but shortsighted pundits. It was first specified within IBM as early as 1953 and released to customers in 1957. Since then there have been a number of significant updates and the latest, FORTRAN 77, makes some slight concessions to modern ideas of structured programming. One of the acknowledged shortcomings of FORTRAN on mainframe computers was its clumsy handling of stored text. On byte-oriented microcomputers the introduction of the short integer type (Section 3.3) has rectified this to a great extent.

FORTRAN's antagonists point out that it is not a 'structured language'. In the sense that PASCAL is structured this is true. However, this does not mean that one cannot write structured programs in the language. A FORTRAN program consists of a set of independent modules (subroutines and functions), any of which can communicate through parameter lists with any other. It is entirely possible to write very strictly structured programs in

FORTRAN, but it is up to the programmer to discipline himself. To misquote Shakespeare: 'Some are born to structure, FORTRAN programmers attain structure, and PASCAL programmers have structure thrust upon them.' Which is the language of those who are 'born to structure' is debatable – I suspect it may be FORTH!

FORTRAN is almost as easy to learn as BASIC, and there is much evidence to show that it is still a viable language for programs of any complexity. Outside the field of commercial data processing, where COBOL reigns supreme, there is no doubt that the majority of large systems are implemented in FORTRAN. This is particularly true of simulators which of course have much in common with simulation games.

Computer magazines and user groups frequently publish the results of benchmark tests (see for example Back [12]). A group of small programs, each written in a number of languages, are run and carefully timed, often on a range of different computers. It would indeed be a biassed person who could deny that FORTRAN produces faster object code than other high level languages.

However, this speed of execution is bought at a price. FORTRAN cannot perform any cross-checking of parameter lists when the various subprograms are linked to produce the final object code. Parameters may be of the wrong type or be present in the wrong numbers, and the only clues to such faults arrive when the execution crashes in some catastrophic way.

If you plan to write a games program using a tree searching algorithm, such as the α–β algorithm described in Section 8.3, then speed is essential and FORTRAN is strongly recommended unless you fancy writing in an assembly language (see later). However, where FORTRAN is used it is very important to complete the design stages properly before coding starts. FORTRAN punishes sloppy programming severely.

ASSEMBLY LANGUAGES

Every microprocessor has its own assembly language, sometimes several. Modern assembly languages have many features in common and having learnt one it is a relatively easy matter to learn another. Each assembly language statement corresponds to one instruction in the object code of the machine. The format for a statement is fairly constant from one assembler to another. The line is divided into four fields holding an optional label, an operation code, a small set of operands, and an optional comment of no significance to the assembler itself. The label, if present, assumes a value equal to the address of the memory location where the instruction is stored. The operation code, or 'op-code', is a mnemonic specifying the type of machine instruction, and the operand field indicates the data involved in the operation. Typical operands are machine register identifiers, memory addresses usually referred to by labels, and literal values such as integers and character-strings. The comment field is for the programmer's convenience only. Certain statements do not lead to a stored instruction but merely set labels to values given in the operand field. Such labels play the part of program variables in a high level language, though in a somewhat indirect manner.

Assembly language coding is nowhere near as difficult as its reputation suggests. Assemblers now offer many helpful facilities and should not be compared with the old-style machine language coding. However, it is essential for the programmer to be familiar with the architecture of his machine. The necessary facts are always presented in the first few pages of the assembly language manual.

Self-contained pieces of assembly language code can be incorporated with most high level languages for the purpose of improving program performance in critical areas. These are almost always subprograms exchanging data with the calling program through the use of pointers held in the machine registers. The rules for this are determined by the high level language and are usually buried away in a hard to get 'User Guide' for the language. Naturally they cannot be regarded as part of the language manual when the language may be implemented on many different machines.

If a program demands the highest possible efficiency in execution then an assembly language must be used. For programs of any size it is a great advantage to use a *macro-assembler*. Such assemblers allow the programmer to name a group of instructions rather in the manner that subprograms are named. Such a group of instructions constitutes a *macro* which may be copied into the object code wherever its name is quoted in the assembly code. Macros may have parameters like subprograms but these are evaluated at the time the macro is inserted in the object code. Because statements invoking macros look somewhat like subprogram calls some people talk of macro calls. However this is misleading because no true calling is involved. A macro should be thought of as a shorthand aid. Devise a sufficiently powerful set of macros and you will have created a high level language!

If you decide to write in an assembly language it is essential to write or otherwise obtain a good library of supporting software. No microcomputer, at the present time, has machine level instructions for floating point arithmetic. If your game uses real numbers you will need subroutines for addition and multiplication, and for either subtraction and division, or negation and reciprocation. You may also need functions for taking a square root, calculating sines and cosines, and so on. Writing these from scratch is no small task. However, they are readily obtainable on the market. Input and output software will also be required.

Efficient coding
We conclude this section with hints on some coding techniques which can lead to faster execution of programs written in almost any high level language. In fact the programmer should take some account of these techniques at the design stage. They have been included at this point partly to avoid adding to that already overloaded section, and partly because it is not too late at the coding stage to make the necessary adjustments.

(a) *Economise on array dimensions*. It takes longer for a program to determine the location of an array element with many indices than it does to locate an element with few indices. As an example consider a program which must store the coordinates of ten spaceships. These objects travel in space rather than along railway lines so the position of each is determined by three numbers which could be stored in an array declared as:

```
REAL COORDS(10,3)
```

The first index identifies the spaceship and the second identifies the particular coordinate. Thus to move spaceship number 5 a distance of N lightyears in the Y direction (the second coordinate axis) the program might contain a statement:

```
COORDS(5,2)=COORDS(5,2)+N
```

Whenever a reference is made to an element of COORDS the program must find the base address for the specified column then augment this by the row index. These base addresses are set up by the language processor in a separate list, itself an array.

A more efficient mode of storage is to use three one-dimensional arrays thus:

```
REAL X(10),Y(10),Z(10)
```

The required move can now be represented by the statement:

```
Y(5)=Y(5)+N
```

which executes considerably faster than its equivalent using COORDS. Statements such as this frequently occur inside loops where the program spends much of the time. In such places apparently minor savings can lead to big improvements in the overall performance of the program.

(b) *Economise on array references.* A particular array reference might occur in a number of statements in some area of the program in which the actual element remains unchanged. The programmer should adopt the habit of transferring the element to a single local variable (a *scalar*) by inserting a simple assignment such as:

```
Y5=Y(5)
```

This produces a saving comparable to that obtained by replacing two indices by one.

(c) *Economise loop bodies.* Consider the following nested loop in PASCAL:

```
FOR I:=1 TO N DO
    FOR J:=1 TO N DO
        IF J>I THEN
            MAT(I,J)=MAT(I,J)-R*MAT(I,I);
```

This essentially alters the elements of a square array named MAT if they lie to the right of the main diagonal. These elements are decreased by an amount equal to R times the value of the element on the diagonal in the corresponding row.

Notice that the inner loop does nothing at all when J is less than or equal to I. Hence we may start the inner loop not from 1 but from $I+1$. Similarly, no action will be taken when I is equal to N, so we may terminate the outer loop at I equal to $N-1$.

The value $R*MAT(I,I)$ does not change whilst the inner loop is being executed. A considerable improvement in speed will result if this is evaluated outside the inner loop and set in a scalar variable, say W, thus:

```
FOR I:=1 TO N-1 DO
    BEGIN
    W:=R*MAT(I,I);
    FOR J:=I+1 TO N DO
        MAT(I,J)-W
    END
```

The BEGIN and END are needed because the body of the outer loop is now a compound statement.

Unfortunately the elegant mathematical statement of many published algorithms fails to coincide with the most economic computer code, and reorganisation such as that illustrated is often advantageous.

(d) *Avoid real variables.* The disadvantage of using real variables has already been remarked upon but the matter warrants some expansion. There are, of course, situations where real variables are essential. They are necessary whenever the range of values assumed by a variable is large or unpredictable. However, many programmers declare a variable to be real merely because the quantity it represents has a fraction part.

Before the advent of floating point hardware in the late 1950s programmers had recourse to two options. They could use library floating point software, just as most microcomputers do today, or they could represent real numbers as integers with an implied scale factor. In fact the two options are two manifestations of the same technique. In floating point representation the scale factor is some power of 2, 4, or 8 and the exponent is carried with the argument which is interpreted as a binary fraction. In the scaled representation the whole of one or two integers is assigned to carry the argument and the scale factor is understood to be some constant value, usually a suitable power of ten.

The latter technique leads to faster code in general. The idea is to conduct all possible computations in integers and to convert to real numbers at the latest possible moment. Let us consider an example.

A simulation game has to attenuate a quantity representing the visibility of each member of a large set of different objects. The attenuator to be applied to each object depends upon the simulated time of day, the weather, the size and aspect of the object, its state of motion, and upon whether it is currently under observation or not. All attenuators lie in the range 0.0 to 1.0. Bearing in mind the realities of the situation being simulated it is decided that an accuracy of two decimal places is sufficient. Thus the attenuators take values of 0.00, 0.01, 0.02, . . ., 0.99, 1.00. Hence there are only 101 different values. The astute programmer stores these for each combination of object and condition as short integers (type BYTE, INTEGER*1, etc.) with an assumed scale factor of 0.01. This saves 75% of the memory required for the storage of real attenuators, and the calculations are executed much more rapidly.

3.5   Language processing

Language processing is the conversion of the source code into executable object code for the machine being used. This work is carried out automatically through the action of various programs one of which reads the source code as input data. There are two distinct approaches, and one which could be said to be a blend of the first two. Most high level languages adopt only one of these approaches, but a few give the user a choice.

Interpretation

This is the method used for most programs in BASIC. The computer memory is notionally divided into four areas or partitions.

(a) *The interpreter partition.* This holds the actual language processor – the *interpreter*. It controls all the operations to be decribed in what follows.

(b) *The source code partition.* The user's source code is read into this area under the control of the interpreter. Some compression is normally performed to economise on space. For example, commonly recurring words such as READ, WRITE, PRINT, FOR, THEN, and so on are stored as single characters. If a program listing is required the interpreter translates these back into recognisable words.

(c) *The data partition.* In this area space is reserved for all the program variables. Certain parts are assigned to serve as input–output buffers in which data is received or assembled when the program communicates with the user or with backing store files.

(d) *The execution partition.* At the time when the user types RUN, or some equivalent command to start execution, none of the program exists in the form of object code. As each statement is due for execution the interpreter collects the source code and *compiles* it to object code in the execution partition. Most of this object code consists of subprogram calls to library routines held permanently within the interpreter. At the end of the compiled statement the interpreter inserts some code which will cause a return to the interpreter, then transfers control to the start of the compiled statement. Every statement is handled this way.

Different interpreters organise memory in different ways and use different terminology.. The foregoing is intended only to give a general idea of the mode of operation. Of course, the user need know nothing of these details, but some important effects should be noted.

First, it should be clear that the overall execution speed of the program will be far slower when interpreted than when the whole program is compiled into object code. The execution of every statement is preceded by a considerable amount of preparatory work.

Second, the interpreter must be resident within memory whilst the program is running and typically uses up about 6K bytes. Certain computers are *dedicated* to one language, usually BASIC. Such machines, which can run programs in no other language, often have very large interpreters which are allocated separate memory never available to the user and which is not included in a specification of the available memory size.

Third, the user can interrupt the execution of his program to make amendments with minimal delay. He can delete and insert statements without the need to reprocess the remainder of the program. He can even alter the values of variables directly from his terminal, then continue execution of the program. Thus an interpreter is a powerful development aid.

Compilation and link-editing

This is a two-stage process which starts with source code and finishes with object code for the whole program which may then run without further action by a language processor. Most programs used in scientific work, industry, and commerce are prepared in this way. Software embedded in games playing devices, such as dedicated Chess machines, is also prepared in this way. However the average home computer programmer usually works with an interpreter. If he wishes to produce genuinely interesting games which run at an acceptable speed he must shake off the restrictions imposed by an interpreter, and come to terms with a compiler. It is not difficult as we now hope to show.

All programmers make mistakes and need to amend parts of a program during the testing phase. If it were necessary to recompile a whole program each time an amendment was made everyone would use interpreters! Fortunately, all modern compilers can process separate parts of a program. As might be expected these separate parts are the named modules – subroutines and functions in FORTRAN, procedures and functions in PASCAL, and so on.

To avoid having to type in COMPILE commands for each subprogram compilers are organised so that they can compile a whole file of subprograms. Obviously to put all subprograms in one file would be tantamount to recompiling the whole program each time an amendment was made. Having one file for each subprogram would also be somewhat inefficient. There is a happy medium easily derived during development work.

The facility for compilation of separate parts has two important results. First, the output from the compiler is 'not quite' object code because several things cannot be absolutely decided, or *resolved*, at this stage. The compiler has no means of knowing where in memory the part it is compiling will be stored. There might be other groups of subprograms to be stored at lower addresses and, as the different compiler runs are independent, it cannot know how large these are. Hence the compiler produces *relocatable code*. This means that the output from the compiler must be accompanied by some additional information defining how the code can be made to work at any location in memory.

For the same reason the compiler cannot resolve the location of subprograms called by the part being compiled. Nor can it resolve the locations at which certain variables will eventually be stored. The solution, however, is very simple. All unresolved references are stored in a list of data called a *symbol table* which accompanies the relocatable code. The symbols of the title are the names of subprograms and variables which must have locations assigned to them when everything is put together to produce the final object code.

The 'putting together' of the various pieces of relocatable code is performed by the *link-editor* (see below).

The second consequence of separate compilation is that a program can be constructed from parts written in different languages provided the different compilers produce the same sort of relocatable code and store their symbol tables in the same format. Usually if more than one language is involved one of them is an assembly language introduced at some critical point for the purpose of achieving the highest possible speed of execution.

The link-editor is a program completely separate from the compiler (though both are normally purchased as a single package). The task of the link-editor is to read a set of file-names identifying the files holding relocatable code, and then to link these together in memory to produce the final object program. Whilst it does this it also resolves all the references in the symbol tables. If it fails to resolve all these *external references* by the time it has processed the last file of relocatable code it will, if it is a good link-editor, search library files associated with the language looking for subprograms with the requisite names. If there are still unresolved external references the link-editor run will report the fault and terminate.

Unresolved external references are quite common in the early stages of program testing. They mean simply that something is missing from the original source code, or possibly that a call to a library subprogram has used the wrong name. In some languages the omission of a terminating 'END' from a subprogram will cause the compiler to completely miss the next subprogram name from the symbol table. The 'END' for the missed subprogram then terminates the first subprogram in a syntactically correct manner, so the compiler thinks all is well!

As the ideas presented in this subsection are very important we have summarised them in Figure 3.5 which is, in effect, a system flowchart for the action of a compiler and a link-editor. The symbols used are the same as those employed in Figure 3.2. The circles represent files which may or may not reside on a single disc or cassette tape. Lower case words relate to data of an ephemeral nature.

The top quarter of the diagram shows the initial input of the source code under the control of a program called EDITOR. EDITOR handles character data only, and must not be confused with the link-editor. I am not trying to be difficult! On many systems such a program really is named EDITOR, and the editing function concerned is 'insertion' into an initially empty file. The source code file S may be one of several required for the storage of the whole program.

In the second quarter we show a source file being amended, again under the control of EDITOR. The output file will normally be physically distinct from the input file which might be retained for a short while in case the amendments are mistyped. This, and subsequent computer runs are likely to be repeated many times during the development of a program.

The third quarter of the diagram shows a compiling run in which a source file S is input, and a new file R containing relocatable code is output. REL is an abbreviation of 'relocatable'. A typical program may require three or four files of relocatable code.

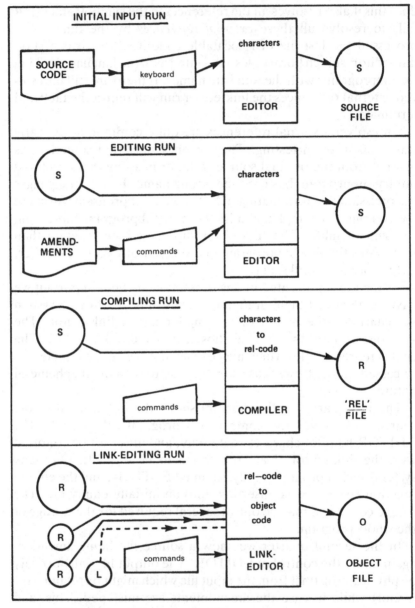

Fig. 3.5. Language processing.

In the final quarter of the diagram all the different REL files are being read and converted into object code within memory. The file marked L represents the file of library subprograms supplied with the language. This is in relocatable form and will be searched if, as is usual, the program needs to load any of them. At the end of the link-editing run the memory will contain the object code for the complete program. In many cases, this *memory image*, will be output to an object code file O from which the program may be directly loaded into memory whenever execution is desired. Alternatively the program may be executed in situ when the link-editor has completed its work.

The VDU, teletype printer, or whatever, which conveys progress reports and error messages to the user has not been shown in the diagram for reasons of space.

P-code processing

Some languages, notably PASCAL, provide the option of compiling into an intermediate language known as P-code (pseudo-code). This may be thought of as the assembler language for some fictional machine. Although P-code is relocatable in a sense, it is not as near to object code as that produced by true compilers. To execute the program the P-code representation may either be interpreted or further compiled into true object code. This depends on whose PASCAL is being used and which computer it runs on.

Some computers have been built to execute P-code directly. These machines are picturesquely entitled 'Pascal engines'.

On general purpose microcomputers P-code interpreters run faster than source code interpreters but not as fast as true object code. They may be regarded as providing a compromise between the various disadvantages of interpreters and the advantages of true compilers whilst enhancing program portability between different machines.

3.6 Program testing

Whilst program design is best conducted top–down, program testing is best conducted bottom–up. If the parts are faulty the whole cannot function correctly! This should be very obvious but just as there are those who attempt bottom–up design, there are those (in all probability the same people) who test their programs by running them in toto.

Let us suppose, for a moment, that you adopt this strategy in testing your program. You accordingly prepare some test data, which might comprise some predetermined moves for a games program, load the program and, wonder of wonders, it works! What have you learnt? Unfortunately, very little.

It may be possible to deduce that certain subprograms, because they have functioned correctly once, will function correctly under all circumstances. In most cases, though, the operation of a subprogram will depend on the data supplied to it, and running the program as a whole is unlikely to guarantee that every circumstance will be tested.

The rational way to test a program is to check out the lowest level subprograms first through the use of test beds. A test bed is a section of program with two simple functions only. It must generate a range of parameters for the subprogram under test, and report the results after each call to the subprogram. On moving to the next higher level only tested subprograms may be included at lower levels. However, as with program design, practicalities intrude. The methods one should adopt for testing a program of great importance, one on which human lives may depend for example, may not be justified for a games program. One should balance the means against the end. To some extent the testing procedure will depend upon degrees of confidence.

If a subprogram is particularly simple and uses a well-tried technique it may be sufficient to test it manually. This is sometimes called executing a 'dry run', or 'playing computers'. On a large sheet of paper write all variable names in ink, then work your way through the subprogram statement by statement writing values in pencil on the work sheet. Only use an eraser when there is no more space for new values assigned to a variable. If you erase the old value each time a variable changes you will find it hard to backtrack when you make errors, as you will.

Debuggers
On mainframes many high level compilers include *trace* facilities. The idea is that the programmer can direct the compiler to include various output options in selected areas of the program. These options vary widely from one language to another. A typical trace output might include the names of all called subprograms in the order in which they were called. More sophisticated traces might include the values associated with all assignment statements. As object code 'knows' nothing about the programmer's source code names a trace facility must obviously insert a lot of additional information between each statement. Thus the object code becomes bulky and runs rather slowly. Such trace facilities are not normally available for microcomputers though there are some. For

example, one implementation of PASCAL is noted for its symbolic debugger which is a trace facility able to recover the programmer's variable and procedure names.

For interpreters the production of a trace is easier because the interpreter regains control after the execution of each statement, and the source code is always present.

Many microcomputers, or more specifically, operating systems, include non-symbolic debuggers for use with assembly language programs. These demand some expertise on the part of the programmer, and are very difficult to use with object code generated from a high level language.

When something goes wrong during the execution of a program written in a high level language the main problem is to discover where the fault occurred. One simple technique which the author uses is to include at the start of every subprogram a statement which will print a single letter. This is made conditional on the value of a switch, an integer taking the value zero for 'trace-off' and non-zero for 'trace-on'. At various points in the program the user is requested to set, or unset, the value of the switch. The letters, or other characters, output are unique to each subprogram, and are not accompanied by any carriage-return or line feed. Trace output can be very voluminous, especially if the program is working well, and full use should be made of the output medium. By omitting any carriage control character one avoids getting miles of output with only one character on each line. The approach relies on the output device supplying an automatic newline when a line is full. For some languages, such as FORTRAN, this technique requires the provision of a low level (assembly code) routine for outputting a single character because the usual language facilities always precede output with some carriage control character.

Programming techniques for games

4.1 Introduction

Practically all games programs share common features and need common capabilities. These are outlined below.

(a) *Command input*. The program must read and interpret commands from the players to execute specific moves, or to change the mode of operation of the program.

(b) *Text handling*. To recognise words used in the commands and to communicate with the player in other ways, the program must store and retrieve text.

(c) *Random sampling*. To simulate the effect of the 'unknown' the program may have recourse to probability calculations which frequently involve the production of random variables satisfying some distribution law.

(d) *Simulating motion*. Most programs record and update the positions of discrete objects such as pieces. In many cases it must be possible to alter these positions at a controlled rate to simulate motion.

(e) *Sorting alternatives*. Where there is choice of action the program will have to rank alternatives according to some measure of their 'merit'. Generally, the program must perform a sorting procedure before making a selection because what may appear to be good at one level of the program may be rejected at another.

The purpose of this chapter, and the next, is to present a variety of useful techniques which can be incorporated in your programs to carry out tasks associated with these features. The present chapter deals with (a) and (b) for which the problems are mainly organisational. The following chapter (Chapter 5) continues with the more mathematical matters which arise in handling (c), (d) and (e).

Notation

To help distinguish between variables used in sample program code and the symbolic quantities used in mathematical statements we shall employ italic typeface for the latter. For example,

A=B+C*D

is an assignment statement setting a program variable named A equal to B plus C times D, whereas

$$A = B + C^*D$$

is a mathematical statement saying that the quantity A is equal to the quantity resulting from the evaluation of $B + C^*D$.

The difference between the two kinds of statement could be summarised as that between 'convenience' and 'truth'. The program statement represents a convenience, perhaps temporary, whilst the mathematical statement represents an actual or assumed fact. In another part of the program the variable named A might legitimately be used for a completely different purpose. On the other hand, in a mathematical argument we may not use the symbol A for any other purpose without an explicit note explaining how the notation has been changed.

As to the language we use for showing samples of program code, this is initially a blend of BASIC and FORTRAN. This has been chosen to illustrate the use of parameter lists, variable type declarations, etc. in a manner which should be easily understood by those who have hitherto programmed only in BASIC. Later examples of code have been presented in FORTRAN to facilitate transfer to actual games programs. FORTRAN is undoubtedly the most efficient high level language for the games programmer and compilers are widely available for practically all home computers.

Game independence

Having written one successful games program it is probable that you will want to write another. Here is some good advice.

As far as possible write subprograms which are independent of the particular game for which the program is intended.

This means, for example, that a subprogram for sorting a hand of seven playing cards into some order of precedence should be written so that it could equally well sort a hand of 13 cards. It is a question of defining the right set of modules, and of allowing flexibility through the use of parameter lists. Game-independent subprograms may be used in more than one game, and so reduce programming effort. As a rule try to constrain game-dependent program to the higher levels of a program so that the lower level modules can constitute a library for use in other programs.

4.2   Reading items of data

With the exception of automata (Section 2.5) all games programs must be able to read a player's commands and act upon them. Such commands vary from simple symbolic inputs like P-K4 for a Chess program to complex sentence-like constructions such as:

```
MOVE PARA-2 15 NW AT 0600 IN CM
```

Such a command, in a battle simulation program, might be interpreted as: 'Move the unit named PARA-2 a distance of 15 km. in a north-westerly direction starting at 6 o'clock in the morning and proceed in column of march.'

Like statements in a computer language commands must abide by rules of syntax. The more relaxed the syntax the harder it is to write a program which will understand what a player means by his commands. On the other hand, if the syntax is too rigid it may simplify the programming at the expense of game playability. The constituent items of a command must also obey rules of syntax stating which characters may be used in forming words such as MOVE and PARA-2, and numbers such as 0600. In this section we shall be concerned with reading and recognising the items of a command. In Section 4.3 we proceed to assemble these into commands.

The material is based upon several successful programs exploiting the idea of an *item-oriented* input facility. Most languages are provided with a means of reading integers, real numbers, and character-strings, but they assume that the type of data to be read at a given point in the program is known in advance. Just as this is not the case for a language processor reading source code, so it is not the case for a games program reading a player's commands. We shall describe an approach to data input which, though it may be implemented by the programmer with a little effort, could usefully be made an integral part of any computer language. The idea is simple. On executing an input operation the program reads one item of data, then indicates what it has read. We define what constitutes an item, with greater precision, after we have established a foundation.

CHARACTERS

Every character has a representation inside the machine which occupies one byte. For example, in the ASCII code normally used by microcomputers, upper case letter A is stored as the eight binary digits 01000001. However, not every character has a simple symbolic representation outside the machine. For example, the internal character carriage-return has to be written out as such, or abbreviated to (RET) or something similar. All this may sound very familiar but masks a common misconception.

Users of home microcomputers get so used to seeing each typed character appear immediately on the screen that they often associate the keyboard and the screen more closely than they should. A typed character is first read by the program which happens to be in control at the time. It is then up to the program to *echo* the character to the screen. This is not always as direct as it may seem. If you hit the (RET) key, for example, the program receives the single character carriage-return but it will normally respond by outputting two characters to the screen. The first is the echo of carriage-return, and the second is the character line-feed supplied as an extra. To echo only the carriage-return would cause the next line of input to overwrite the preceding line.

A further example is afforded by backspace. If you hit this character the program receives the single backspace character but may well respond by outputting the three characters backspace, space, backspace, so that the previous visible character is apparently erased from the screen.

Character input–output

To write a flexible item-oriented input facility it is essential to be able to read a single character from the keyboard and echo it properly. Many language implementations provide character I–O in a programmer-accessible form. Before describing this let us consider what happens at the hardware level when a character is to be transmitted.

Most microcomputers use an unclocked *handshaking* procedure. If you type in a character at the keyboard it is stored in an *input port buffer* and, at the same time, the machine indicates that a character is waiting to be read by altering the contents of an *input port status byte*. The character itself occupies the whole of the buffer, but the fact that a character is present is indicated by setting only one bit of the status byte. So far this is independent of the program being run.

Now suppose the program needs to read a character from the keyboard. If it merely executed a machine code input instruction to take a character from the keyboard port buffer there are two possible outcomes. If the character has been keyed before the input instruction is reached all is well and the character is success-fully read by the program. However, when he keys in the character the operator cannot know exactly what point the program has reached, and he may be late. In this case the input instruction will have already been executed and will have read whatever happened to be present in the buffer at the time. Obviously, then, it is necessary to examine the port status and to wait until it indicates that a character is ready. After the character has been read by the program is it necessary to 'unset' the port status? Yes – but this is done automatically by the hardware when the buffer is read. This exchange of indicators between hardware and program is known as handshaking.

Here is a piece of assembly language source code for reading a character from the keyboard. The particular language used is that for the Intel 8080 microprocessor which may or may not be familiar to you. If it is not, the comments to the right of the semicolons explain what is going on. We have assumed that the status port number is 3, and that the buffer is filled from port number 5. The 'ready' bit which is tested in the status byte is assumed to be the third bit from the least significant end of the byte. This is bit number 2 if we number the bits 0, 1, 2, . . . from the least significant end, and a 1 at this bit position has the value 4 in the conventional binary notation. The label CONIN represents 'console input', the console being comprised of the keyboard and the principal output device.

```
CONIN:  IN    3        ;READ THE STATUS BYTE TO
                       ;REGISTER A THE ACCUMULATOR
                       ;OF THE INTEL 8080
        ANI   4        ;SET ALL BITS OF A TO ZERO
                       ;EXCEPT FOR BIT NO. 2
                       ;WHICH IS UNALTERED
        JZ    CONIN    ;JUMP BACK TO FIRST
                       ;INSTRUCTION IF A IS ZERO
                       ;(BIT NO. 2 NOT SET TO 1)
        IN    5        ;BIT NO. 2 OF A WAS SET
                       ;TO 1 SO CHARACTER READY IN
                       ;BUFFER. READ IT TO A.
```

Character output works in the same way as input. Before the program can send a character to the output port it must test a status 'ready' bit. If the character is output when the device is not ready the character will be lost. We show an appropriate piece of assembly language code for character output below. The port numbers are assumed to be the same as above. On many machines they are the same because, as one buffer is for input and the other is for output, there can be no ambiguity. However, the 'ready' bit for output must obviously be different from that for input as both will lie in the same status byte. We assume it to be bit number 0 (the least significant bit). We also assume that the character to be output is waiting in register B.

```
CONOUT: IN    3        ;READ THE STATUS BYTE TO
                       ;REGISTER A
        ANI   1        ;SET ALL BITS OF A TO ZERO
                       ;EXCEPT BIT NO. 0 WHICH
                       ;IS UNALTERED
        JZ    CONOUT   ;JUMP BACK TO FIRST
                       ;INSTRUCTION IF A IS
                       ;ZERO (BIT NO. 0 NOT SET
                       ;TO 1)
        MOV   A,B      ;DEVICE IS READY. TRANSFER
                       ;CHARACTER FROM REGISTER
                       ;B TO REGISTER A
        OUT   5        ;OUTPUT CONTENTS OF
                       ;REGISTER A TO PORT NO. 5
```

We have started by giving examples of assembly-code character I–O for two reasons. First, they show clearly how character I–O works, and second, your high level language may not provide any other facilities for this purpose. If this is the case it will be necessary to write assembly language subprograms like those above with the addition of several instructions to transfer the character to or from an actual parameter quoted in the subprogram call statement in the high level source code. It will also be necessary to identify CONIN and CONOUT as subprogram names by means of an assembly language pseudo-operation such as ENTRY CONIN,CONOUT. Information on linking assembly language subprograms can usually be found in an appendix to the language manual or in a 'User Manual'. The port numbers are hardware dependent so will not normally be specified in any of the language literature. They should be found in the documentation for the particular machine.

Now let us briefly consider how to handle character I–O in high level languages which do provide the appropriate facilities. Input is normally performed by a library function named INP, INPUT$, INKEY$, GET or something similar. It is important to establish whether the character is automatically echoed to the console VDU or not. Output is executed by calling a library subprogram named OUT, COUT, or similar. Depending on the machine and the language to be used it may or may not be necessary to quote port numbers as parameters and test the 'ready' status. As a rule BASIC is tailored for the machine on which it runs and the programmer can leave everything to the interpreter. However, some BASIC's provide an INP function which does require attention to port numbers, status bits, and 'ready' loops. This function is not suitable for keyboard input because BASIC reads the input buffer between statements in order to test for the control-C character used for interrupting a run. Thus, unless the key is depressed precisely as the execution of INP is started the 'ready' bit will indicate that there is nothing to be read.

DATA ITEMS

As stated earlier the aim is to produce a facility able to read an item of data from the keyboard and then to report what has been read. An item consists of a string of characters with a recognisable beginning and end. The item may be preceded by a string of 'ignorable' characters, normally space characters used for layout purposes, and is ended by a *terminator*.

If this were a book for computer scientists and compiler writers we could devote several chapters to the generalities of this approach to data input. Instead, we will explain the ideas through the medium of a specific set of items and terminators which have proved adequate for many games programs, and indeed for numerous other applications. Tables 4.1 and 4.2 list all terminators and

Table 4.1. *Terminator table*

Character	Represented as
Carriage-return	(RET)
Space	Δ
Comma	,
Escape character	(ESC)

Table 4.2. *Item table*

Type no.	Item	Examples (with terminator)
1	Null	Nothing typed except (RET) or comma
2	Cancel	Any item terminated by (ESC)
3	Fault	Any item not of type 1, 2, 4, 5, 6, or 7
4	Name	FREDΔ APPLE, Z56(RET) MOVE-OUTΔ
5	Text	'TITLE', '6/11/84'(RET) '3A2 & ETC.'Δ
6	Integer	25Δ 15427, 0(RET) −99Δ +1, 0001(RET)
7	Real	2.5Δ +.0003, −66.07(RET) 0.0, 1234.Δ

types of item, and will be followed by a short discussion. When the program has read an item typed in at the keyboard the type number for the item is returned in an integer variable named TYPE so that the program knows what has been read and where it is stored. First though, let us become familiar with the various items.

The *null* item results from hitting (RET) or comma without previously typing anything else. It is used to indicate 'no data'. Possibly the program will assume some default item in its place. The *cancel* item is anything containing (ESC). The program might interpret this as 'no good – type the item again'. A *fault* is anything not recognised as anything else! The item 5ABC is a fault because it is neither a number nor a name for example.

We now come to the informative items. A *name* is a string of characters starting with a letter (upper or lower case). It may contain any other characters excluding the terminator which ends it. A *text* is anything enclosed in apostrophes though apostrophe itself may not occur inside a text. An *integer* is a number in the range $(-32768, +32767)$ not containing a decimal point, and optionally preceded by a sign + (plus) or − (minus). A *real* is any number containing a decimal point, or an integer outside its specified range. As they are stored in floating point format real numbers have a very large range. No allowance is made for typing in real numbers with an exponent (for example, as 1E-4 in place of 0.0001).

Data is input in a free format, and any item may be preceded by a string of one or more spaces to facilitate layout. The space character is not regarded as a terminator until an item character has been encountered.

Table 4.3. *READIT parameters table*

Variable-name	Variable-type	Description
TYPE	INTEGER	Receives a value in the range (1,7) to indicate the item type
NCH	INTEGER	Holds the number of characters in the item excluding terminator
CHARS	CHARACTER	A character-string for holding the characters of the item excluding the terminator
INTEG	INTEGER	A 16-bit integer for returning the value of an integer item
REALV	REAL	A real variable for returning the floating point representation of any numerical item (integer or real)

The item input subprogram READIT

At any point where the program is to read an item there is a call to a subprogram named READIT. Some other name might have been chosen, but names such as READ and INPUT are often reserved words of the language. The parameters of READIT are set out in Table 4.3. If you program in a BASIC having no integer variables it is perfectly feasible to implement READIT using ordinary BASIC real variables because computation speed is not a major factor where keyboard input is concerned.

In relation to the character-string CHARS it should be noted that it is easier to handle backspace and rubout characters if the apostrophes of a text-string are regarded as part of the item. Of course the program could remove them from CHARS at a later stage.

All parameters of a BASIC program are global variables so a call to READIT will be merely a GOSUB statement. In FORTRAN we could read an item by executing a statement such as:

```
CALL READIT(T,N,CHS,INT,RVAL)
```

where T, N, etc. are the actual parameters (Figure 3.4) corresponding to the formal parameters TYPE, NCH, etc. When READIT must be called from many places in the program it is more convenient to communicate via COMMON store. As each item is read it will almost certainly be stored in some game-dependent variable so there is no disadvantage in using a single set of global parameters on each call to READIT. In a PASCAL program it might be better practice to employ actual parameters as shown above.

We now turn attention to how READIT actually converts the characters read into recognisable items.

There are two phases of operation. In the first the characters are read, stored in CHARS, and some syntax checking is carried out. In the second, the syntax checking is completed, and the characters are compiled into the finished item. We shall explain an amazingly simple and powerful technique for carrying out these tasks. It is used in both phases of READIT and, with a little imagination, you will see that it could also be used in many other programming tasks having the same general structure.

Symbol-state tables

A symbol-state table is a rectangular array of numbers in which the rows correspond to some identifiable eventuality such as the occurrence of a character in data, and the columns relate to the current state of the program.

As READIT treats all letters in the same way, and all digits in the same way, it is not necessary to have a separate row for each character which could be typed in from the keyboard. Instead we assign the characters to *character classes*. That is, on reading a character READIT first establishes which class the character belongs to, then uses the class number as the row index when extracting an entry from the table.

The *state* of the program (specifically of READIT) is represented as a small integer identifying what is going on. The various states of READIT are described in a table below.

The entries of the symbol-state table each contain two pieces of information held in a *packed* form. One is the new state number representing a change in the mode of operation if it is different from the current state number. The other is a small integer specifying what action the program is to perform immediately. The format of an entry is:

```
TABLE ENTRY = 100*NEW STATE NUMBER + ACTION NUMBER
```

To unpack an entry it is necessary to carry out an integer division by 100, then to set the state equal to the quotient and the action number equal to the remainder. It is possible to avoid packed entries by having separate tables for state and action numbers but

Table 4.4. *Table of character
classes (phase 1)*

Class	Character(s)
1	Carriage-return (RET)
2	Escape (ESC)
3	Space Δ
4	Comma ,
5	Backspace (BCK)
6	Rubout (RUB)
7	Apostrophe '
8	All other characters

execution speed is not critical whereas saving memory space almost always is important. Note however that if short integers are available as a variable type we can obtain the best of both worlds because the packed entries will certainly require two bytes each whereas state and action numbers, being less than 255, can be fitted into single byte variables.

The packing-constant of 100 has been chosen to aid readability but any other value greater than the largest action number would suffice. Sometimes a power of two is chosen so that the integer division can be performed as a shift operation in assembly language programs.

We now describe the two phases of READIT, together with the relevant definitions of character classes and state numbers. Phase 1 is concerned with reading characters into CHARS until a terminator is reached. Backspace or rubout may be used to make amendments whilst the item is being typed. The character classes are listed in Table 4.4.

READIT PHASE 1

In Table 4.5 the reason for distinguishing between states 1 and 2 is to facilitate the handling of backspace and rubout. We do not wish to echo backspaces which would carry the cursor back beyond the start of the current item. It should be noted that backspace and rubout are here regarded as alternatives. If both are used in a single item the display will be spoiled although the internal representation of the item will be correct.

At some points in the symbol-state table, Table 4.6, a new state

Table 4.5. *Table of states (phase 1)*

State	Description
1	No character has yet been read by READIT
2	One or more leading spaces (ignorable) have been read but no significant character has been read
3	One or more characters associated with an item which is not a text-string have been read
4	A text-string is being read
5	The terminating apostrophe of a text-string has just been read

number of zero is specified. This means merely that the state is irrelevant because the action about to be performed includes a return to the calling program.

To complete the description of phase 1 it remains only to list the actions (Table 4.7). One additional action (numbered 0) must be included to initialise the state and the character counter NCH. This is executed on entry to READIT and also if the use of backspace or rubout makes it 'appear' that READIT has just been entered. Most actions include an entry to some other action. As the actions are *open coded* (that is, they are not subprograms) ordinary GOTO statements are used.

The class of a character is set by a function named CHCLS1 the parameter being the character itself. A character is echoed by a call to a subprogram named ECHO, again with the parameter being the character itself. ECHO automatically supplies a line-feed when carriage-return is output.

Table 4.6. *Symbol-state table (phase 1)*

State	1	2	3	4	5
Character class 1	004	004	009	006	010
2	005	005	005	005	005
3	202	202	009	403	010
4	004	004	009	403	010
5	101	207	307	407	407
6	101	208	308	408	408
7	403	403	303	503	006
8	303	303	303	403	006

Table 4.7. *Actions table (phase 1)*

Action no.	Program description

0	```NCH=0```
	```STATE=1```
	```GOTO ACTION 1```

1	```Input next character to CH```
	```CLASS=CHCLS1(CH)```
	```ENTRY=SST1(CLASS,STATE)```
	```STATE=ENTRY/100```
	```N=ENTRY-100*STATE```
	```GOTO ACTION N```

2	```ECHO(CH)``` ```GOTO ACTION 1```

3	```NCH=NCH+1```
	```CHARS(NCH)=CH```
	```GOTO ACTION 2```

4	```ECHO(CH)```
	```TYPE=1```
	```RETURN```

5	```ECHO(CH)```
	```TYPE=2```
	```RETURN```

6	```ECHO(CH)```
	```TYPE=3```
	```RETURN```

7	```IF NCH=0 THEN GOTO ACTION 0```
	```ECHO(BCK)```
	```ECHO(SP)```
	```ECHO(BCK)```
	```NCH=NCH-1```
	```IF NCH=0 THEN GOTO ACTION 0```
	```GOTO ACTION 1```

8	```IF NCH=0 THEN GOTO ACTION 0```
	```CH=CHARS(NCH)```
	```ECHO(CH)```
	```NCH=NCH-1```
	```IF NCH=0 THEN GOTO ACTION 0```
	```GOTO ACTION 1```

9	```ECHO(CH)``` ```Enter phase 2 of READIT (see below)```

10	```ECHO(CH)```
	```TYPE=5```
	```RETURN```

We assume that the symbol-state table is stored in an array named SST1. Several working variables are used as follows:

STATE — The current state number.
CLASS — The class of the character read.
ENTRY — An entry taken from SST1.
N — An action number extracted from ENTRY.
BCK — A character variable holding backspace.
SP — A character variable holding space.

READIT PHASE 2

In phase 2 the characters are taken not from the keyboard but from the character-string CHARS. As CHARS contains no terminators, leading spaces, backspaces, or rubouts it should hold a 'clean' item representing a name, integer, or real number.

Phase 2, of course, uses different character classes and states from phase 1 and these are shown in Tables 4.8 and 4.9 respectively.

The symbol-state table is shown in Table 4.10. Again, a new state of 0 is indicated if the action about to be performed includes a return to the calling program.

Table 4.8. *Table of character classes (phase 2)*

Class	Character(s)
1	Plus +
2	Minus −
3	Point .
4	Digit $(0, 1, 2, \ldots$ or $9)$
5	Letter (upper or lower case)
6	All other characters

Table 4.9. *Table of states (phase 2)*

State	Description
1	No character yet processed
2	Processing integer part of number
3	Processing fraction part of number

Table 4.10. *Symbol-state table (phase 2)*

State	1	2	3
Character class 1	201	002	002
2	204	002	002
3	306	306	002
4	205	205	307
5	003	002	002
6	002	002	002

As for phase 1 there is an additional action (numbered 0) executed on entry to phase 2. This initialises the state and several other variables. The phase 2 actions are listed in Table 4.11. Note that a numerical item is first compiled in REALV. Just before the return from READIT the integer part is copied to INTEG. If the real value lies outside the range specified for integers the value of INTEG will be spurious and TYPE will indicate that a real number has been read.

We assume that the symbol-state table for phase 2 is stored in an array named SST2. The following working variables are used:

STATE — The current state number.

CLASS — The class of the character being processed. This is set by the function named CHCLS2.

PCH — A pointer running from 1 to NCH used for picking up a character from CHARS.

ENTRY — An entry taken from SST2.

N — An action number extracted from ENTRY.

SGN — An integer variable set to $+1$ or -1 according as a numerical item is positive or negative.

VDIGIT — The integer value of a digit derived from a digit-character.

F — The exponent of 0.1 used in compiling the fraction part of a number. For example, if $F = 3$ the clause $0.1 \wedge F$ will produce the result 0.001.

This concludes our presentation of an item-oriented input facility. If you program READIT (under that name or some other of your choice) you will have acquired a valuable addition to your library and will have liberated yourself from the constraints of language-provided input facilities some of which hark back to the days of 80-column punched cards. Another advantage which may result from using READIT is that it will occupy far less memory

Table 4.11. *Actions table (phase 2)*

Action no.	Program description
| 0 | ```
PCH=0
STATE=1
SGN=+1
REALV=0.0
GOTO ACTION 1
``` |
| 1 | ```
IF PCH=NCH THEN GOTO ACTION 8
PCH=PCH+1
CH=CHARS(PCH)
CLASS=CHCLS2(CH)
ENTRY=SST2(CLASS,STATE)
STATE=ENTRY/100
N=ENTRY-100*STATE
GOTO ACTION N
``` |
| 2 | ```
TYPE=3
RETURN
``` |
| 3 | ```
TYPE=4
RETURN
``` |
| 4 | ```
SGN=-1
GOTO ACTION 1
``` |
| 5 | ```
VDIGIT=CH-48
REALV=10*REALV+VDIGIT
TYPE=6
GOTO ACTION 1
``` |
| 6 | ```
F=0.0
TYPE=7
GOTO ACTION 1
``` |
| 7 | ```
F=F+1.0
VDIGIT=CH-48
REALV=REALV+VDIGIT*(0.1∧F)
GOTO ACTION 1
``` |
| 8 | ```
REALV=SGN*REALV
INTEG=INT(REALV) (Integer part function)
IF REALV≤-32769.0 THEN TYPE=7
IF REALV≥+32768.0 THEN TYPE=7
RETURN
``` |

space than the language input facilities which generally have to cater for all manner of seldom used formats. We say 'may result' because in some languages these will be loaded whether you use them or not.

The particular features of READIT as detailed above may not
```

exactly match your requirements but, provided you have understood the principle of symbol-state tables, you should have little
difficulty extending them to recognise additional item types.

Should you wish to further your knowledge of symbol-state
tables and their uses you should consult Day [13]. Now here is a
question for you to ponder. How does the use of symbol-state
tables relate to top–down program design?

4.3   Reading game commands

Equipped with a means of reading data items we now move
on to consider how to read a succession of such items as a
command.

In assembling items from their constituent characters we were
concerned only with matters of syntax. That is, no particular
meaning was attached to the items read – an item either conformed
to the grammatical rules, or it did not and was flagged as a fault. At
the command level we could continue the same approach by
checking that each item is of the expected type before interpreting
the command in the context of the game. However in most cases
this would carry game independence too far, and would result in
gross inefficiency. For example, a particular item might not only
have to be a name, but one drawn from a set of admissible names.
If the command is to be faulted because this name has been
mis-spelled it is better that the player is informed as soon as the
item has been keyed in, rather than wait until the whole command
has been typed. This requires that the command processor should
take some account of semantics from the start. An analogous
situation occurs in a language processor which must take account
of reserved words such as FOR, UNTIL, BEGIN, and END.
Where such reserved words are used in the syntax definition of a
computer language they are, in effect, being recognised as distinct
items in their own right. Some of the semantic rules have been
forced into the syntax.

SYNTAX DIAGRAMS

The most economic way of expressing rules of syntax is in
the form of a diagram. Readers of books on PASCAL will have
encountered these, but for some reason they are less often presented for other languages. They appear as networks with the
elements of the language sited at the nodes which are joined by
directed branches to indicate what may follow what. It has become

Real number :

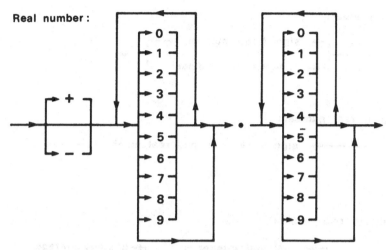

Fig. 4.1. Syntax diagram for a real number.

fashionable to smooth away all sharp corners in the branches and call the result a 'railway chart'. Perhaps the intention is to avoid any similarity with flowcharts, though anyone who could confuse the two might be well advised to take up knitting rather than programming!

To illustrate the basic concepts let us briefly return to the character level. Figure 4.1 shows the syntax diagram for a real number as recognised by the subprogram READIT (Section 4.2).

Any succession of characters encountered by starting at the left of the diagram and following the arrows constitutes a valid real number. Note that the item terminator is not included. A more useful representation of the same information is shown in Figure 4.2. Here the syntax has been modularised to reduce the complexity of the branching and to enable small sections of the syntax to be referenced by other parts of a larger syntax diagram. Although Figure 4.2 requires more space than Figure 4.1 big savings result from modularising the syntax for a complete computer language.

Figure 4.1 admits a single decimal point as a real number, as do the symbol-state tables of Section 4.2. READIT interprets such a real number as having the value 0.0, however this mode of representation invites error and some languages do not permit it. PASCAL, for example, demands that the decimal point be preceded by at least one digit, and its syntax diagram omits the dotted branch in Figure 4.2.

Real number:

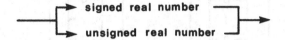

Signed real number:

Unsigned real number:

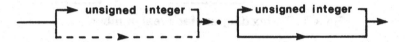

Unsigned integer: **Sign:**

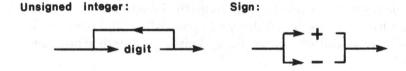

Digit:

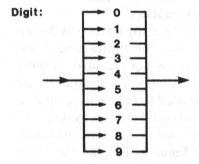

Fig. 4.2. A modular syntax diagram.

Where the diagrams of Figures 4.1 and 4.2 have single characters the syntax diagram for a game command has complete data items. As explained at the start of this section, we are interested not only in matters of grammatical syntax but also in attaching some meaning to the items. Thus names might be characterised as piece-names, unit-names, place-names and so on. At this point it must be emphasised that the term 'name' is used generically to mean an item starting with a letter. Many such names will not, in fact, be used as identifiers but will be words such as MOVE, REPORT, RESIGN, etc. Thus it is necessary to distinguish between items identifying the members of a class and those which are used as they stand – as literal constants. This is done by the use of brackets. If an item in a syntax diagram is enclosed in brackets it stands for one member of the indicated class. For example, (PLACE-NAME) shows that when issuing a command the player must substitute one name from the class of recognised place-names. Similarly (INTEGER) means any valid integer. An item not enclosed in brackets must be typed in as it stands.

A further useful modification is to incorporate any program-generated prompts in the diagram. Commands for many games, particularly simulation games, can be quite lengthy and the inclusion of prompts greatly improves the chance of typing a valid command. Well-chosen prompts make a games program 'player-friendly'!

Figure 4.3 presents the syntax diagram for the commands of an actual game simulating movement and pursuit across a terrain model (Chapter 7). Each side has a number of mobile 'units' assigned names in another program which creates a *database* for the game.

The term 'database' has become familiar to the public in the context of company and police records, and the associated problems of data privacy. The headline-hitting databases are very large and complex. However, size and complexity do not enter the definition of what constitutes a database, which is merely a set of stored operational data. The term 'operational' is used to distinguish the contents from input data and output data though, at some earlier stage, much of the contained data will have been input data. The database for the game in question is quite small by corporate standards but contains eveything defining the scenario for the game including the terrain model and a representation of the syntax diagram. We shall describe the latter after a short commentary on the material of the diagram.

Although it is not essential to an exposition of syntax and how it can be represented in computer memory, it would be somewhat insensitive to pass on without a description of what the commands

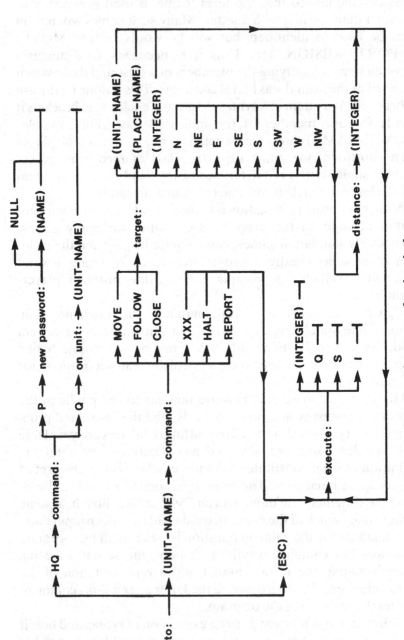

Fig. 4.3. Command-syntax of a simulation game.

embodied in the diagram actually achieve when the program is running.

The game proceeds in a series of phases in which the two players issue commands, the orders represented by the commands are communicated to the units concerned, orders currently in execution are continued if necessary or new orders are initiated, various reports are generated by the units, and these reports are communicated back to the players. The simulation is intended to be realistic and everything takes time. It takes time to issue an order, it takes time for an order to reach its destination unit, and it obviously takes time for most orders to be executed especially where they involve movement to some other part of the map. The units of the game may be vehicles, bodies of men, flocks of sheep, or anything suitably defined in the database. In addition each player has a special unit named HQ (headquarters) which performs administrative duties. In fact, HQ is sited within one of the mobile units, but the name HQ is used only when issuing commands related to security and advice.

A command starts with the prompt *to:* (all prompts are in lower case and finish with a colon) to which the player responds with HQ, a unit-name, or just hits the escape key (ESC) to end his phase of command input. If he hits (ESC) in any item other than the first his current command is abandoned and the machine again prompts *to:*. If the player has specified HQ he may hit either P or Q in response to the prompt *command:*. Hitting P enables him to reset his password which is used to prevent his opponent from issuing counter-productive commands on his behalf (see Section 3.2). One permissible response to the prompt *new password:* is the null item (READIT item type 1) which suspends the password checking. The response Q causes HQ to supply him with the latest estimates concerning the status and location of the named unit. The most accurate information comes from reports issued by the units themselves, but even this may be a little out of date because time is allocated to communications.

When the player responds to the prompt *to:* with the name of one of his units he may instruct it to move to a specified point; follow another unit; close with an opponent's unit (provided the latter is under observation) in order to catch it; or halt. The command XXX is used to cancel all uncompleted and pending orders received by the unit, and the REPORT command causes the unit to issue a report on its status and location. For an order involving movement there are many ways of specifying a target location. It may be another unit, a named place such as a village, a map reference given as a four-digit integer, or it may be a position relative to the current location of the unit when the order is initiated. The last method requires the specification of a compass bearing and a distance in metres.

The last clause of a command directed to a unit specifies when the order is to be initiated. An actual time within the next 24 hours may be given directly as an integer. For example, if the unit receives the order at 7 o'clock in the morning a time given as the integer 0600 would imply 6 o'clock on the next morning, whereas 1300 would mean 1 o'clock that afternoon. If the player hits Q in response to the prompt *execute:* the order is queued and will be initiated when all earlier orders for the unit have been completed. The response S means that the order will be initiated when the order currently being executed has been completed. The response I means: 'Drop everything and execute this order immediately on reception.'

The syntax diagram allows a few meaningless orders. For example, an XXX order is pointless if it is to be a queued order. Some allowances of this kind simplify the syntax.

The objective of the game is very flexible. The aim may be the capture of the opponent's HQ unit, the completion of a specified tour of named places, or it may be a cross-country race game.

It is hoped that the foregoing will satisfy the reader's curiosity about the nature of the game reflected in Figure 4.3. Let us now return to the matter of representing syntax within the machine.

INTERNAL REPRESENTATION OF SYNTAX

The representation of structured data, such as that pictured by a syntax diagram, is a big subject and one offering great scope for ingenuity. Deriving such representations is perhaps one of the most enjoyable of all programming tasks, and the efficient solution of problems associated with memory space and access time is central to the theory of language processing and database technology.

The data defining the syntax of a game (specifically of its commands) is generally static. That is, most games do not modify their own syntax. In a working database on the other hand the data grows or contracts as new information is gathered or old data is purged. Static data structures pose relatively few problems for the programmer, though it should be remembered that what will be static in its final form may well be dynamic during development. In this section we suggest one method of storing an internal definition of the syntax illustrated in Figure 4.3. After this, we take a more general view of structured data because the ambitious games programmer is certain to encounter plenty of it.

Let us remind ourselves of the purpose of an internal representation of command syntax. It has three functions:

(a) It must enable the program to validate the type of each item as it is keyed in by the player.

(b) It must invoke such program actions as are needed to carry the validation process into the area of semantics. In other words, it must determine if the command is meaningful in the context of the game.

(c) It must cause the relevant data to be stored in game-dependent variables to represent the internal form of the command – the *order*.

It is beginning to sound as though we have discovered a further use for symbol-state tables, and indeed they can fulfil the functions listed above. However the numbers of distinct inputs and program states are such as to demand a rather large table. Furthermore many of the entries are unused except for the purpose of reporting a 'wrong item' fault. We can do better by devising a *command control list*, which we name CCL, of the following form.

The integer array CCL is declared to have three columns, and in which each row corresponds either to a prompt to be output or to the player's response. The first column is associated with the actual I–O item. If it specifies a prompt then the second column indicates the number of alternative data items from which the player may select his response, and the third column is unused. If the first column relates to an input item then the second column contains a *pointer* giving the row index of the row holding the 'next' prompt, and the third column contains an action number.

The pointers and action numbers are perfectly straightforward, but the definition of an I–O item is a little more subtle. There are four kinds of I–O item.

(a) Prompt-texts for output.

(b) Input items of a specified type (see item table in Section 4.2).

(c) Input items which must exactly match some specified item (literal constants).

(d) Input items which must belong to a specified class of items such as unit-names, place-names, etc.

In Section 4.4 we discuss the storage and retrieval of text but for the present let us take it that any text, which may be a READIT text-string or name or a prestored prompt-text, is identified by a single integer *text-number*. We use the text-number directly to identify prompts and literal constants, but to specify only the type of an item we use the type-number. Clearly we must make sure that the ranges do not overlap. Items of a specified class have a *context-number*. For example, unit-names have context-number 1, place-names have context-number 2, and so on. To distinguish these from item type-numbers we add 100 to them before storing them in CCL. Here we have assumed that we require no text-numbers greater than 100.

Presented below are four tables (Tables 4.12–4.15) relating to the syntax diagram of Figure 4.3. Only Table 4.15, CCL itself, is complete. The actual game requires other texts, other item classes identified by additional context-numbers, and the actions table gives only a brief summary. However they will suffice to illustrate the main ideas.

The table for CCL is divided by horizontal lines to show the groups of rows associated with a single prompt and its admissible responses.

Use of the command control list

To use the array CCL for reading and checking a command the program executes a loop with one pass per clause of the command. A pointer variable P keeps track of the current row of CCL starting with P equal to 1 at the beginning of the command. The prompt text-number is given by CCL(P,1) and this is used to locate and output the prompt. The number of alternative player

Table 4.12. *Table of text-numbers (for relevant texts only)*

11	N	42	HQ	70	to:
12	NE	43	P	71	command:
13	E	44	Q	72	new password:
14	SE	45	S	73	on unit:
15	S	46	I	74	target:
16	SW	47	MOVE	75	distance:
17	W	48	FOLLOW	76	execute:
18	NW	49	CLOSE		
		50	XXX		
		51	HALT		
		52	REPORT		

Table 4.13. *Table of context-numbers*

1	UNIT-NAMES
2	PLACE-NAMES
3	PLAYER-NAMES
4	PASSWORDS
5	COMPASS DIRECTION (see later note)

Table 4.14. *Table of program actions*

1	No action
2	Record unit to receive this order
3	Terminate command input phase for the current player
4	Set new password for current player
5	Mark HQ-report on named unit due for output (soon)
6	Record type of order
7	Find location of named unit and store it as target
8	Find location of named place and store it as target
9	Store grid coordinates (map reference) as target
10	Record compass direction no. ($N = 1$, $NE = 2$, ..., $NW = 8$)
11	Convert distance and compass direction to grid coordinates (relative to unit location at some later time)
12	Mark order for execution at stated time
13	Mark order as queued (Q), soonest (S), or immediate (I)
14	Cancel current command
15	Issue assembled order. This action is automatically performed when the pointer (P) is zero, and after any other action indicated in the CCL row

Table 4.15. *Command control list – CCL(45,3)*

Row index	I–O	P	A	Comments
1	70	3	0	to: – prompt
2	42	5	1	HQ
3	101	16	2	(UNIT-NAME) by context no.
4	2	0	3	(ESC). End command input phase.
5	71	3	0	command: – prompt
6	43	9	1	P
7	44	13	1	Q
8	2	1	14	(ESC.) Cancel this command.
9	72	3	0	new password: – prompt
10	1	0	4	(NULL)
11	4	0	4	(NAME)
12	2	1	14	(ESC). Cancel this command.
13	73	2	0	on unit: – prompt
14	101	0	5	(UNIT-NAME) by context no.
15	2	1	14	(ESC). Cancel this command.
16	71	7	0	command: – prompt
17	47	24	6	MOVE
18	48	24	6	FOLLOW
19	49	24	6	CLOSE
20	50	40	6	XXX
21	51	40	6	HALT
22	52	40	6	REPORT
23	2	1	14	(ESC.) Cancel this command.
24	74	12	0	target: – prompt
25	101	40	7	(UNIT-NAME) by context no.
26	102	40	8	(PLACE-NAME) by context no.
27	6	40	9	(INTEGER) Map reference.
28	11	37	10	N
29	12	37	10	NE
30	13	37	10	E
31	14	37	10	SE
32	15	37	10	S
33	16	37	10	SW
34	17	37	10	W
35	18	37	10	NW
36	2	1	14	(ESC). Cancel this command.

Table 4.15. (*cont.*)

Row index	I–O	P	A	Comments
37	75	2	0	distance: – prompt
38	6	40	11	(INTEGER)
39	2	1	14	(ESC). Cancel this command.
40	76	5	0	execute: – prompt
41	6	0	12	(INTEGER) Clock time.
42	44	0	13	Q
43	45	0	13	S
44	46	0	13	I
45	2	1	14	(ESC). Cancel this command.

responses from CCL(P,2) is set in a counting variable N. READIT is called to accept an input item and the program then performs comparisons as prescribed by the values CCL(P + 1,1), CCL(P + 2,1), . . . , CCL(P + N,1) in succession until either a match is found or the alternatives are exhausted. In the latter case a fault message ITEM NOT RECOGNISED is output, and the player is asked to reinput the item. When a match is found, say at the Ith attempt, action number CCL(P + I,3) is performed, then P is reset to equal CCL(P + I,2). if the new pointer P is zero the end of the command has been reached, and the order assembled in various buffer variables is 'issued' to its destination unit.

To highlight the value of item classes identified by a context number we have deliberately withheld their use in respect of the compass directions N, NE, E, etc. Figure 4.3 included each of these as a literal constant but it should now be clear that they could be grouped together as a class in the same way as unit-names and place-names. In the presentation of the command control list this is evident from the fact that pointer and action numbers for each direction are the same.

4.4   Structured data – a general view

An experienced programmer might raise several objections to the somewhat ad hoc representation of command syntax described in the previous section. The most serious of these would be that changes in the command control list, such as arise during development and program enhancement, entail troublesome adjustments to pointers and option counts. In the following survey we discuss, with almost inexcusable brevity, some of the concepts and terminology used in the scientific treatment of structured data. These will suggest how we might better organise a representation of command syntax.

In describing syntax diagrams we used the word 'network'. This is a rather imprecise term with many other connotations, and information scientists borrow certain terms from mathematics to describe such networks.

Graphs and digraphs

A *graph* is a set of elements, together with a set of pairs of these elements. The elements can be represented by points, or *nodes*, and the element-pairs by lines, or *branches*, drawn between the appropriate pairs of nodes. If the order of the elements in a pair is significant the corresponding branch has an implied direction. This is indicated by drawing an arrow on the branch, and a graph containing such *directed branches* is known as a *directed graph* or *digraph*. Data of various kinds can be associated with the nodes and branches and the result is then called a graph, or digraph, *with assignments*.

These constructions are without doubt the most valuable abstractions of 'things' and 'relationships' and are used throughout computer science, operations research, physics, and many other disciplines. Theorems which have been proved for graphs (we understand the term to include digraphs as well as undirected graphs) can be carried over into the fields of applied mathematics and computer science and frequently enable us to handle problems in the real world with mathematical economy and insight.

Typical of the areas where graph theory has been used to model structured data is the analysis of flow in networks. Data assigned to the branches may represent actual and limiting flow-rates in terms of vehicles per hour for a traffic network, or in gallons per minute for a fluid distribution system. In the latter case node assignments might be used to represent the fluid pressure at pipe junctions.

Applied graph theory is a subject of great interest to the 'games-hunter', and makes quite modest demands on mathematical ability. Busacker & Saaty [14] provide a thorough and entertaining intro-duction to the subject.

The relationships expressed by a graph are *binary relations* – a branch has only two ends. What happens if the data assigned to a node depends upon a combination of the data assigned to two or more other nodes? Structured data might in general embody ternary or higher relations. Fortunately it is not necessary to move into higher dimensions because, by introducing additional nodes and branches, we can represent the conjunction of data and make it appear that all relations are binary. It is this ability to add or remove nodes and branches which gives flexibility to a representation of structured data.

Representing graphs in computer memory

Whilst we represent structured data as graphs with assignments, we must find a way to represent the graphs in computer memory. (Chains of representations again!) If, as is usual, a graph is to grow and contract it is highly desirable to allocate a fixed amount of memory space to each node and branch. Then, if it is necessary to remove a branch, or perhaps a node together with all of its branches, the space can be reused when new nodes and branches are introduced. The memory space allocated to a node is called a *node cell*, and that for a branch is called a *branch cell*. Each cell is divided into fields of two types – *pointer fields* and *data fields*.

The pointer fields contain pointers which enable the program to find its way around the graph. These are analogous to the pointers stored in column 2 of the command control list CCL described earlier. The data fields 'might' hold the actual data which has been assigned, but more often they hold further pointers. These enable the program to find the data in a separate area of memory. By using data pointers we avoid the potential dangers of mixing different variable types in a single array. This is, in any case, not permitted by many languages. It also guarantees that we can make all cells the same size. If necessary a single integer data pointer can be used to address another structured list holding an assortment of pointers addressing the data directly.

Figure 4.4 shows one method of representing a graph with assignments – a digraph in this instance. Four nodes are shown as shaded circles, and each of the five branches bears a bold arrow. The cells are superposed on the diagram, but are actually stored in a single integer array within the computer.

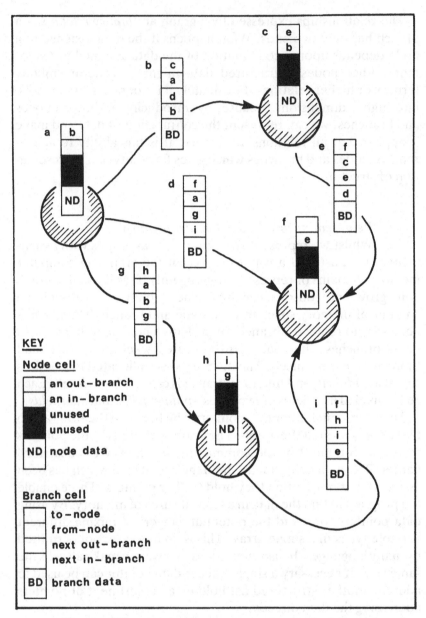

Fig. 4.4. Memory representation of a general digraph.

The letters a, b, c, . . . , i represent the addresses of the initial
memory locations for each cell. Thus, the node cell for the node at
the left of the diagram starts at address a. The following points
should be noted:

(a) To make all cells the same size two locations of a node cell are unused.

(b) A node cell refers to 'one' branch directed away from the node (an out-branch), and to 'one' branch directed towards the node (an in-branch). Which branches are chosen is not generally significant. Unused locations are left blank in the diagram – they might contain zero in the memory representation.

(c) A branch cell refers to the nodes at its two ends, to 'one' branch originating at its start-node, and to 'one' branch entering its end-node. Thus a branch belongs to two 'families' of branches – those leaving its start-node and those entering its end-node. The branch references form a circular list in each family. Hence if a family contains only one member – the branch itself – the branch cell refers to itself. When searching the branches in a family it is necessary to keep a record of where the search started so that it can be terminated.

(d) No counters of any kind are required, and the cells may be stored anywhere in the graph array in memory provided, of course, that the pointers are set accordingly.

The method of representation illustrated in Figure 4.4 is of a very general kind. It makes no assumptions about any special features which the graph may possess, and the program can use the pointers to gain access to any part. In many types of structured data, however, such omniscience is superfluous. It is fairly uncommon, for example, to need to look back at nodes whose out-branches are in-branches for a specific node. Usually one is more inclined to ask: 'Where am I going?' than 'Where have I come from?' This is the case for a syntax diagram which expresses a simple order-relation. The value of the general scheme shown in Figure 4.4 is that it offers a good starting point from which to 'tailor' a method to suit particular data structures. Let us at least begin this process for the command syntax hitherto represented by the command control list CCL. We shall not, however, present the finished article.

First, we must decide where to assign the data. Prompts must obviously coincide with nodes to avoid repetition. This suggests that players' responses should correspond to branches. However, every branch must end at a node, so we must introduce a terminal node for the whole command.

As we shall need to move forward from a node the node cell must include an out-branch address. In-branch addresses are of no interest here. The data field for the node cell must include a reference for the particular prompt – the actual prompt-text number would suffice. Several actions are more properly associated with nodes than with branches. These include the initialisations preceding the command input, and the operations involved in 'issuing' a complete command. Hence we include space in the node data field for an action number. This gives a total of three integer locations for each node cell.

A branch cell must include a to-node address so that we can find the next prompt if the player's response matches the data descriptor for the branch. Again, there is no requirement to get back to the start node so we can omit the from-node address. If the player's response does not correspond to the data descriptor it is necessary to find the next branch in the family of out-branches originating at the start-node for the current branch. We therefore include an out-branch address in the pointer field. We can omit any reference to a member of the in-branch family though it is worth noting that in some places the two families have common branches. For example, the nodes corresponding to the prompts *command:* and *target:* are linked by three branches corresponding to MOVE, FOLLOW, and CLOSE. The data field will include a data descriptor of the type listed under I–O in the table showing CCL. Also there must be an action number. This gives a total of four integer locations for each branch cell. To make all cells of equal size we 'pad' the node cells with one unused integer location.

For comparison with the general scheme of Figure 4.4 we summarise the node and branch cells for the syntax digraph below. In both, the first two locations constitute the pointer field, and the last two constitute the data field.

Node cells	Branch cells
Out-branch address	To-node address
Unused location	Next out-branch address
Prompt number	Data descriptor
Action number	Action number

If you feel moved to redraft the whole of CCL in this new form you will discover that it requires somewhat more memory space. However this is compensated for by the potential for easy modification, and the simplification of the programming. Should you be fired with enthusiasm for structuring your data, or wish to develop a database for a large scale simulation game you will find that Pfaltz [15] contains a great deal of practical advice replete with examples.

4.5   Storage and retrieval of text

Preceding sections have referred to text-numbers as a convenient way of identifying names and other character-strings. In this section we explain how such numbers are assigned and used. For brevity we refer to any stored character-string as a *text* – a slightly more general use of the term than that sometimes adopted.

A common problem arising in games programming, and one faced also by the compiler-writer, is to discover if a given text is present in a list of 'known' texts and, if so, to determine its text-number. If the given text cannot be found it may have to be added to the list and assigned a text-number for future reference.

For the compiler-writer these texts will be the names of variables and subprograms. They occur in large numbers and demand very efficient handling. For the games programmer they will be piece-names, place-names, command-codes, and so on. For him the problem is less acute because most texts can be recognised during the interactive phase of the program. Computation involved in searching for a text is effectively lost in the player's thinking time where the difference between delays of, say, 0.1 seconds and 0.001 seconds is hardly noticeable. Thus the techniques for handling texts in a language compiler are not normally required in a games program. There are several exceptions however. Adventure games (Section 2.5) frequently have to recognise players' textual responses in some profusion, and several word games need to ascertain if a word is present in a prestored lexicon, or has occurred at some earlier stage of play.

We describe three methods which are representative of the main approaches to text recognition. However, it is emphasised that there are literally hundreds of variations on these, each catering in different ways for variations in the quantity and nature of the texts concerned, and each attempting to strike the right balance between memory space and execution speed.

For many games the first method – simple linear storage and search – will suffice. Where there is a large number of texts the second method – hashing – should be considered. The third method, which might be called partitioned linear storage and search, is particularly applicable to games in which the texts belong to various classes, or occur in certain 'contexts'.

In each method we assume that the texts are stored in a single character array or vector named VEC. This is dimensioned to accommodate VMAX characters where VMAX is an integer variable initialised to some suitably high value. Other variables common to each method will be introduced once only, on their first occurrence.

(Some modern BASIC interpreters offer powerful facilities for addressing and comparing character-strings. In particular the elements of a dimensioned string variable can each hold a complete text. In respect of the methods about to be described this simplifies the programming a little, but does not invalidate the fundamental principles.)

Depending on the nature of the program and the inclinations of its programmer the texts stored in VEC could be read as input and stored whilst the program is running, they could be read from an external file, or they could be initialised directly in the source code by means of DATA statements or, in PASCAL, by constant definitions.

In presenting each method we assume that the text to be found has been read into the character array CHARS defined in Section 4.2, and has length NCH.

Method 1 – linear storage and search

Each text is addressed by the index of its first character in the text vector VEC. This address is **not** the text-number. That is the index of an element in another array holding the text addresses. This address array, named ADD, is of type INTEGER (two bytes per element). A further array named LEN holds the length of each text. Provided no text has a length greater than 255 characters LEN could be an array of type BYTE (one byte per element).

Let us assign the integer variable T to be the text-number which we wish to determine for a text stored in CHARS, and having length NCH.

Several other necessary variables, all of type INTEGER are listed below:

TMAX – The maximum number of texts permitted.

TNEXT – The next available text-number which will be assigned to the next text to be stored in VEC. If

VEC were empty then TNEXT would take its
initial value of 1.

VNEXT – The index of the next available element of VEC.

A – A working variable holding a text address.

C – A working variable holding a character pointer.

All this is summarised in the top half of Figure 4.5 which shows
the state of the arrays VEC, ADD, and LEN when three texts
PLAY, WIN, and GO are present in the list of known texts. T is
assumed to be equal to 2 in the diagram and might be used to pick
up the length LEN(2), equal to 3, for the text WIN whose address
is given by ADD(2), namely 5. The text itself starts in VEC(5).

The linear search for a text matching that supplied in CHARS is
illustrated by the bottom half of Figure 4.5. We have taken this
opportunity to show a simple program flowchart employing the
loop control symbol introduced in Section 3.2 and used in its 'while'
mode. For reasons of space (some might suggest lack of draughts-
manship) the condition associated with a test lozenge has been fully
written out against only one of the branches leaving the symbol.
The condition appropriate to the other branch is 'suggested' by a
single symbol. Whatever its shortcomings this is a form of contraction widely used in program flowcharts so it is as well to be aware
of it.

Using the linear search method an unknown text will require
TNEXT-1 comparisons most of which will involve only the length
test.

On exit from this piece of program T will be set equal to the
text-number of the text in CHARS provided that it occurs in VEC.
If it is an unknown text then T will be set equal to TNEXT, which
would facilitate its inclusion should that be necessary.

Method 2 – hashing

When the number of stored texts is large, or when it is
important to recognise an input text as rapidly as possible, the
linear search method is inefficient. In such cases the hashing
technique should be considered. The general idea is that the text
itself is used to give an 'intelligent' estimate of the text-number. If
this estimate is wrong it at least gives a good starting point for a
linear search. Obviously hashing is useless unless the known texts
have already been stored in accordance with the hashing system to
be used.

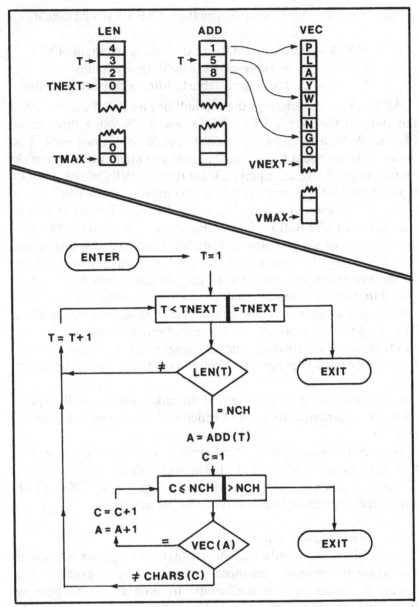

Fig. 4.5. Linear text storage and search program.

What we want is some method of transforming a text into an integer in the range 1 to TMAX. The relation is embodied in a *mapping function* which may well be programmed as a function subprogram implicitly called by a statement such as:

```
H=MAP(CHARS,NCH)
```

where H is the *hash-number* (the estimated text-number), MAP is the name of an integer function, and CHARS and NCH are the actual parameters of the function call. The operation of converting a text to its hash-number is usually called *hashing*.

Whatever method is used within MAP for hashing it should aim to satisfy the following criteria:

(a) Any given text should produce the same hash-number.

(b) Any two slightly differing texts should produce widely differing hash-numbers.

(c) Considering the entire collection of texts which will eventually be stored, they should produce an even spread of hash-numbers.

(d) The mapping function should operate rapidly.

Requirement (a) effectively precludes the use of random numbers in the mapping function – the same text must always map to the same hash-number. It is requirement (b) that gives the technique its name – we want the relation between texts and their hash-numbers to look as 'scrambled' as possible. If we can satisfy (b) we increase the chance that (c) will be satisfied. However, it is not in general possible to guarantee that two different texts will always result in two different hash-numbers. This should be evident when it is remembered that there is an astronomical number of possible texts whilst TMAX may be a quite small number – at any rate less than the memory capacity of the machine. When two texts do in fact produce the same hash-number a *collision* is possible. We shall return to the matter of collisions after suggesting the form of the mapping function.

In searching for a particular text the mapping function is evaluated once only so a reasonable degree of sophistication may be tolerable. However, we must be careful not to defeat the original purpose of hashing – high speed. Requirement (d) should be understood to mean that the time to evaluate a mapping function should be very small compared to the time needed for a full linear search (method 1 above).

The most generally useful method of hashing is *hashing by division*. First an *initial key* is derived directly from all or part of the text. This is an integer value lying in some range other than (1,TMAX). Second, this number is forced into the range (0,TMAX − 1) by taking the remainder after division by TMAX.

Finally, the result is augmented by 1 to bring the hash-number into the range (1,TMAX).

In the first step it is desirable to derive as large an initial key as possible subject to the ability of the machine to execute the subsequent division. Suppose, for example, that the initial key was derived simply as the value of the first character of the text. For ASCII this would lie in the range (1,127). As TMAX may be somewhat larger than 127 some potential hash-numbers would be unused and requirement (c) would not be satisfied. In practice most texts will start with a letter having an ASCII value in the ranges (65,80) for upper case, and (97,122) for lower case. This would reduce the quality of the mapping function still further.

A common expedient for obtaining a large (and random-looking) initial key is *folding*. Characters from the left-hand and right-hand ends of the text are added to an initially cleared integer variable. To enhance the contribution from the right-hand end of the text the byte order can be reversed. However we must be careful not to take bytes from outside the text. It will not do, for instance, to use CHARS(NCH − 1) if the text consists of a single character only! Furthermore, the matter of signs demands attention. The most significant bit of the internal representation of an ASCII character is zero so the equivalent short integer value (byte value) is positive. But if two such characters are added in a single-byte short integer, or to the most significant byte of a two-byte integer, the sign may be changed. It will be sufficient to conclude the calculation of the initial key with a call to the IABS (integer absolute value) function.

Having obtained the initial key in an integer variable, say K, we complete the derivation of the hash-number with a statement such as:

```
MAP=1+K-TMAX*(K/TMAX)
```

Notice that the assignment is made to a variable named MAP because the statement occurs within the function subprogram named MAP. The term (K/TMAX) represents an integer division.

In the academic computer literature a great deal of attention has been given to the problem of finding good mapping functions. Where the number of texts is very large, and where they must be stored on some backing medium such as magnetic disc, the matter is of great importance. However, the method described above should be adequate for most applications of home computers.

Now let us set the scene for a collision! An incoming text resides in CHARS in the usual way, and has length NCH. The mapping function is executed to yield a hash-number in H. To discover if H is in fact the correct text-number we first compare the respective text lengths NCH and LEN(H). If these are different we have a collision unless LEN(H) is zero. The latter eventuality indicates that no text has previously been stored under text-number H. Therefore the incoming text is not known and may require to be stored. If the two lengths agree it is necessary to compare the two texts character by character. Complete agreement indicates that the incoming text has been found and we may set the text-number T equal to H. Any discrepancy indicates a collision.

When a collision has occurred it becomes necessary to conduct a search. This could be a linear search similar to that used for method 1 with the difference that, because it starts with text-number H, the search must be circular. That is, texts $H + 1, H + 2, \ldots$ TMAX, then texts $1, 2, \ldots, H - 1$ are examined in this order. Again, it is emphasised that the procedure used for text storage must be identical to that used for pure search if inefficiency is to be avoided. In practice, the same piece of program can perform either function.

Clearly, we want the search to be as short as possible. The trouble is that, unless our mapping function is very good, we shall encounter 'clumps' of collisions. Suppose that a new text due for storage hashes to text-number 15 which we find to be already assigned to some other text. If the linear (circular) search procedure is employed we next try text-number 16. If this is assigned we try 17, and so on. It will be evident that, if there is the slightest bias in the mapping function as it operates on the particular texts of the dictionary, future searches will encounter a lot of collisions.

One method of reducing the tendency to clumping is to employ a non-linear search procedure. For example, the trial text-number might be increased successively by $1, 2, 3$, and so on. However, this is an area fraught with danger. It is essential that, in the worst case, every stored text will be examined once only. This can only be achieved if we accept constraints on the possible values of TMAX. Day [16] describes one technique in which TMAX may assume any value which is a prime number of the form $4n + 3$, the successive increments to the trial text-number being the absolute values of $2 - \text{TMAX}, 4 - \text{TMAX}, 6 - \text{TMAX}$, and so on. The derivation of non-linear search methods calls for some quite sophisticated number theory and the ordinary home computer user might be well advised to stick to a simple linear (circular) search.

Whatever search method is used it is important to be clear about its terminating condition. If no previously stored texts are ever removed from the dictionary the search may terminate as soon as an unused text-number is found. This would be indicated by an associated text length of zero. This is because if the incoming text were already present it would have been assigned this text-number, or one of those already tested in the search. On the other hand, if texts can be removed from the dictionary during the course of the run it will be necesary to continue the search either until the text is found or until the trial text-number is equal to the initial hash-number.

Method 3 – partitioned linear storage and search

It is often the case that an incoming text is associated with information additional to that provided by its characters alone. For example, it may be known that the text is, or should be, a piece-name. If through some error the text is in fact a place-name, that is of no great interest to the program, or to us. All we need to be told is that it is not a valid piece-name. The introduction of some simple pointer lists enables the program to limit its search to those stored texts which have the expected *context*.

The idea is that the set of all texts having the same context is assigned a *root text-number*. This is stored in an integer array called ROOT which has one element per context. Given a context-number X the search always starts with the text-number given by ROOT(X). Successive texts with context-number X are linked by a chain of pointers held in an array named LINK. A search ends when the required text is found, or when the current text-number is equal to the root text-number.

Figure 4.6 pictures an early stage in the construction of a dictionary which currently holds only three texts DOG, BITE, and CAT. The animals have text-number 2, and the verb BITE is the sole representative of context-number 1. ROOT contains the root text-numbers and has space for XMAX elements. LINK contains the succession of pointers for each context set. Note that these are organised in a circular fashion to facilitate the termination of any fruitless search. As context-number 1 consists of only one text its LINK element points to itself. All other lists are identical to those used in Figure 4.5.

The piece of program code at the bottom of the diagram is a subroutine for searching for an input text. If the text is found its text-number is returned in T. If the text is not found T is set equal

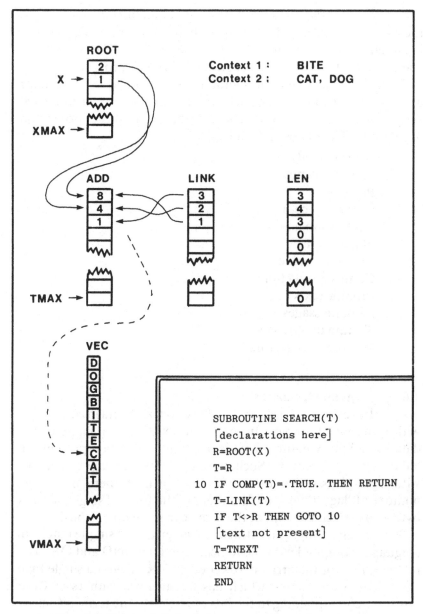

Fig. 4.6. Context-linked storage and search.

to TNEXT. We have assumed, for compactness, that the scope of the text lists covers the subroutine so that they are not needed as parameters. COMP is the name of a logical (or Boolean) function which returns the 'value' .TRUE. if the input text matches text T, and .FALSE. otherwise. COMP would contain code identical to the body of the main loop shown at the bottom of Figure 4.5. Comments have been enclosed in square brackets. The symbol <> stands for 'not equal to' as recognised in BASIC programs.

The author has found this method of text storage very useful for a number of simulation games. It may help those writing such programs to list some typical contexts. Not all of these correspond to texts which could occur as input items.

> *Some typical contexts*
> Players' names
> Passwords
> Unit or piece-names
> Unit-group names
> Place-names
> Command codes
> Compass directions
> Prompt-texts
> Fault messages
> Terrain descriptors
> Weather descriptors

4.6   Flags and bit-masks

In Section 4.2 we met the idea of packed data in connection with symbol-state tables. In other contexts it often happens that data has a binary nature. That is, each item of data represents an 'all or nothing' situation. Such items are known as *flags* by analogy with signal flags which may be 'up' or 'down'. If there are a large number of flags it pays to store them in the form of single bits in a byte array. Each element of the array can store up to 8 bits.

Setting, unsetting, and extracting a given bit is a simple matter in languages equipped with the logical functions AND and OR. The relevant byte of the array is AND'ed or OR'ed with a single byte variable – a *bit-mask* – which has been preset with 1s or 0s at positions corresponding to the bits of interest. The term 'bit-mask' is often loosely applied to any variable or array containing bit-flags whether it is used in logical masking operations or not. Assembly languages and microcomputer FORTRAN implementations have this capability, but many other languages do not. If your language has logical AND and OR functions their use will be explained in the programming manual, and here we shall concentrate on overcoming the problem posed by their absence.

Throughout we assume that the flags are stored in a one-dimensional array named FLAG. The bits within FLAG are numbered 1, 2, 3, . . . , 80 starting with the least significant bit of FLAG(1) and ending with the most significant bit of FLAG(10).

Testing a bit

Suppose we wish to determine if bit N is 1 or 0. First we must calculate the index of the appropriate byte within FLAG as:

```
I=1+(N-1)/8
```

using integer division.

Now let us assign local bit-numbers relative to the least significant bit of FLAG(I), which is numbered 1. The local bit-number is computed as:

```
J=N-8*(I-1)
```

We now want to test local bit-number J of FLAG(I).

The sign bit of an integer is the most significant bit, and the easiest to test. Thus, after copying FLAG(I) to a working integer variable K, we shift bit J up to the sign position. If J is equal to 8 the bit already occupies this position, but if J is less than 8 we must effectively multiply the integer by 128, 64, 32, 16, 8, 4, or 2 according as J is 1, 2, 3, 4, 5, 6, or 7 respectively. We say 'effectively multiply' because on a microcomputer it is considerably more efficient to use repeated addition to double the integer the required number of times. Thus,

```
K=K+K
```

shifts the entire bit pattern in K up one place, a zero bit being inserted at the least significant end.

After completing the shift operation(s) on K we simply test the sign of K. If K is less than 0 the bit of interest is a 1, otherwise it is a 0.

Setting or unsetting a bit

Without logical functions it is always necessary first to test the bit concerned. If we wish to set it to 1 when it is already 1 no operation must be performed. Similarly if we wish to unset it no operation must be performed if it is already 0. To change the bit we add or subtract a single byte bit-mask containing a 1-bit at the appropriate position. For this purpose it is useful to use a preset array of 8 bytes named MASK. MASK(1) contains 1, MASK(2) contains 2, MASK(3) contains 4, and so on to MASK(8) which contains 128. Thus to change bit J we add or subtract MASK(J) to or from FLAG(I).

Mathematical techniques for games

5.1 Introduction

This chapter concludes the discussion of particular techniques of general value which was started in Chapter 4. We now turn our attention to the features outlined in (c), (d), and (e) at the beginning of that chapter. These are more mathematical than logical in nature. Readers who have skipped Chapter 4 are referred to the comments on notation and game independence in Section 4.1.

5.2 Elements of probability

By their nature games involve uncertainty. Games programmers should therefore have some familiarity with the elementary calculations entailed in assessing the odds.

A *probability* is a number expressing the degree of certainty that some event will occur. By convention a probability lies in the inclusive range (0.0, 1.0). A value of 0.0 implies that the event cannot occur, whilst a value of 1.0 implies that the event is certain to occur.

A working interpretation of the meaning of a probability is afforded by statistics. Suppose that some event E can occur under a certain set of conditions. If these conditions were to be repeated a very large number of times – say, in some experiment – then the probability of E represents our estimate of the ratio:

$$\frac{\text{No. of times that E will occur}}{\text{No. of times that E could occur}}$$

For example, we might conduct an experiment ten times and obtain some specified result three times, seven of the experiments yielding some other result. We could then say that the probability for the occurrence of the specified result is 0.3. Supported by only ten experiments we would have little confidence that this is an accurate value for the probability. By performing many more experiments it is possible to obtain a more accurate value for the probability. That is, confidence in our ability to predict the results of future experiments would be increased.

It is sometimes convenient to express probabilities as percentages. This simply requires us to multiply each value by 100. However, probability calculations must always be conducted with values in the proper range (0.0, 1.0). We may convert to percentages only for the purpose of stating results.

Mutually exclusive events

Suppose that we throw a six-sided die. From the foregoing definition we know that the probability for throwing a particular value is 1/6. What is the probability that we will throw a number greater than or equal to 5? There are two ways of achieving the specified event – we could throw either a 5 or a 6. We cannot throw 'both' a 5 and a 6 in a single throw, they are mutually exclusive events, but their probabilities may be combined by addition. We calculate the probability of throwing a 5 'or' a 6 as 1/6 + 1/6, that is, 1/3.

More generally, the probability for the occurrence of one of three mutually exclusive events A, B, C having probabilities P_A, P_B, P_C respectively, is given by:

$$P_{A \text{ or } B \text{ or } C} = P_A + P_B + P_C$$

It is not hard to see that this addition law may be applied to any number of events provided they are mutually exclusive.

Complementary events

Every event E is associated with one particular event known as its complement. This is the 'event' **not** E. Obviously E and **not** E are mutually exclusive – at least, in our everyday experience! We know that the probability for the occurrence of one of these events must be 1.0. Therefore:

$$P_{E \text{ or } (\text{not } E)} = P_E + P_{\text{not } E} = 1.0$$

from which we see that the probability for the occurrence of the complementary event is given by:

$$P_{\text{not } E} = 1.0 - P_E$$

Independent events

Reverting to our die, suppose that we want to know the probability that two throws will each produce a 6. The result of each throw is completely independent of the other throw and we can combine the single-throw probabilities by multiplication. Hence we obtain $1/6 \times 1/6$, that is, $1/36$. More generally, the probability for the occurrence of 'each' of three independent events A, B, C having probabilities P_A, P_B, P_C, respectively, is given by:

$$P_{A \text{ and } B \text{ and } C} = P_A P_B P_C$$

As for the addition law relating to mutually exclusive events, the multiplication law may be applied to any number of events provided they are completely independent. However, the definition of what constitutes a set of independent events is more subtle than many people realise. It is not sufficient that every pair of events be independent. In fact every subset of events must be independent of every other subset. If you find this hard to believe consider this example:

Two coins are tossed. The three events 'first coin shows heads', 'second coin shows heads', and 'both coins show the same face'. Any pair of these events is independent, but one of them is not independent of the other two taken together.

5.3   **Random numbers and their use**

There is no such thing as a solitary random number. The number 517287, for instance, is no more random than the number 20. A number is random only in relation to a sequence of associated numbers every member of which lies in a predetermined range. To underline the importance of the range condition consider the sequence 17, 2, 98, 33, 35, 82, 49. Intuitively this appears to be a reasonably random sequence of integers. If, however, we are told that all members of the sequence are constrained to lie in the range (0,1000000) our opinion might change. We would be rather suspicious of the fact that all the members so far seen lie in the first ten thousandth part of the range. Should there not be an equal probability that any number of the sequence would lie in any other ten thousandth part of the range? Yes – provided that we are dealing with *uniformly distributed* random numbers. This is what people understand by the term 'random number'.

PSEUDO-RANDOM NUMBERS

Almost all computer languages provide a library function for producing a sequence of uniformly distributed pseudo-random numbers. The term 'pseudo-random' is used because each number in the sequence is generated from the number which preceded it. Thus each number is *dependent* on its immediate precursor. This is emphatically not the case for a sequence of *strictly random* numbers.

It is very difficult to produce a device which will generate strictly random numbers. Some machines which amplify electronic random noise have been built for the purpose, and are used in the selection of winning lottery tickets. ERNIE (electronic random number indicator equipment), used for drawing premium bonds, is a well-known specimen. But you will not be able to generate strictly random numbers on your home computer however cleverly you program it. Furthermore you will not need to. A sequence of pseudo-random numbers is far more useful because it enables development runs to be repeated under controlled conditions. During tests you will often need to be able to predict every member of a pseudo-random sequence of moderate length. By running a short program consisting of a loop for calling the random number function and printing the result, you can arm yourself with the necessary list. When running the test you must be careful to start the random number function at the same point of course.

Since we shall not be using strictly random numbers we will use the term 'random' to imply 'pseudo-random' from now on. As to the methods used for producing these random numbers, we shall not devote space to them here. Those few who use a language which is not equipped with the relevant function are referred to Tocher [17].

Range and type conversions

Language-provided random number functions produce a uniformly distributed random sequence of REAL numbers in the range (0.0, 1.0). More usually the games programmer requires random integers in some other range. Some care is needed in the conversion. It is surprisingly easy to obtain results which look satisfactory at first sight, and then to discover that an integer at one end of the range is never generated.

The following integer function produces random integers in the range specified by the parameters MIN and MAX. The range is *closed*. That is, the function is capable of returning a result equal to either parameter. The third parameter INV specifies an interval between numerically adjacent results. Hence the number returned by the function is drawn from the set MIN, MIN + INV, MIN + 2*INV, MIN + 3*INV, . . . , MAX − INV, MAX. The calling program must ensure that the range-size, MAX–MIN, is an integer multiple of INV.

```
INTEGER FUNCTION IRAND(MIN,MAX,INV)
INTEGER MIN,MAX,INV
INTEGER N,K,INT
REAL W,RAN
N=1+(MAX-MIN)/INV
W=N*RAN(1.0)
K=INT(W)
IF K=N THEN K=K-1
IRAND=INV*K+MIN
RETURN
END
```

N, W, and K are local working variables. RAN(1.0) represents a call to the random number function, and the parameter 1.0 is included because such functions do generally demand a parameter to specify whether the current sequence is to be continued, or a new sequence started. INT(W) represents a call to the 'integer part' function.

Typical calls to IRAND would be:

```
DELTA=IRAND(-1,+1,2)
```
Set DELTA to −1 or +1 with equal probability.

```
PERCNT=IRAND(0,100,1)
```
Produce a random percentage.

```
DIE=IRAND(1,6,1)
```
Simulate the throw of a die.

```
DIR=IRAND(1,8,1)
```
Select a random direction from the eight principal directions of a square grid.

```
DIR=IRAND(1,7,2)
```
Select a random direction from amongst the four orthogonal directions of a square grid.

If it is known that INV will always be equal to 1 the speed of IRAND can be increased by removing INV from the parameter list, removing the division in line 5, and removing the multiplication in line 9.

DISTRIBUTION OF A RANDOM VARIABLE

Up to now we have referred only to random numbers. A *random variable* is simply a variable assigned to hold a succession of random numbers. The concept is somewhat more general than the idea of a program variable, and the term is often used without reference to computers. We cannot know 'everything' about a random variable X unless we generate all of its values, say x_1, x_2, x_3, . . . This is obviously impractical in most cases, so we have to make do with a *sample* comprising some of the x-values. The degree to which the sample represents the behaviour of X depends on the size of the sample, and is the focus of much statistical attention amongst opinion-pollsters and their critics!

To investigate a sample we can plot a *frequency distribution*. This takes the form of a histogram, each block of which corresponds to a subrange Δx of the random variable. The height of each block is proportional to the number of occurrences of values within its associated subrange. In Figure 5.1 we show a typical frequency distribution for a random variable uniform in the range (1.0, 5.0).

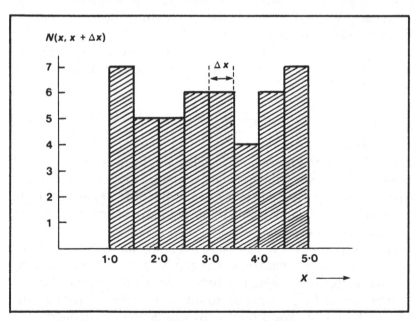

Fig. 5.1. A (uniform) frequency distribution.

The subrange size Δx has been chosen to be 0.5. If the histogram was produced from a very large sample it would have a much flatter top. For this reason a uniformly distributed random variable is sometimes described as being *rectangularly distributed*.

It is not so much the overall size of the sample which is important as the number of values falling within any block of the histogram. For example, we might subdivide the range even further until each histogram block contained only one or two values. Once again the top of the histogram would look jagged.

At this point let us distinguish between random variables which are *discrete* and those which are *continuous*. For a discrete random variable, such as that whose values are produced by calls to IRAND, there is a limit to the subdivision of the range. Strictly speaking this would be true for values produced by calls to a function such as RAN whose results are 'allegedly' real numbers in the range (0.0, 1.0). In fact a computer can represent real numbers to only a limited accuracy – certain values cannot be represented. Thus RAN, and all other real functions, produce 'pseudo-continuous' results. Nevertheless we regard them as continuous, and are prepared to indicate their behaviour with the use of smooth graphs. This continuous approximation of discrete quantities is very common in applied mathematics and statistics, but it can mislead the newcomer. We shall return to this topic when discussing another frequency distribution.

It is not always practical or necessary to draw a frequency distribution. There are more economic ways of characterising a random variable.

Mean and variance

Everyone knows how to calculate the average of a set of numbers. Because mathematicians recognise a number of different types of average they tend to use somewhat different terminology. What most people understand by an average is called an *arithmetic mean*, or simply a *mean*.

Let us suppose that ten measurements are made on the horizontal error in aiming a field gun. The gun is supposed to be pointing at some target but, owing to wobbly gunsights and an inebriated gunner, might be pointing up to one degree left or right of the target. We might expect these errors to be uniformly distributed between $(-1, +1)$ degrees, and the actual measurements result in:

$$(-0.9, -0.9, -0.7, -0.6, -0.3, +0.1, +0.1, +0.1, +0.8, +1.0)$$

For convenience the values have been sorted into increasing order. (If the measurements were in fact produced in this order we would suspect a *systematic* error rather than a purely random error.) We note with satisfaction that there are as many negative values as positive ones. Let us denote the random variable by X and the values it assumes in the 10 measurements by $x_1, x_2, x_3, \ldots, x_{10}$. The mean may be calculated as:

MEAN(X) = Sum of the 10 x-values divided by 10

It is very useful to have a symbol meaning 'sum of', and we use capital sigma (Σ) for this purpose, thus:

$$\text{MEAN}(X) = \sum_{i=1}^{10} x_i/10$$

This is read as 'the mean of X is equal to the sum of its values x_i (i running from 1 to 10) divided by the number of values, that is, 10'. Note that there is no ambiguity needing to be resolved by the use of brackets. We could calculate the sum first then divide by 10, or divide each value by 10 first then add the results together.

Completing the calculation we find that the mean is -0.13. For a series of only ten measurements this is not significantly different from zero so we might begin to have some confidence in an assertion that the angular errors are distributed about zero. Now we need to find out more about how the various measurements relate to the mean.

We define a number called the *variance* to characterise the spread about the mean. A somewhat old-fashioned term for the variance is *mean square deviation* which gives an idea of how it is calculated. We start by finding the difference between each value and the mean calculated above. These differences are squared so that we obtain a set of positive numbers, and finally we calculate the mean of these using the formula already described. Algebraically we can write this as:

$$\text{VAR}(X) = \sum_{i=1}^{10} (x_i - \text{MEAN}(X))^2/10$$

Evaluating this quantity for the sample errors we obtain a variance of 0.405. If in fact the ten values were uniformly distributed across the range $(-1, +1)$ the mean would be exactly 0 and the variance would be about 0.41.

The mean and the variance are the two principal parameters characterising a distribution but they do not uniquely determine it. Certainly the extreme values, -0.9 and $+1.0$, are of interest.

Standard deviation

The positive square root of the variance is known as the *standard deviation* of the sample. It gives us no more information than the variance of course, but it is often more convenient to work with. The symbol lower case sigma (σ) is normally used to represent the standard deviation. Another term commonly used for the standard deviation is *dispersion*.

The normal distribution

We have discussed uniform or rectangular distributions at some length. Now let us consider another distribution which occurs throughout nature and is of great interest to games programmers. This is known as the *normal distribution*. It appears when a measurement is subject to independent errors from a number of sources. The total error is the sum of the constituent errors, and takes values near some mean more often than elsewhere. In other words the total error is not uniformly distributed. A good example of this is afforded by the results of throwing a pair of dice. A single die gives a uniform discrete random value, but the sum of two dice gives a triangular distribution peaking at the value 7.

The form of the normal distribution is shown by the *normal frequency function* presented in Figure 5.2. We use the term

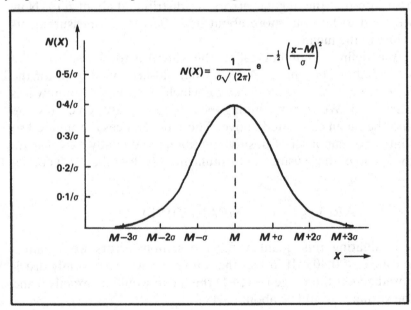

$$N(X) = \frac{1}{\sigma\sqrt{(2\pi)}}\, e^{-\frac{1}{2}\left(\frac{x-M}{\sigma}\right)^2}$$

Fig. 5.2. The normal frequency function.

'function' because we have assumed a continuous distribution which can be represented as a smooth curve specified by an equation.

It may seem strange that such a complex-looking equation can arise through the addition of simple uniformly distributed quantities. In part, it results from the fact that the normal distribution is exact only in the limit when the number of contributory terms tends to infinity. Where infinite series occur it is not so surprising that e (the base of the natural logarithms) appears. Other quantities involved in the equation are M the mean of the distribution and σ the standard deviation. The equation is given in its *normalised form* which effectively scales the values of $N(X)$ so that the total area under the curve is equal to 1.0.

$N(X)$ gives a continuous approximation to a normal frequency distribution which, in practice, would consist of discrete quantities. The histogram for the frequency distribution would follow the curve in a stepwise fashion. Suppose we were to take sample values from a normal random variable. $N(x)$ is not to be interpreted as the number of occurrences of the value x, but as proportional to the expected number of occurrences of a sampled value in a small subrange centred on x. Of course, if a larger subrange is used the quality of the approximation deteriorates.

Note that the curve is *asymptotic* to the line $N(X) = 0$ (the X-axis). That is, it gets closer and closer but never actually reaches the line. The area under the curve outside the range $(M - 3\sigma, M + 3\sigma)$ gives the probability that a sample value will differ from the mean by more than three standard deviations. It is useful to remember that this has the value 0.003 approximately. That is, three sample values in a thousand would be expected to differ from the mean by at least that amount.

Sampling from a random normal distribution
We know how to sample a uniform random variable – but how can we sample from a normal distribution? This is a common problem for the programmer of a simulation game in which certain events are subject to a large number of small errors. Such errors affect events such as the arrival of a vehicle at some specified point, and the fall of shot in gunnery.

The first essential is to decide upon the mean and standard deviation. For an arrival time problem the mean represents the result of an ideal journey affected neither by holdups nor by specially favourable intervals. In gunnery the mean would represent a direct hit. In many cases the standard deviation has to be derived by trial and error – starting with guesswork.

We present two methods – one of them fast but approximate, and the other slower but exact.

(a) *Approximate method.* Using the fact that the sum of a set of uniformly distributed variates tends to become normally distributed as the size of the set increases, we simply call a random number generator a number of times and add the results. If we add N such numbers, each in the usual range $(0,1)$, the mean tends to $N/2$ and the standard deviation tends to $\sqrt{(N/12)}$. (The derivation of the latter term is not given here but note that the 12 comes from the standard deviation of a single uniform variate in the range $(0,1)$ which is $1/12$.)

In practice, a good approximation can be found with N as low as 10 and this is the value adopted in the function RANORM below. The parameters MEAN and SD are the mean and standard deviation for the random normal distribution sampled on each call to RANORM. RAN(1.0) represents a call to the language-provided random number function as described for IRAND above.

```
REAL FUNCTION RANORM(MEAN,SD)
REAL MEAN,SD
REAL A,RAN
INTEGER I
A=0.0
FOR I=1 TO 10 DO A=A+RAN(1.0)
RANORM=1.095445*SD*(A−5.0)+MEAN
RETURN
END
```

(b) *Exact method.* This method was developed by G. E. P. Box & M. E. Muller, and is fully described in Tocher [17]. We cannot discuss the derivation here but would note that our presentation below amends a small misconception concerning operating speed (in Tocher), and takes about twice as long to produce its result as method (a).

```
REAL FUNCTION RANORM(MEAN,SD)
REAL MEAN,SD
REAL PI,A,B,ALOG,COS,SQRT
DATA PI/3.141593/
A=RAN(1.0)
```

```
A=-ALOG(A)
B=RAN(1.0)
RANORM=SQRT(A+A)*COS(PI*B)*SD+MEAN
RETURN
END
```

The function ALOG(A) produces the natural logarithm of its parameter A. COS is the cosine function, and SQRT is the square root function. These are provided in practically every language. Note that we have assumed that RAN never produces a value exactly equal to zero. If it did the call to ALOG would result in a run-time error, and it would be necessary to insert a test for A equal to zero after the first call to RAN, jumping back one statement if the test were satisfied.

5.4 Random walks on a square grid

Many simulation games are played over an area of ground represented within the machine as a *terrain map*. These maps are discussed in detail in Chapter 7. To facilitate the identification of points on the map it is considered to be overlaid by a square grid each intersection being addressed by two integers i (a row number) and j (a column number). A common problem is to generate a succession of points (i, j), each one step removed from its neighbours in the sequence but subject to random changes of direction.

Random walks are a topic of considerable interest in operations research and physics and in general involve some quite fearsome mathematics. However, none of this need concern the average games programmer. His random walks are of a simple kind and all he needs to know is how to generate steps efficiently and how to estimate some basic characteristics of a completed N-step walk.

Figure 5.3 shows a small portion of a square grid and some associated directional data. Surrounding the grid are the direction numbers adopted throughout this book. Thus north is identified as direction number 1, north–east as number 2, and so on. These numbers are used as row indices to locate the corresponding increments Δi and Δj in a small two-dimensional array named INCS.

To produce an *unbiassed* random walk of N steps we choose a starting point (i_0, j_0) and call a random integer function such as IRAND (see earlier) to generate a succession of uniformly distributed direction numbers in the range $(1, 8)$. As each new direction

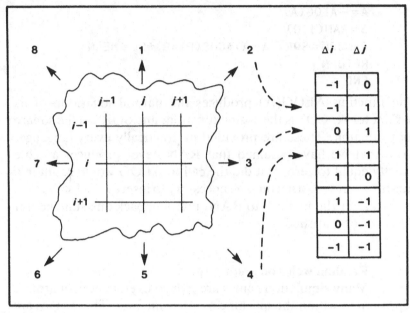

Fig. 5.3. Direction numbers and increments.

number is generated we increment the current point (i, j) to $(i + \Delta i, j + \Delta j)$, Δi being obtained from INCS(D,1) and Δj from INCS(D,2) where D is the current direction number given by IRAND. Of course it is necessary to ensure that the random walk stays within the limits of the grid.

In an *unrestricted* random walk the current point (the 'object' which is walking) may revisit points reached earlier in the walk, whilst in a *restricted* random walk this is precluded. Clearly a restricted walk may reach a dead-end before the requisite number of steps have been completed. At any stage the points which have been visited are surrounded by a *minimal rectangular envelope* – the smallest rectangle with sides parallel to the main grid lines which may be drawn around the points of the walk. The length of the longest side of this envelope is called the *diameter* of the walk, and the ratio of visited points to all points in the envelope is the *density* of the walk. It is useful to have some idea of the size of these various parameters when programming random walks. The values in Table 5.1 were obtained as averages in an extended series of trials and accord reasonably well with theoretical predictions. Note that they relate to an effectively infinite grid – the grid boundaries were not encountered.

Table 5.1. *Random walk parameters table (approximate values)*

	No. points visited	Diameter	Density
UNRESTRICTED WALK	$N/2$	$N/20$	0.29
UNRESTRICTED WALK (ORTHOGONAL STEPS)	$N/3$	$N/25$	0.33
RESTRICTED WALK	230	37	0.29
RESTRICTED WALK (ORTHOGONAL STEPS)	100	20	0.33

In the table N is the number of steps executed. For restricted walks a dead-end was reached after the specified number of steps on average. The second and fourth lines of entries relate to walks in which every step was made in an orthogonal direction (direction numbers 1, 3, 5, and 7). Note that the densities are independent of whether the walk was restricted or not!

Biassed random walks

For an unbiassed random walk the direction of each step is chosen from those allowed with equal probability. However, it is often useful to favour one direction or another. For example, when choosing the course of a river in setting up a terrain model one would favour the direction giving the greatest decrease in ground level.

Prior to executing each step of the walk we can set up a *probability vector* with eight elements, one per direction. The value assigned to an element gives the probability that the corresponding direction will be chosen. In a normalised probability vector the sum of the elements will be equal to 1.0. To select the direction for the next step of the walk we generate one uniformly distributed random number and perform a sequence of comparisons against the *cumulative* probabilities comprising the first element of the vector, the sum of the first two elements, the sum of the first three elements, and so on. When one of these exceeds the random number generated the stage reached indicates the direction to be chosen. No test is necessary after the 7th comparison because we know that direction number 8 must be selected.

5.5 Distance approximations

A common task performed by programs which simulate movement is to determine the distance between two points. A simulation game may have to execute code for this purpose many millions of times, and clearly it should be efficient. In many instances it is unnecessary to calculate distance to the full floating point accuracy of the machine. In such cases approximations may be used, and these can yield considerable savings in time.

First consider the accurate computation of the distance between two points whose coordinates are held in the variables X1, Y1, and X2, Y2. Most programmers would be quite happy to include a function subprogram DIST of the following form:

```
REAL FUNCTION DIST(X1,Y1,X2,Y2)
REAL X1,Y1,X2,Y2,DX,DY,SQRT
DX=X2-X1
DY=Y2-Y1
DIST=SQRT(DX*DX+DY*DY)
RETURN
END
```

This code evaluates Pythagoras' formula to the normal accuracy allowed by the machine. When distances are required at only a few places in the program it is more efficient to *open code* the assignment statements (insert them directly where they are needed) rather than call the function DIST. Whether DIST is called or not, there are two subtractions, an addition, two multiplications, and a call to the SQRT function. The latter might typically execute eight or nine additions and a similar number of multiplications.

The distance resulting from this formula is known as the *Euclidean distance*. We take this to be the 'true' distance between two points on a flat Euclidean plane in which the coordinate axes are embedded.

The Euclidean distance is not the only distance function known to science. One variant is the 'Manhattan distance', defined as the sum of the X and Y separations of the two points. This is the distance function of most concern to someone travelling across an American city with its rectangular 'block' layout. As an approximation to the Euclidean distance, it is poor. However, it suggests the form of an improved approximation.

Let us denote the coordinates of the points by $(X_1, Y_1), (X_2, Y_2)$. The positive separations are:

$$X = |X_2 - X_1|$$
$$Y = |Y_2 - Y_1|$$

Let U denote the greater of these two quantities, and V the lesser.

If X is equal to Y it does not matter which goes to U and which to V. The Euclidean distance E may then be approximated by a quantity D, having the form:

$$D = \alpha U + \beta V \quad (U \geq V)$$

where α and β are numerical coefficients chosen to minimise the *maximum absolute relative error* of the approximation. Let us consider the meaning of this.

Wherever the two points are situated we have derived two positive separations U and V, which represent 'projections' of the line joining the points onto the coordinate axes. We are interested in the error of the approximation as V goes from 0 (zero) to U.

Error

The *error* ϵ is defined as $E - D$; the *relative error* ρ is $(E - D)/E$; and the *absolute relative error* is simply the absolute magnitude of ρ, denoted $|\rho|$. It is convenient to express $|\rho|$ as a percentage. Thus, if $|\rho|$ is 0.5, we say that the *percentage absolute relative error* is 50%. As this is the only measure of error which we shall use, we abbreviate it to the *percentage error*.

First consider the Manhattan distance, which has $\alpha = 1$ and $\beta = 1$. The percentage error is zero when $V = 0$, but grows rapidly as V tends to U. When $V = U$ it reaches a value of 41%. If we set β to some positive value less than one, we can reduce the rate at which the percentage error increases. When $\beta = \sqrt{2} - 1$ we obtain exact agreement between E and D when $V = 0$, and when $V = U$. The maximum percentage error then occurs when V is somewhat less than $U/2$, and has a value of about 8.3%. By further reducing β we introduce some error when $V = U$, but decrease the maximum percentage error. The minimum of the maximum percentage error occurs when β takes a value of 0.336358. At this point our approximation $(D = U + 0.336358V)$ never varies from the Euclidean distance by more than 5.5%.

Next, we obtain another approximation by allowing α to vary. By reducing α we can obtain a better approximation at the expense of introducing some error when $V = 0$, that is, when $E = U$. The derivation of the optimal coefficients, α and β, may be carried out in a number of ways, but none is sufficiently short to be included here.

Table 5.2 summarises the various approximations, their maximum percentage errors, and speed improvement factors

Table 5.2. *Distance approximations table*

Number	Approximation formula	Maximum % error	Speed factor
(1)	$E = \sqrt{((X_2 - X_1)^2 + (Y_2 - Y_1)^2)}$	0.0	1.0
(2)	$D = U + V$ (Manhattan)	41.4	0.12
(3)	$D = U + 0.336358V$	5.5	0.19
(4)	$D = 0.960434U + 0.397825V$	4.0	0.25
(5)	$D = 0.9874U + 0.4501(V^2/U)$	1.7	0.43

obtained from trials run in FORTRAN on a Zilog Z80 based microcomputer. In addition to the linear approximations described above one non-linear formula is included. It is emphasised that the timings take into account the code needed to derive U and V.

Approximation (4) may be the most 'cost effective' for the purposes of simulation games. Note that the timings were made with a FORTRAN program. If an interpreter such as BASIC were used the savings in execution time would be smaller because the SQRT function is provided fully compiled – as object code.

Toleration of error

In the context of numerical analysis the errors resulting from the above approximations are large. However, they are acceptable in some circumstances. A simulation game may frequently have to determine the distances between two positions on a map in order to discover such information as:

(a) Whether town A is nearer to a given point than town B.

(b) Whether object A can be seen by object B.

(c) Whether unit A is within range of some weapon associated with unit B, or not.

For such purposes an error of about 4% may be tolerable.

Extension to three dimensions

In the foregoing discussion we have assumed that only the horizontal distance is required because the fact that two points may be at different vertical levels would have little effect on the true distance between them. Obviously, if the difference in level approaches the horizontal separation, all three components must be taken into account. This eventuality is unlikely in a game played on terrain, unless we have chosen a truly Alpine scenario. For space games it is clear that three dimensions must always be used.

We may extend the earlier approximations to three dimensions by simply applying them twice. First we approximate the distance in two of the three dimensions, then use this in conjunction with the third component of the separation. The order in which the components are used is important. Where we had two of these before, U and V ($U \geqslant V$), we now have three, U, V, and W ($U \geqslant V \geqslant W$). Let us apply approximation (4) as an example.

$$D = 0.960434U + 0.397825V$$
$$A = 0.960434D + 0.397825W$$

where A represents the required distance approximation. Substituting the expression for D into that for A we obtain:

$$A = 0.922434U + 0.382085V + 0.397825W$$

This approximation has a maximum percentage error of 7.8%, which is not very good. Furthermore, there is little saving in execution time. The moral is, 'don't use distance approximations in three, or more, dimensions'. In two dimensions, however, they are well worth consideration.

5.6   Simulation of motion

Most simulation games involve the movement of objects – people, vehicles, spaceships, etc. – across space. In many cases the space concerned is two-dimensional, or *locally two-dimensional*. By this we mean that an object is confined to an ordinary two-dimensional plane in its own neighbourhood. If it moves to a remote point it will still be confined to a plane, though one which is not necessarily parallel to that in which it started. It is a question of approximation. The object might actually lie on a curved surface, but to an acceptable degree of accuracy small changes in position are assumed to occur in a flat Euclidean plane. To allow for curvature large movements are compounded of a number of smaller steps, each of which is restricted to a 'local' plane.

Some games demand a genuinely three-dimensional treatment of space. Examples are aerial dog-fight games and certain space-travel games. In such cases the three coordinates of any point must be immediately available to the program, and the calculations use all three in equal measure. In other words, no direction is more 'important' than any other.

Apart from a few abstract games played on, or in, cubes three-dimensional games are not easy to play and require a lot of computer time for geometrical calculations. Wherever possible the games programmer should separate out two of the dimensions so that most the work relates to a plane with occasional 'interruptions' from the third dimension. This approach is particularly fruitful for games played over a computer model of terrain – a *digital terrain model* or *DTM*. The creation and storage of DTM's are subjects discussed in Chapter 7, and for the present we require no special knowledge of the techniques employed for these.

In this section we describe methods for simulating motion across a plane. Often this will correspond to a real horizontal plane superimposed upon a terrain surface. We shall regard the two coordinates necessary to locate a point in this plane as the 'main' coordinates, and the third coordinate specifying ground level (height with respect to some datum such as sea level) as a subsidiary value entering the calculations less often. Such an assumption is justified only if the terrain is reasonably flat with, say, no slopes exceeding 1 in 10.

Although we shall be concerned with planar motion this should not be interpreted to mean that the game is played over a feature-less plain. We shall certainly need to handle impassable ground and other obstacles.

COORDINATES

As described in Section 5.4 it is convenient to associate a square grid with the area of ground to be represented so that points can be identified by their coordinates. Figure 5.3 showed a portion of such a grid in which grid points were identified by row and column index numbers (i, j). These are, of course, coordinates of a restricted kind. They take only integer values and, if we regard the rows as running across the page with row number 1 at the top, are not arranged in the manner usually adopted for Cartesian coordinates. The Cartesian coordinates (X, Y) are normally expressed as actual distances (REAL values) with X relating to distance across the map-page and Y relating to distance up the page. The origin is usually chosen to lie at the south-western corner of the page. In some applications X and Y are referred to as *eastings* and *northings* respectively.

Thus we might consider that there are two systems of coordinates covering the same area of ground. The first could be termed the 'array system' and the second the 'Cartesian system'. There is, of course, no material reason why we should not view a two-dimensional array as having its first index i relating to array columns, and

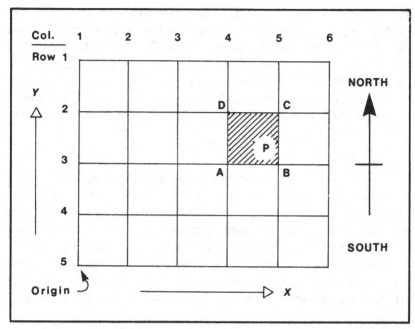

Fig. 5.4. Rectangular coordinate systems.

its second index j relating to rows numbered from the bottom of the page. The machine needs no information about how we write out an array on a sheet of paper. This would make the *sense* of the two systems correspond, and only two differences would remain. First the origin of the array system would be denoted (1, 1) rather than (0, 0). (In fact some languages such as BASIC and PASCAL permit array indices to run from zero.) Second there will generally be a difference of scale. To increment an index by 1 might correspond to some change other than 1 in the value of X or Y.

Most simulation games require to use both systems and Figure 5.4 summarizes the situation. The diagram incorporates the author's preference for viewing arrays in the conventional way. The grid points A, B, C, and D and the intermediate point P are included for future reference.

It is advantageous to impose a limit on the accuracy with which a point can be located. This enables the program to treat all coordinates as integers. An object can then be moved only between identifiable points. However, these need not necessarily be grid points. It is common practice to use a relatively coarse grid with each grid cell being subdivided by a finer grid. Under this system the position of a point could be specified in the form $(I, i: J, j)$ where (I, J) locates the south-west (or bottom-left) corner of a grid cell, and (i, j) locates the point within the cell in terms of an imaginary fine grid superimposed upon the main grid square. I, J, i, and j would each be held in an integer variable. In essence this is the map reference system used by the Ordnance Survey. They use a fine grid of dimensions 10 by 10 to facilitate visual interpolation.

MOVEMENT

To simulate the movement of an object is simply to amend its coordinates so that its new position reflects its speed and direction of travel over a specific length of time. The complexities arise because certain positions are forbidden and because the nature of the terrain might cause variability in the object's speed.

It is emphasised that we are concerned with overall movements of a 'reasonable' size such as may result from a player's command. For example, using the command syntax of Figure 4.3, he might specify:

to: JONES *command:* MOVE *target:* CARDIFF *execute:* I

The words in italics are program prompts, and the command says: 'Move Jones to Cardiff starting immediately.' It would not be realistic to immediately set Jones's coordinates to those of the place named Cardiff. Each cycle of the simulation will take a certain length of time – the *activity period* (see Section 6.2) – and Jones must be advanced by the correct distance each time the program deals with the matter of motion. Cardiff may be a long way from the current position of Jones when the command is initiated and much could happen to him on the way. In particular he may have to pick his way around Welsh mountains and avoid crossing rivers except by bridges. For the player to be responsible for all such 'minor' changes of course would be a prescription for tedium! What is needed is a reasonably intelligent movement algorithm which will continue without player interaction until the command has been completed. Of course, a well-designed program will allow the player to interrupt with new commands if he so desires.

We present a movement algorithm which goes a long way towards fulfilling the non-intervention requirement. First, however, we cover some preliminary ground-work.

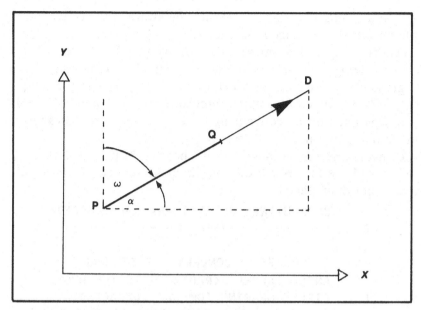

Fig. 5.5. Object moving from P towards D.

Directions and destinations

Every movement has a direction. However, we must distinguish between the overall *course* of the moving object and its *current direction*. The course is that direction which leads the object towards its destination 'as the crow flies'. The current direction is that taken by the object at any instant of time. The two may differ as a result of impediments which the object must avoid, or because the course is not a *feasible* direction in the immediate neighbourhood of the object. A direction which is not feasible (an *infeasible* direction) is one not permitted for mathematical reasons. For example, a direction which would immediately lead the object out of the area represented by the DTM is infeasible.

A direction may be specified in one of the following ways, each of which is briefly discussed with reference to Figure 5.5.

(a) *As an angle.* In the diagram α denotes an angle measured anticlockwise from the X axis. This is the angle normally used in trigonometric calculations. The units are 'radians', and α lies in the range $(-\pi, +\pi)$ by convention. However, the SIN and COS functions of a computer language will work correctly even when the angle lies outside this range. For example, $\alpha = -\pi/2$ is equivalent to $\alpha = 3\pi/2$. A programmer must be aware of the convention when using the arctangent function (see (d) below).

Another angle sometimes used to specify a direction is the *whole circle bearing*, denoted ω in the diagram. This is measured in degrees clockwise from north (the Y axis), and lies in the range (0°, 360°) by convention. Whole circle bearings are commonly used in navigation, and are convenient for representing direction angles in input and output operations.

Conversion from one angle to the other may be performed by the following FORTRAN subroutine, which is intended to be illustrative rather than efficient.

```
      SUBROUTINE CONVRT(ALPHA,OMEGA,MODE)
C     ---------- ------------------------
C
C     IF 'MODE'=1 CONVERT THE STANDARD
C     ANGLE 'ALPHA' (RADIANS) TO THE WHOLE
C     CIRCLE BEARING 'OMEGA' (DEGREES).
C     IF 'MODE'=2 CONVERT 'OMEGA' TO 'ALPHA'.
C
      REAL ALPHA,OMEGA,PI
      INTEGER MODE
      DATA PI/3.14159/
C
      GOTO (10,20),MODE
C
C     ALPHA TO OMEGA
C
   10 OMEGA=(PI/2.0-ALPHA)*(180.0/PI)
      IF (OMEGA.LT.0.0) OMEGA=OMEGA+360.0
      RETURN
C
C     OMEGA TO ALPHA
C
   20 ALPHA=(90.0-OMEGA)*(PI/180.0)
      IF (ALPHA.LE.-PI) ALPHA=ALPHA+2.0*PI
      RETURN
      END
```

(b) *As a compass bearing*. Compass bearings, N, NE, E, SE, etc. provide a convenient method for specifying a direction in the input data (player's commands), but must be converted to angles through the use of a look-up table.

(c) *As direction cosines.* These express the relative components of the direction along each of the axes. For a direction in the horizontal plane, the direction cosines are:

$$\delta_X = \text{Cos}\,(\alpha) = (X_D - X_P)/l_{PD}$$
$$\delta_Y = \text{Cos}\,(\pi/2 - \alpha) = \text{Sin}\,(\alpha) = (Y_D - Y_P)/l_{PD}$$

where l_{PD} denotes the distance from P to D.

Note how the sign of one of the direction cosines changes as point D moves north, east, south, or west of point P.

(d) *As a destination.* Here the direction is given implicitly. It has to be calculated from the coordinates of the object and its destination. Some care is necessary. FORTRAN includes a two-argument function ATAN2(Y,X) which will calculate α in the standard range $(-\pi, +\pi)$ when X is set to $X_D - X_P$, and Y is set to $Y_D - Y_P$. However, some languages provide only a single-argument arctan function which gives a result in the range $(-\pi/2, +\pi/2)$. The argument must be set to $(Y_D - Y_P)/(X_D - X_P)$ when the denominator is non-zero. When the denominator is zero, α is set to $\pm \pi/2$ according to Table 5.3) which also shows how the angle returned by the function must be amended to lie in the correct range.

Under (a), (b), and (c) no destination is known, and movement may continue, perhaps for many cycles, until it is interrupted for some reason. Under (d), a direction may be calculated as described above. We may convert forms (a), (b), and (c) into form (d) by

Table 5.3. *The arctan function*

$X_D - X_P$	$Y_D - Y_P$	New α
<0	<0	$\alpha = \alpha - \pi$
<0	=0	$\alpha = +\pi$
<0	>0	$\alpha = \alpha + \pi$
=0	<0	$\alpha = -\pi/2$
=0	=0	Indeterminate
=0	>0	$\alpha = +\pi/2$
>0	<0	No change
>0	=0	$\alpha = 0$
>0	>0	No change

creating a *pseudo-destination*. This is a point lying on the specified course, but at an effectively infinite distance away from the current position of the object. Using the direction cosines, we set $X_D = X_P + L\delta_X$ and $Y_D = Y_P + L\delta_Y$, where L is a suitably large value of distance, perhaps somewhat greater than the distance between the two most separated points of the DTM.

Of the various forms for specifying the course of an object, (d) is the most useful. Programming is easier if every moving object has a real, or pseudo-, destination.

We now present two methods for simulating motion. These are the *unit time step method* and the *unit distance step method*. In the first we calculate the new position of the object after a fixed interval of time has elapsed. In the second the object is moved a fixed distance, and the time required for the step is then calculated. In both methods the step-time will normally be much smaller than the activity period – the time over which motion is simulated in any one visit to the movement segment of the program. That is, on each visit to the movement segment, each moving object will execute a number of unit steps. This is because the activity period for movement will usually be too long to allow an adequate single-step simulation of the effects of local obstacles and changing terrain.

Unit time stepping

Let us denote the activity period by T, and the time step constant by t. T must be an integer multiple of t thus:

$$T = nt$$

where n is an integer constant initialised at the start of the simulation. For each moving object, the activity segment will execute at most n steps.

Referring to Figure 5.5, an object at P moves towards a destination point D. Before updating the coordinates of the object, the program must find its speed at P which may depend on many factors such as the type of terrain at P, the slope of the ground, the weather, and the state of fatigue. Let the speed be denoted v_P. The point Q indicates the position reached after time t. The coordinates of Q are given by:

$$X_Q = X_P + v_P t \delta_X \qquad Y_Q = Y_P + v_P t \delta_Y$$

where δ_X, δ_Y are the direction cosines described in (c) above. Note especially that the coordinates, and all other quantities, must be held in real variables.

Before the next step, a new speed must be calculated appropriate to point Q. After each step, a check must be made to find if the destination has been reached.

For implementation on microcomputers, this method has several disadvantages. Coordinates must be permanently stored in real variables, whereas in the unit distance step method to be described it is generally possible to use integer coordinates for much of the time. A severe shortcoming is that the task of avoiding obstacles, which involves changing the current direction, and the task of determining if the destination has been reached, require a great deal of computation. The unit distance method deals with these easily and efficiently.

Unit distance stepping

In this method all movement is conducted as a series of steps between neighbouring points of the fine grid described earlier. This grid is deemed to overlay the main DTM grid and will normally have a smaller interval than the latter. For most games it is convenient to use ten fine grid intervals per main grid interval.

Two types of step are allowed. Using the same system of direction numbers shown in Figure 5.3 we have *orthogonal steps* in the odd directions, and *diagonal steps* in the even directions. Orthogonal steps are of length d (the fine grid interval), and diagonal steps are of length $\sqrt{2}d$. After a step, from point P say, the program calculates the time required as:

$$t = kd/v_P$$

where v_P denotes the speed of the object at point P, and $k = 1$ for orthogonal steps, $k = \sqrt{2}$ for diagonal steps.

During each phase of movement these step-times are accumulated in a real variable T. When T exceeds the activity period the object is 'frozen' at its current position and the program moves on to treat the next object. The imbalance between the total movement time T and the activity period is called the *residual time*, and is used to initialise T before the object is again due to be moved. Put another way, residual time is time 'stolen' from the next activity period and used for the additional movement necessary to ensure that the object reaches an 'allowed' position at a fine grid point. This time must be subtracted from the next activity period for the object concerned. Thus each object must have its own residual time variable. In certain situations it is possible for the residual time to exceed the activity period. When this happens the residual time is reduced by an amount equal to the activity period but the object remains stationary until the residual time is less than the activity period.

Now, although d is used in the calculation of the step-time t, it is not a relevant parameter for operation of the movement algorithm. We shall therefore assume that the fine grid has a unit interval for this purpose.

The movement algorithm is a combination of two basic procedures introduced first.

(1) *The minimal distance procedure.* Suppose that the object starts at a point S and is ordered to move to a point D (the destination). During the journey the object may be forced to deviate from the straight line joining S and D. To attempt to move back onto the original course would be unrealistic and inefficient. At any stage it is preferable to move along the best route between the 'current position' denoted P and the destination D.

One obvious stepping strategy is to move the object to the neighbouring fine grid point which lies closest to D. Each pair of *unit increments*, shown in Table 5.4, is applied in turn to the coordinates (x_P, y_P) of P, to execute a trial step. For each new trial point we calculate the distance to D, perhaps using one of the approximation techniques described earlier. We obtain a (real-valued) distance for each of the eight basic directions in this way. These are then sorted (Section 5.7) in order of increasing magnitude. If the direction corresponding to the first element of the sorted list is feasible, and if the trial point lies on acceptable terrain, a step is executed. If the first direction is unsuitable, the second is tested, and so on.

A typical route resulting from the application of this method (over clear terrain), is shown at the centre of Figure 5.6. It is easy to see that such a route will sometimes deviate considerably from the original course.

(2) *The maximal projection procedure.* A second strategy is to execute each step along the direction which is most nearly parallel to the line joining P and D. Again, we construct a vector of eight real quantities, one for each direction. However, this time these are the *projections* of the line from P to D onto each of the basic directions, and the sorting is carried out in the opposite sense to that used in the 'distance' method. The direction which yields the

Table 5.4. *Direction numbers and increments*

Direction number	Δx	Δy
1	0	1
2	1	1
3	1	0
4	1	−1
5	0	−1
6	−1	−1
7	−1	0
8	−1	1

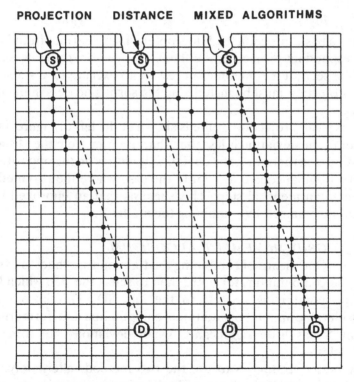

PROJECTION   DISTANCE   MIXED ALGORITHMS

Fig. 5.6. Performance of the stepping methods.

Table 5.5. *Direction cosines*

Direction number	δ_x	δ_y
1	0.0	1.0
2	$+1/\sqrt{2}$	$+1/\sqrt{2}$
3	1.0	0.0
4	$+1/\sqrt{2}$	$-1/\sqrt{2}$
5	0.0	-1.0
6	$-1/\sqrt{2}$	$-1/\sqrt{2}$
7	-1.0	0.0
8	$-1/\sqrt{2}$	$+1/\sqrt{2}$

greatest projection is the preferred direction, and will be used unless it is infeasible, or leads to unsuitable terrain.

To calculate a projection we use a pair of direction cosines drawn from Table 5.5. For any direction we select the corresponding δ_x and δ_y and evaluate:

$$PROJECTION = (x_D - x_P)\delta_x + (y_D - y_P)\delta_y$$

When a basic direction leads to a point which is further from D, the corresponding projection is either negative or zero. However, as will be seen, it is sometimes necessary to execute such steps, and the projection must be included in the sorting process in the usual way.

A typical 'projection' route is shown at the left of Figure 5.6. In general, the deviation is less than that resulting from the 'distance' method. Furthermore, the deviation is always on the opposite side of the original course, except in the case where the two methods indicate an identical step. This suggests that an improved route might be obtained by combining the methods.

GRID MOVEMENT ALGORITHM

One means of combining the foregoing methods is to carry out the computations for both, then to select the step which leads to the point lying nearest to the line SD. This introduces a considerable amount of additional computation and, furthermore, point S has little significance when deviations are forced by obstacles.

A better strategy is to use the two methods alternately. This produces an 'average' route, but deviations resulting from the 'distance' method still predominate.

Analysis has shown that the best approach is to execute a sequence of cycles each consisting of a 'projection' step, a 'distance' step, and a further 'projection' step. Denoting the two methods PROJ and DIST, the object moves according to the progression PROJ, DIST, PROJ, PROJ, DIST, PROJ, and so on.

A typical route for the 'mixed' algorithm is shown at the right of Figure 5.6. It should be noted that the line SD (the original course) has been chosen to lie at the angle which gives almost the worst performance of the two basic methods and, incidentally, almost the best performance of the 'mixed' algorithm. For many course angles, all three methods yield the same route.

Avoiding obstacles

There are many types of impediment to the progress of a moving object. Most vehicles cannot cross water, others may be prohibited from entering forest because of their size, and some may be confined to roads. There may be limits to the slope which can be climbed. In war games the 'objects' may be complete 'units' comprising many vehicles and large numbers of men. If the fine grid interval is small (100 metres is typical), the objects are, themselves, mobile obstacles.

The presence of all such obstacles must be tested **after** the sorting procedure has found an order of precedence for the eight basic directions.

Consider what might happen when a route is impeded. It may be that a considerable number of the directions from the current point P cannot be used, and the program must choose the best of those that can. Having executed a step from P, it is quite possible that the next step will return the object to P. Such loops can comprise any number of steps, so it is not sufficient merely to test whether the last point is about to be revisited. Without accumulating a growing mass of route data there can be no guarantee that looping will not occur. (See the note on shortest-route algorithms below.) However, it is possible to reduce its likelihood by discouraging sharp changes in direction. This can be achieved very simply.

As each step is made the program records its direction number in an integer variable. Before the next step is made, and before the sorting of the eight-element vector is commenced, the elements are *weighted* by the addition of suitably large values. The element corresponding to the reverse direction receives the largest weighting, the two directions adjacent to this reverse direction receive the

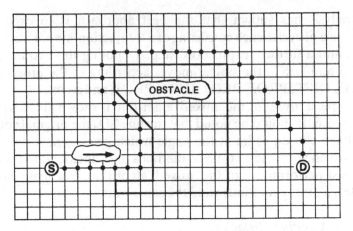

Fig. 5.7. Semi-intelligent route finding.

next largest weighting, and the two directions at right angles receive the smallest weighting. The particular weights used must be determined by trial and error during program development. In fact the task can usually be carried out with pencil and paper. Weights of 4000, 2000, and 1000 are usually adequate for most purposes.

Whilst the weighting approach cannot eliminate all looping, it does endow mobile objects with something which might be termed 'semi-intelligence'. A typical route around a large obstacle, obtained in an actual computer run, is shown in Figure 5.7.

Shortest-route algorithms

Some readers may be aware that there are powerful algorithms for finding the shortest route between points of a network such as a square grid, without any danger of looping. In principle these are applicable to the problem of simulated motion, but they have not been described for several reasons.

First, the network representing the fine grid superimposed on a DTM is normally very large. The methods so far described do not require an explicit representation of the fine grid, but the storage demands of a shortest-route algorithm would be beyond the capacity of most microcomputers. Second, to use such an algorithm is to assume that each mobile object has complete information about all areas of the terrain. This is often an unrealistic supposition in the context of a simulation game.

Despite such difficulties there is scope for ingenuity in reducing the size of the fine grid network, and for finding 'approximately' shortest routes. Should you wish to investigate such an approach the most efficient shortest-route algorithm is, for most purposes, Dijkstra's method which is presented in most books on optimisation (see for example Dreyfus [18]).

5.7 Sorting small lists

Every programmer needs, from time to time, to rearrange a list of numbers in order of decreasing (or increasing) numerical magnitude. Although this is not a particularly 'mathematical' operation it is included here to support the material of the preceding section.

The term *sorting* is applied to the operation of ordering a set of data according to some criterion. In most cases the final (sorted) order depends upon the numerical magnitude of a *key* associated with each group of items in the data. The keys are usually held in a list separate from the rest of the data, and are accompanied by pointers enabling the program to access the data associated with each key. Less frequently the keys are stored with the data and the sorting procedure physically rearranges both the keys and the data.

Figure 5.8 shows two representations of sorted data using separate key and pointer lists. The diagram does not illustrate any particular method of sorting – just the result of applying some sorting procedure.

The data groups, denoted ABC, D, EFG, and HI, have deliberately been given different sizes to emphasise the value of the data pointer list. Using data pointers enables the data to remain undisturbed – a great advantage if the volume is great or if it is held on some backing medium. The actual data pointers shown in the diagram are symbolic only. Typically they will be memory addresses or values for an array index.

In (a) the keys are sorted into numerically decreasing order, and the data pointers undergo exactly the same rearrangement. In (b) a new list of pointers is created to indicate the sorted order of the keys, but the key list and the list of data pointers are left in their original order. Obviously (b) demands more memory space than (a) but, for some methods of sorting, it facilitates faster operation. When programming a sorting procedure (a *sort* in the customary computer jargon) both representations should be considered.

Sometimes it is necessary to sort lists with no associated data! Or rather, the data consists only of the keys. An example of this was

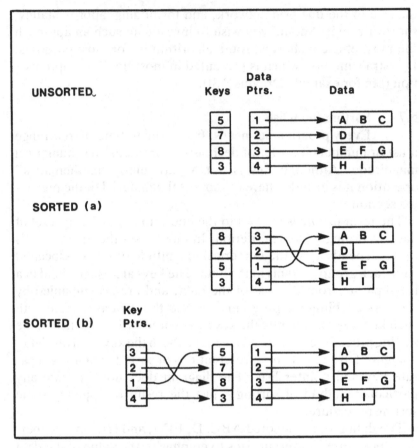

Fig. 5.8. Two representations of sorted data.

seen in the previous section where it was required to sort a list of real numbers in which the nth element measured the desirability of moving in a direction numbered n. The data items were the direction numbers $1, 2, 3, \ldots, 8$ 'implied' by the initial order of the keys, but not stored explicitly.

Three elementary methods

There are many methods of sorting. Those used in commercial data processing applications, where key lists can be very large and where each key may itself comprise more than one item, are often sophisticated and difficult to understand. However, for games programs, where key lists are practically always short, we can confine the choice to one of three or four simple methods.

Each method has its strengths and weaknesses which depend essentially on whether the initial key list is almost, partially, or completely unsorted. We shall give several of these methods no more than a passing mention, and will concentrate on a detailed presentation of one particular method – the *tournament* sort – which has certain advantages for the games programmer.

We assume that, in every case, there are N keys to be sorted, and that we wish to sort them into numerically decreasing order. To execute a sort in the opposite sense is simply a matter of changing a 'less than' test into a 'greater than' test, or vice-versa. Many sorts use the concept of *machine infinity*. This is a number greater than any element in the list of genuine keys. If all keys were 16-bit integers the programmer might choose 32767 as his infinity. Some sorts gradually replace sorted keys with infinities to guarantee that they stay at one end of the list or the other. Machine minus infinity is similarly defined as a number less than any genuine key, say -32766 for 16-bit integers.

The simplest, but least efficient, method of sorting is the *exchange* sort. The program makes $N - 1$ passes of the key list each of which results in at most one exchange of keys. Let us use MAX to denote the index of the largest key found during a pass. At the start of the first pass MAX is initialised to 1, then the program scans through the key list looking for a key greater than that held in KEY(MAX), where KEY is the name of the array holding the keys. As soon as one is found the value of MAX is changed to the index of the key concerned. At the end of pass 1 the keys held in KEY(1) and KEY(MAX) are exchanged, together with their associated data pointers if they exist. At the start of the second pass MAX is initialised to 2 and the pass starts at the third element of KEY. In general the Pth pass starts by initialising MAX to P, and the first element tested is KEY($P + 1$). It ends with the exchange of KEY(P) and KEY(MAX). The exchange method requires $1 + 2 + 3 + \ldots (N - 1) = N(N - 1)/2$ comparisons.

The exchange sort is economic with memory and quite adequate when sorting is executed only infrequently. Furthermore the code is very compact.

The *bubble* sort is equally economic with memory and is much more efficient provided much of the key list is already in the right order at the start. On the other hand, if the order of the keys happens to be the reverse of the required sorted order the bubble sort is just as inefficient as the exchange sort. If the keys are in a random order the bubble sort is about twice as fast as the exchange sort. The idea is to make repeated passes through the key list exchanging pairs of adjacent elements if they are in the wrong order. The sort is complete when a pass results in no exchanges.

The first pass will carry the smallest key through to the end of the key list. The second pass will carry the next smallest through to the last-but-one element position, and so on. Each pass may therefore be terminated one element before the last element of the preceding pass.

The *tournament* sort simulates a 'knock-out' context between the keys. Each pass consists of a complete tournament which finds a single winner – the largest unsorted element of the key list. In round one the keys are paired off KEY(1) versus KEY(2), KEY(3) versus KEY(4), and so on. In round two the winner of match 1 plays the winner of match 2, the winner of match 3 plays the winner of match 4, and so on. Eventually an overall winner emerges and his index number is recorded in a key pointer list (see Figure 5.8). For the next pass he must be eliminated from the tournament. This is done by resetting his key value to machine minus infinity so that he is a guaranteed loser!

All who have participated in knock-out tournaments will know that things get awkward when the number of competitors is not a power of two. Then, byes are necessary to ensure that the second round does involve a number of players equal to some power of two. For small lists we simplify matters by padding the key list up to the next power of two greater than N with machine minus infinities.

The important feature of the tournament sort is that after a winner has been found in any pass the next pass need examine only those matches which involved the winner – the result of every other match will be unchanged. The number of comparisons in a complete tournament sort is about $N \log_2 (N - 1)$.

This method may well be the best choice for the games programmer as it is efficient, and its performance is predictable and independent of the initial order of the keys. A disadvantage is the extra memory space needed for the key pointer list, a working list of results and, perhaps, a copy of the original key list which will be progressively invaded by minus infinities.

Tournament sort (FORTRAN code)
We present a subroutine in FORTRAN for executing a tournament sort on a list of 1, 2, 4, 8, or 16 keys. It is assumed that

the calling program will have provided any necessary padding of the key list. All keys are real numbers greater than −1000000.0 which is taken as the minus infinity. The key pointer list is named SORTED, the key list named KEY, and RESULT is a temporary working list local to the subroutine. There are N keys in KEY.

One reason for presenting this subroutine is to illustrate a trick ('technique' seems too grand a title!) concerning the use of RESULT. This simplifies the coding and speeds the execution.

As the sort proceeds RESULT is used to hold key pointers indicating the result of each match, but the tournament matches are numbered from N + 1, not from 1. It is supposed that there has been a 'qualifying' round of N matches which provided the N keys to be sorted. Thus the first N entries of RESULT are permanently set to 1, 2, 3, . . . , N. As there will be N − 1 tournament matches RESULT must be declared to have dimension 2N − 1. This enables first round matches to be handled by the same code used for later rounds.

```
      SUBROUTINE SORT(N,KEY,SORTED)
      IMPLICIT INTEGER (A-Z)
      DIMENSION SORTED(16),RESULT(31)
      REAL KEY(16),MINFIN
      DATA MINFIN/-1000000.0/
C INITIALISE RESULT VECTOR
      DO 10 K=1,N
   10 RESULT(K)=K
C SET MATCH-NUMBER LIMITS
      N1=N+1
      N2=N+N-1
C START PASS-LOOP
      DO 40 PASS=1,N
      I=-1
      J=0
C START MATCH-LOOP
      DO 30 M=N1,N2
      I=I+2
      J=J+2
      IF (PASS.EQ.1) GOTO 20
      IF (RESULT(M).NE.W) GOTO 30
   20 RI=RESULT(I)
      RJ=RESULT(J)
      RESULT(M)=RI
      IF (KEY(RI).LT.KEY(RJ)) RESULT(M)=RJ
```

```
      30 CONTINUE
   C  END OF MATCH-LOOP
         W=RESULT(N2)
         KEY(W)=MINFIN
         SORTED(PASS)=W
      40 CONTINUE
   C  END OF PASS-LOOP
         RETURN
         END
```

For those unfamiliar with FORTRAN we remark that the second line of code is a 'blanket' declaration stating that, with the exception of the REAL variables declared in line 4, all variables starting with the letters A, B, C, . . . , Z are of type INTEGER. The DATA statement in line 5 merely initialises the minus infinity MINFIN. The variables RI and RJ are introduced only because FORTRAN (in common with other languages) does not permit array elements to be used directly as array indices. Note that the winner of any pass always wins match number 2N − 1 (the final), hence his key pointer is always set in RESULT(N2).

5.8   Functions and interpolation

Function subprograms were introduced in Section 3.3 and have reappeared frequently thereafter. From time to time we have also referred to mathematical functions such as the normal frequency function without necessarily implying that they must be implemented through function subprograms. A mathematical function maps, or transforms, one set of numbers into another. For the mathematician this is not the whole story however. He has to consider functions which map single numbers (scalars) into single numbers, sets of numbers (vectors) into single numbers or into sets of numbers, and so on. He is also interested in functions which operate upon a single *independent variable* yet produce a whole family of distinct results. The square root function is a simple example of such a 'multi-valued' function because every positive number has two distinct square roots – one positive and the other negative. The SQRT function of a computer language produces only the positive value of course.

The functions of a computer language are of a quite restricted kind. Each produces only a single numerical (or logical) result. If it is desired to emulate mathematical functions of a more general nature it is necessary to use other types of subprogram, FOR-TRAN or BASIC subroutines, for example, with the results being communicated via a parameter list.

Computer scientists classify functions according to how they produce their results. There are two main classes.

A *formal symbolic* function is one which can be written as a single expression using the 'formal notation' of ordinary algebra, calculus, etc. FORTRAN and BASIC *statement-functions* are examples of this kind of function. The language processor normally handles these as macros (see Section 3.4 – notes on assembler coding). That is, the relevant code is copied into the program wherever the statement-function is used.

A *procedural* function is one which cannot be written out as a single algebraic statement. Functions involving condition tests are clearly of this kind. The majority of program functions are procedural either by nature or by choice. It is often easier to code a formal symbolic function as a procedural function to avoid long and complex program statements.

A type of procedural function which is particularly important in simulation games is the *tabular* function. Here the function is defined in terms of its values at fixed 'points'. Tabular functions arise when the mathematical form is unknown or involves lengthy computation. The tabulated points correspond to 'observed' function values, or they may have been worked out in some earlier computer run.

Let us denote the independent variable by x and its function value by $f(x)$. (Most tabulated functions are functions of a single variable. Functions of two or more variables often demand too much memory space for the table approach.) The tabulated points are denoted $(x_1, f(x_1))$, $(x_2, f(x_2))$, and so on. These are commonly represented as two one-dimensional arrays – the first holding values of the independent variable x and the second holding the corresponding function values. If the function is tabulated for regular increments of x the first array may be replaced by three scalar variables holding the initial and final values of x and the size of the increment. We note in passing that, if the function is tabulated at regular intervals, it may be feasible to handle functions of two variables in the form of a two-dimensional array. Digital terrain models (Chapter 7) store ground levels in this way.

The central problem facing the programmer is this. Given a value of x which does **not** correspond to one of the tabulated points, find a value of $f(x)$ consistent with the tabulated values. If x lies within the range of the table, (x_{min}, x_{max}) say, this process is called *interpolation*, if not it is called *extrapolation*. For most functions extrapolation is clearly an inaccurate procedure.

Linear interpolation
The simplest interpolation technique assumes that $f(x)$ may be taken as equal to the value of the function at the closest tabulated point. Thus a graph of the function comprises a series of steps. When the function varies rapidly this is a very crude method. The next simplest technique assumes that the function can be adequately represented as varying linearly between adjacent tabulated points. The two 'bracketing' points corresponding to the two values of the independent variable lying respectively closest below and closest above x must be found. Let us denote these by x_1 and x_2. The interpolated value is obtained as a linear combination of the two tabulated function values thus:

$$f(x) = \alpha f(x_1) + (1 - \alpha)f(x_2)$$

where α represents the ratio:

$$\alpha = (x_2 - x)/(x_2 - x_1)$$

Note that $f(x)$ will be equal to one of the tabulated values when $x = x_1$ or $x = x_2$. This is a fundamental requirement of any interpolation technique. For data which is subject to random error (noise) there exist *smoothing* techniques which relax this requirement. However, these are rarely of interest to the games programmer, and will not be discussed here.

Quadratic interpolation
If the tabulated function is known to vary smoothly an improved interpolation may be obtained by using the curvature information implicit in three tabulated values. Ideally these should be adjacent points lying on either side of x – two points on one side and one on the other. The following interpolation formula effectively fits a parabola to the three chosen points at x_1, x_2, and x_3.

$$f(x) = \frac{(x - x_2)(x - x_3)f_1}{(x_1 - x_2)(x_1 - x_3)} + \frac{(x - x_1)(x - x_3)f_2}{(x_2 - x_1)(x_2 - x_3)} + \frac{(x - x_1)(x - x_2)f_3}{(x_3 - x_1)(x_3 - x_2)}$$

where we have abbreviated $f(x_1)$ to f_1, $f(x_2)$ to f_2 and $f(x_3)$ to f_3.

It should be evident that this can be programmed efficiently by collecting the x-difference terms in temporary working variables.

If the table increment is constant the denominators are constant terms. Note also that the formula is independent of the order of the points. That is, it does not matter if x_1 is greater than x_2, x_2 greater than x_3, etc.

Polynomial interpolation

The formula given above is the three-point case of Lagrange's interpolation formula which may be used to fit any polynomial in x (an expression having the form $a + bx + cx^2 + dx^3 + \ldots$, where a, b, c, d are constants) to a set of data points. If the polynomial is of order n (the highest power of x) there must be exactly $n + 1$ data points used in the formula.

Sometimes it is useful to fit a polynomial to many of the data points in the table, and we therefore give the general form of Lagrange's interpolation formula below. This is followed by an explanation of the, possibly, unfamiliar symbols.

$$f(x) = \sum_{k=1}^{n} \frac{\Pi_{i \neq k} (x - x_i)}{\Pi_{j \neq k} (x_k - x_j)} f_k$$

The capital sigma means the sum of a series of terms the form of which is indicated on the right. The successive terms have $k = 1$, $k = 2, \ldots, k = n$. Each term consists of a numerator equal to the product of x-differences denoted by $(x - x_i)$ excluding the case when i is equal to k. The capital pi symbol denotes a continued product. The numerator is multiplied by its corresponding tabulated function value f_k. The denominator consists of a similar continued product excluding the case when j is equal to k. If the notation is unfamiliar to you compare the formula with that given above for the case of $n = 3$.

The general formula may be compactly coded with a loop for the summation enclosing two loops for the continued products. However, if n is fixed the code can be made much faster by ad hoc programming without loops.

6

Simulation games

6.1   Introduction

A simulation is an 'exercise' employing some mechanism which mimics the behaviour of a part of the real world. Let us distinguish between *research simulations* and *simulation games*. The objective of the former is to discover facts about some design or process (the *real system* under simulation) which might otherwise demand lengthy observation, after which it may be too late to rectify faults. Research simulations are normally run many times, the results being subjected to statistical analysis. Depending on the quality of the simulation and the number of trials performed the results may suggest improvements in the design of the real system.

Any research simulation can be the basis of a simulation game. The only necessary requirements are that human decisions influence the behaviour of the real system and its *model*, and that the players are interested in the subject concerned. In such a game the player is presented with problems which parallel those faced by a participant in the real system. He makes decisions which affect the state of the model, and these changes produce further problems requiring attention. Each player has a goal which corresponds to some terminal state of the model, the winner being the first to attain his goal. Obviously, the necessity for repeated runs and statistical analysis of the results are absent from a simulation game except, possibly, during development of the model.

Much of the fascination of a simulation game resides in the player's curiosity to discover how he might perform in situations that he is unlikely to encounter in real life. Would he make a good astronaut, a good Napoleon, or even a good pig farmer – and if not, why not? Clearly, to enjoy the game to the full there should be considerable confidence in the ability of the simulation to reproduce the behaviour of the real system at the level observable by a human participant. The last point is significant. A good simulation models no more detail than is necessary to give convincing responses. Of course, certain things are very difficult to simulate accurately. Napoleon, for all his faults, was an accomplished persuader of men. Wellington suggested how his effect might be simulated (very badly) when he said that his (Napoleon's) presence on the field made the difference of 40 000 men. Fortunately we can generally avoid these subjective matters. The performance of our pig farmer, for instance, will depend more upon his feeding schedules and less upon his powers of persuasion.

The role of the computer

The subject of simulation has a long history dating from well before the introduction of computing machinery. Let us briefly review the simulation game scene, and see how the home computer is affecting it.

It is generally easy to distinguish between games which simulate a real, or imaginary, world, and those which do not. In the former the player identifies with a role, whilst in the latter his part has more the nature of a system-element – a cog in the wheel. The classical games Chess and Go seem to be essentially abstract. Yet in their formative years they were possibly regarded as simulations. Both are idealised battle games, the latter on a more strategic level than Chess with its origins rooted in ideas of expansion and the acquisition of territory. As the centuries passed the thematic features of these games were displaced by a rising interest in their mathematical and logical characteristics. Thematic games need extensive rules and complex equipment if an adequate simulation is to result, and these inhibit propagation.

In modern times improved communications and market forces have reversed this trend to abstraction. Whilst the classical games retain their popularity, some games inventors have 'borrowed' their principles and mechanics, and have created more overtly thematic games. One published war game, for example, uses Chess pieces and movement rules to simulate a Napoleonic campaign played over a vastly extended chessboard. Other inventors try to be more original.

For a good simulation the logistic and administrative tasks are considerable. Nevertheless, recent years have seen a flood of simulation board games, the majority of which are war games.

Many of these are produced – quite justifiably – to a formula. Different games relate to different scenarios and different historical periods, but employ the same set of rules with minor variations. Enjoyable though they often are, few would claim that these games are easy to play. They generally utilise large numbers of tiny pieces bearing microscopic inscriptions which induce eye strain, and voluminous rule books which are equally liable to induce brain strain. Despite this they have an enormous and enthusiastic following sufficiently active to support three or four regular magazines.

The home computer can change, and slowly is changing, all this. Now, to a great extent, the rule book can be buried in the program. The machine can prompt the player's actions and answer questions about the permitted options. Both the scale and the accuracy of a simulation can be advanced far beyond the limits imposed by a purely mechanical realisation. In short, the computer can render a simulation game painless – for the player, if not for the programmer!

Continuous and discrete simulation

If, being unfamiliar with the topic, you were to visit a technical bookshop or library, you might come away with the impression that there are two different subjects called 'simulation'. One group of books is packed with differential equations, whilst another is far less mathematical and may contain frequent references to simulation languages.

The former group of books deals with the modelling of continuous processes in which the state of the real system changes smoothly with time. The latter group deals with discrete processes in which changes occur, or are presumed to occur, at distinct points in time. In fact the two approaches are much more closely related than might at first appear. The differential equations describing continuous processes are often too difficult to solve by purely analytical methods (algebraic substitution, calculus, etc.) and numerical approximation methods are used instead. Thus continuous systems are very often modelled by discrete processes, explicitly in a step-by-step simulation, or implicitly through the use of finite difference methods. Occasionally the converse applies and discrete systems are modelled by continuous processes if the scale allows, and if the resulting equations are sufficiently simple.

Most real systems exhibit both continuous and discrete modes of behaviour. We shall therefore assume that we are committed to discrete simulation.

Simulation languages

As we have referred to simulation languages let us dispose of them as quickly as possible! Simulation languages are intended primarily as aids to understanding common problems in areas of industrial process control and economics. They are equipped, for example, with means for defining the nature of queues and for simulating the progress of items through a queue. They are concerned with research simulations which are run repeatedly until the results furnish a statistically adequate sample. The necessary statistical tools are often incorporated in the language itself.

As a matter of interest simulation language programs are generally compiled into source code for another high level language such as ALGOL or FORTRAN. The latter may then be amended or augmented to cater for special circumstances before it is, in turn, compiled into object code.

For these reasons, and because simulation language compilers are not readily available for home computers, we shall not refer to them again. Whether there is scope for a 'simulation-game language' is quite another matter – I believe that there is, but the specification of such a language would be a considerable undertaking. We shall discuss this further in the final chapter of the book.

Which language, then, should we use for writing a simulation game? Franta [19] has estimated that around 70% of all research simulations are written directly in FORTRAN. From evidence gained in marketing an overlay system for microcomputers I would suggest that the percentage is even higher where this type of machine is concerned. The features of FORTRAN which make it attractive for this purpose are:

(a) It compiles into very efficient object code.

(b) Segments of code for independent simulation activities can be compiled and tested separately.

(c) The various constituents of the simulation can be assigned meaningful names within the program.

It is a feature of simulation, for research or gaming, that much of the execution time is spent in testing logical conditions. Run-time efficiency problems are not confined to simulations of course, but they can be particularly acute in simulation games because of their interactive nature.

The home computer programmer is therefore recommended to write in FORTRAN for simulation games of any size. Failing this, an assembly language should be used. BASIC and PASCAL interpreters are unsuitable for any but the most trivial simulations. All examples of source code in this chapter are in FORTRAN.

6.2   Time control

A discrete simulation proceeds according to a very simple plan. The program executes a series of *simulation cycles* in each of which a 'clock' measuring simulated time is advanced and then tested against a timetable detailing what activities are due. A simulation activity is an identifiable and distinct part of the simulation. In a large scale war game, for example, the activities might comprise the issue of orders, the transmission of these orders, the execution of movement orders, a combat resolution phase, the issuing of reports, the transmission of reports, the updating of weather conditions, and so on. Within each cycle the execution of activities proceeds independently, but conditions resulting from one activity may necessitate timetable amendments for other activities. In this section we shall discuss time control and the form of the activities timetable.

By the term 'time control' we mean simply the provision and maintenance of time variables used throughout the game. Just as you check your clock to decide if it is time to start a new task the program checks the time variables to decide if a new activity is due. The time variables which measure *simulated time* may vary considerably from the *real time* shown by a real clock. Thus, on your computer, you might play through a simulated expedition along the whole length of the Orinoco before breakfast, but the real time duration of the game may hardly be sufficient to fight off a couple of real anacondas!

If the simulated time is kept in step with real time the process is said to be a *real time simulation*. These find their principal application in training-simulators for pilots and astronauts. Real time simulations require the computer to be equipped with a real time clock accessible to the program. Although a number of home microcomputers are provided with such a clock the area of real time simulation is somewhat specialised, and often relies heavily on interrupt processing. It is therefore considered to be outside the scope of this book.

TIME ADVANCE METHODS

There are two main methods of time control in discrete simulations. These are the *event-driven time advance* method, and the *unit time increment* method.

In the first method the program starts a cycle by examining all possible *events*, which correspond to the initiation or resumption of an activity. The earliest event determines the amount by which the simulated time must be advanced. Thus, if an event is immediately due the time may not be advanced in the current cycle. Clearly, the time increments will not necessarily be constant. This method is inefficient for the simulation of continuous real processes such as motion, and will not be discussed further.

In the second method the cycle starts by executing a time control segment of the program which advances the simulated time by a predetermined constant amount. Later in the cycle the program executes every activity which is due at the current time. To balance the remark at the end of the previous paragraph we should mention that the unit time increment method is less efficient when all the real processes are discrete.

The unit time increment method is recommended for all simulation games.

Many simulations employing the unit time increment method maintain a single time variable T which holds the simulated time elapsed since the start of the run. Time is measured in units appropriate to the scale of the activities. In the time control segment, T is incremented by an amount held in another variable, say DT. The value in DT is often equal to one basic time unit, though this is not always the case. For example, we may have a program which measures time in minutes, but for which the increment is five minutes. DT would be set to 5, T would be initialised to zero and, as the simulation progresses, T would take successive values of 0, 5, 10, 15, and so on. In periods of relative inactivity the value of DT can be increased to improve efficiency, though possibly at the expense of accuracy. For example, the incidence of events may be far greater during daytime than at night. During the daytime it may be necessary to accept player's inputs at frequent intervals, but this could become pointless at night time, and one might wish to increase DT in order to compress the night into a small number of simulation cycles.

A single variable, T, is adequate for simulations which cover a short period of time. Programs which, for example, model an industrial process, or a queuing situation, are not usually concerned with operations lasting longer than a few hours. It may be irrelevant whether the process is carried out during the day or at night, whether it is springtime, or some other season. Games, on the other hand, frequently simulate a considerable span of time.

Even when the simulated duration is short, players may wish to be able to play the game during a (simulated) spring, summer, autumn, or winter when the weather and ground conditions may affect such parameters as vehicle performance, aircraft loading, and visibility. Hence, games programs frequently need a comprehensive set of time variables defining more than clock-time.

Typical time variables
We present here a typical system for time control in discrete simulation games, and discuss how it relates to the activities of the simulation. We define the following time and calendar variables with the indicated ranges which have been chosen to accord with the usual conventions rather than with programming convenience.

Variable name	Meaning and range
YEAR	The current year number (0,32767)
DAY	The current day number (1,365)
HOUR	The current hour (0,23)
MINUTE	The current minute (0,59)
SEASON	The season number (1,4)
DAYPHS	The day phase (1,4)
DT	The fundamental time increment measured in minutes

The season number 1, 2, 3, and 4 represents, respectively, spring, summer, autumn, and winter. The day phase number 1, 2, 3, and 4 represents, respectively, dawn, daytime, dusk, and night time. The following fixed data arrays are used to determine the season and day phase.

Array name and Dimensions	Meaning
SEAST(4)	A vector holding the day number on which each season commences.
DYPHST(4,4)	An array holding, for each season, the minute number within the current day at which each phase of the day commences.

Note that the minute number referred to in the definition of DYPHST is just 60*HOUR + MINUTE.

All the above are integer variables and, in the following
FORTRAN subroutines, are stored in a COMMON block named
TIME. In the time control segment the simulated time is advanced
by a call to the subroutine CLOCK.

```
        SUBROUTINE CLOCK
C       ---------- -----
C
C       ADVANCE TIME BY 'DT' MINUTES
C
        INTEGER DT,YEAR,DAY,HOUR.MINUTE
        COMMON /TIME/ DT,YEAR,DAY,HOUR,MINUTE
C
C       ADVANCE CURRENT MINUTE
C
        MINUTE=MINUTE+DT
C
C       ADVANCE CURRENT HOUR IF NECESSARY
C
     10 IF (MINUTE.LT.60) GOTO 20
        HOUR=HOUR+1
        MINUTE=MINUTE-60
        GOTO 10
C
C       ADVANCE CURRENT DAY IF NECESSARY
C
     20 IF (HOUR.LT.24) GOTO 30
        DAY=DAY+1
        HOUR=HOUR-24
        GOTO 20
C
C       ADVANCE CURRENT YEAR IF NECESSARY
C
     30 IF (DAY.LT.365) RETURN
        YEAR=YEAR+1
        DAY=DAY-365
        GOTO 30
        END
```

Note that subroutine CLOCK assumes nothing about the value of
DT, except that it must be a positive quantity. If it is known that DT
does not exceed 60 (minutes) all the unconditional jumps may be
omitted from CLOCK.

After a call to CLOCK, the program must set the appropriate season and day phase. The season must be set first because the day phase start times depend on the current season. Subroutines SEASET and DAYSET fulfil these tasks.

```
      SUBROUTINE SEASET
C     ---------- ------
C
C     SET CURRENT SEASON (NORTHERN HEMISPHERE
C     ONLY)
C     1=SPRING, 2=SUMMER, 3=AUTUMN, 4=WINTER
C
      INTEGER DT,YEAR,DAY,HOUR,MINUTE
      INTEGER SEASON,SEAST
      INTEGER K
      COMMON /TIME/ DT,YEAR,DAY,HOUR,MINUTE
     A              SEASON,SEAST(4)
C
      SEASON=4
      DO 10 K=1,4
      IF (DAY.LT.SEAST(K)) RETURN
   10 SEASON=K
      RETURN
      END

      SUBROUTINE DAYSET
C     ---------- ------
C
C     SET CURRENT DAY PHASE
C     1=DAWN, 2=DAYTIME, 3=DUSK, 4=NIGHT
C     NOTE: DAYMIN IS THE MINUTE NUMBER
C           COUNTING FROM THE START OF THE DAY.
C
      INTEGER DT,YEAR,DAY,HOUR,MINUTE
      INTEGER SEASON,SEAST
      INTEGER DAYPHS,DYPHST
      INTEGER K,DAYMIN
      COMMON /TIME/ DT,YEAR,DAY,HOUR,MINUTE,
     A              SEASON,SEAST(4),
     B              DAYPHS,DYPHST(4,4)
C
```

```
DAYMIN=60*HOUR+MINUTE
DAYPHS=4
DO 10 K=1,4
IF (DAYMIN.LT.DYPHST(SEASON,K)) RETURN
10 DAYPHS=K
RETURN
END
```

After each time increment, invoked by calls to CLOCK, SEASET, and DAYSET, the program must execute any activities due. We illustrate this for a hypothetical simulation game in which the players issue orders to a fleet of vehicles, and receive reports from the drivers. The program recognises three major activities which are handled by the following three subprograms:

ORDERS – Accept orders to drivers.
MOVE – Execute vehicle movement as directed by the player's orders.
REPORT – Output vehicle position and status reports.

Assume that orders may be accepted from each player at fifteen minute intervals, and that reports are issued every thirty minutes. Although reports are output at half-hour intervals, a driver may prepare a report at any time. For example, he may note the time and position at which his vehicle crosses a river, or reaches a town. He collects his reports and transmits them at the next half-hour report stage. Hence vehicle movement must be simulated with a finer time interval than that used for communication activities. We shall assume that vehicle positions are updated every two minutes. To hold this interval data we use a vector with three elements, one per activity. We also require a similar vector to hold the time elapsed since the previous call to each activity. These vectors are:

APV(3) – Activity period vector.
ETV(3) – Elapsed time vector.

The fundamental time interval DT must be set equal to a value less than, or equal to, the smallest of the activity intervals. Furthermore, it must be chosen so that each activity is a multiple of DT. If it were not, some activities would be subject to delay. A value for DT of one (minute) satisfies these requirements.

Below is a portion of FORTRAN source code from the time control subprogram of the simulation game which, as can be seen, is very simple.

```
....
....
....
C
C     INITIALISE TIME CONSTANTS
C
      DT=1
      APV(1)=15
      APV(2)=2
      APV(3)=30
C
C     INITIALISE ELAPSED TIME VECTOR
C
      DO 10 N=1,3
   10 ETV(N)=0
C
C     ADVANCE TIME
C
   20 CALL CLOCK
      CALL SEASET
      CALL DAYSET
C
C     ACTIVITIES LOOP
C
      DO 60 N=1,3
      ETV(N)=ETV(N)+DT
C
C     SKIP IF ACTIVITY 'N' NOT DUE
C
      IF (ETV(N).LT.APV(N)) GOTO 60
C
C     ACTIVITY 'N' DUE
C
      ETV(N)=0
      GOTO (30,40,50),N
   30 CALL ORDERS
      GOTO 60
   40 CALL MOVE
      GOTO 60
   50 CALL REPORT
C
```

```
C     END OF ACTIVITIES LOOP
C
  60 CONTINUE
C
C     NEXT TIMING CYCLE
C
     GOTO 20
     END
```

The above code includes the initialisation of the time increment DT, and the control vectors APV and ETV. The initialisation of the clock and calendar variables YEAR, DAY, HOUR, and MINUTE are presumed to have been performed at an earlier stage. In fact, it is advisable to initialise all the time, and time-dependent, variables in some sort of game definition database (Section 4.4) prepared in a separate run and loaded at the start of the simulation game. Such an approach obviates the need to amend and recompile the time control segment of the main simulation program each time the game is to be played under different initial conditions.

Notice that the sample of program has no apparent means of stopping. In practice, whatever the objective of the game, execution would cease in one or other of the activity segments when the terminal state is reached, or when the players direct termination in the orders input section.

Residual time

In the example above, each activity is invoked after a fixed period of time specified in the activity period vector APV. If, in the real system, an activity is continuous, then each call to the relevant activity subprogram must simulate action over that length of time. For example, vehicle movement is invoked every two minutes of simulated time, and the MOVE subroutine should simulate just two minutes worth of motion. However, this is not always possible. It is frequently convenient to constrain movement to the points of a rectangular grid at which terrain details can be specified.

In such a case, a travel time of exactly two minutes may leave a vehicle between grid points. To 'round off' by amending the vehicle's position to its nearest grid point is to run the risk, indeed the certainty, of accumulating error. Such error can be noticeable after a few cycles of the movement activity, and very serious thereafter. However, we can reduce error from this source by the use of a *residual time variable* for each vehicle. The movement activity is conducted in the following way, for each vehicle in turn.

The time allowed for vehicle movement is calculated as the activity period (from APV) minus the current residual time for the vehicle. The residual time for each vehicle is, of course, initialised to zero at the start of the game. If this allowed time is less than, or equal to, zero, no movement results, and the residual time is reduced by the activity period. If the allowed time is greater than zero, movement occurs until all the allowed time is used up. However, the actual time used may exceed the allowed time by a small amount. The residual time for the vehicle is then set equal to this discrepancy. In the next cycle of movement this residual time again amends the activity period to yield an allowed time, as described above.

The problem of accumulating error does not occur when movement is simulated with real position variables. However, discrete position variables, held as integers, are often used on microcomputers, which generally have no hardware for floating point arithmetic, and then residual time must not be neglected.

In the example, all activities are *explicitly scheduled*. That is, they occur at known points in time. In most simulations certain activities arise only as a result of some other activity. The subprogram handling this latter action may reset the activity period of the dependent activity so that it is executed in the current, or some future timing, cycle. We say that such a dependent activity is *implicitly scheduled*. Implicitly scheduled activities must have their corresponding periods stored in the activity period vector. However, when the activity is not *pending* the period is set to a very high value which cannot be reduced to zero in the elapsed time vector until it is marked as pending.

Is the sequence of activities within a single timing cycle important? If several activities are due for execution, the results of one may affect the other, and the final outcome may depend on which is done first. In general, the answer is that if the simulation is unduly sensitive to permutation of the activities, then the relevant activity periods must be reduced. Since each activity period must be a multiple of the fundamental increment DT, the latter may also have to be reduced.

Determining sensible values for the activity periods and the time increment DT which yield a good simulation without producing an inefficient program is part of the art of simulation.

6.3   War games

All the evidence suggests that war games are the most popular type of simulation game. That they are used in earnest by all modern armies for training purposes is beyond question. On the recreational front board war games sell in their millions and not only, as the myth goes, to aggressive young males. In the author's experience some of the most expert players are neither aggressive nor young, and by no means all are male. The fact is that a well-designed war game poses the most varied intellectual problems obtainable in a simulation game of any type.

In this section we propose solutions to some of the problems which arise in war games implemented on a computer rather than across a table. Problems of movement, visibility, and fatigue are common to most games played across terrain, so much of the material is relevant not only to war games but to games of pursuit, search, and cross-country race games of all sorts.

Much of the data used by a war game program is highly structured in the sense that one thing affects another, which in turn affects another, and so on. What affects what, and how, can be represented as a graph of relationships (often several disjoint graphs in practice), and the programmer is strongly advised to apply the ideas of Section 4.4 when implementing a war game. The program should be written so that it can be played at a rudimentary level early in its development. The adoption of structured programming practices and flexible data structures will allow the game to grow steadily until it reaches the required level of sophistication.

SIMULATION ACTIVITIES

In accordance with the general plan outlined in Section 6.2 the activities and activity periods of a typical war game for the modern period might consist of:

An orders input phase	– every 5 minutes.
A communications transit phase	– every 1 minute.
A reports output phase	– every 5 minutes.
A movements execution phase	– every 1 minute.
A unit observation phase	– every 2 minutes.
A combat resolution phase	– every 10 minutes.
A weather update phase	– every 60 minutes.
A fatigue update phase	– every 30 minutes.

As the communications transit phase occurs every minute,

orders and reports will arrive at their destinations at times other than those designated for execution and reports output. Clearly the program must be able to queue these for attention when due.

Note that no activity has been specified for the generation of reports from the units. This is because they are produced during the execution of the movement, observation, and combat phases as and when they are necessary. They progress towards headquarters (the player) during the communications transit phase and are queued for output in the reports output phase. It should be remembered that even with modern radio communications there is bound to be some delay before a commander receives the transcript of orders or reports.

It may seem surprising that observations are conducted at two-minute intervals only. This is likely to be the activity demanding the greatest share of computation time. In the least favourable situation it may be necessary to conduct N^2 observation tests where N is the number of units controlled by each player. Each test may involve testing a line of sight. These matters are discussed in later subsections.

OBJECTIVES

War game objectives are no problem except in so far as they are misunderstood by the newcomer. The game need not, perhaps should not, involve wholesale slaughter. Many of the best entail the achievement of geographical objectives – get so many units across a river by some specified time, for example. Neither is it essential for the forces to be balanced. The hidden movement potential of computer war games facilitates games of stealth in which a small force seeks to achieve an objective known only to itself whilst the stronger force attempts to find and destroy or impede the opposition.

UNITS AND UNIT TYPES

It is important to realise that, in the majority of war games, a 'unit' represents a considerable body of men, together with their vehicles and impedimenta. Thus, although we refer to the position of a unit, it may be quite an extended 'object', especially if it is in a dispersed formation. There are exceptions such as naval war games in which the units may represent single ships.

A considerable amount of memory space must be allocated to hold information about units, their status, and their capabilities. In what follows we sketch one approach to organising this data.

Table 6.1. *Unit and unit-type attributes*

	Unit attributes	Unit-type attributes
Constant	UNIT NUMBER Serial no. 1, 2, 3, ... for each player. UNIT NAME Text number (Sect. 4.5) UNIT-TYPE NUMBER	LIST OF ALLOWED FORMATIONS Predetermined e.g. 1 – column of march, 2 – dug in, 3 – open order, ... LIST OF TRANSPORT MODES Predetermined e.g. 1 – on foot, 2 – lorries, ... For each transport mode and formation: BASIC SPEED VISIBILITY ACUITY HEIGHT COMBAT PARAMETERS REDEPLOYMENT TIMES (See notes below)
Varying	POSITION COORDINATES (Sect. 5.5) STRENGTH % Units start at 100%. FATIGUE LEVEL % Fresh units at 0%. CURRENT TRANSPORT MODE Selected from list of allowed modes. CURRENT FORMATION NO. Selected from list of allowed formations. BINARY STATUS Single bits defining: Engaged or not. Bivouaced or not. Under observation or not. RESIDUAL TIME For grid-limited movement. (Sect. 6.2)	NONE

Notes
VISIBILITY and ACUITY are parameters relating to observation (see text).
HEIGHT is the height of an observer in a unit of this type.
COMBAT PARAMETERS depend on the historical period of the game and the methods used (see text).
REDEPLOYMENT TIMES are the times to change formation or, possibly, to change transport. They are normally stored in a 2-dimensional array.

First note that, although many units may participate in the game, there will generally be a limited number of different types of unit. In practice eight different unit types are sufficient for most games.

Table 6.1 lists a reasonably comprehensive set of unit and unit-type attributes. Some may be irrelevant for certain kinds of game. For example, in a battle game – a war game played at the tactical level over a short period of simulated time – units which bivouac would probably be regarded as mutinous!

Many of the quantities listed in the table can be stored in single-byte integers, and the binary status can be stored in a bit-mask (Section 4.6). The unit-type attributes – speed, visibility, etc. – might each be stored in a three-dimensional array with indices corresponding to unit-type, formation number, and transport mode.

Attenuation of parameters

The parameters which determine the performance of a unit at any given time and place are affected by the type of terrain, the state of fatigue, the weather, and so on. If these parameters were to be stored, in tabular form, for every possible combination of circumstances, no computer would have sufficient capacity to hold the resulting multi-dimensional arrays in memory. In practice, we are forced to assume that the various effects act independently.

An additional requirement severely limits the ways in which the program can cater for these effects. This is that it should obtain the same final value for a parameter irrespective of the order in which the effects are applied. This means, for example, that it should not matter whether we consider the weather before the ground slope, or vice versa, in deriving the actual speed of a unit. The effects must *commute*.

There are only two 'simple' ways to obtain such commutative effects. The first is *additive attenuation* in which each effect contributes a constant to be added (or subtracted) from the parameter. This is a crude method which could lead to nonsensical results such as negative speeds in certain situations. The second is *multiplicative attenuation* in which each effect is simulated by a constant *attenuator* which multiplies the parameter. This is the most widely adopted method.

(Strictly, an 'attenuator' reduces the value of the parameter concerned. Depending on the conditions assumed in determining the basic value stored with the unit-type attributes, some effects may actually increase its value. Nevertheless the term has been used in this context for many years, and it does avoid the use of certain overworked words such as 'factor'.)

Like the constant attributes in the table above, the attenuators are set once and for all. Most can be held in arrays of short integers as the percentage increase or decrease of the parameter to be attenuated. Thus, if a denotes an attenuator, and v the initial parameter, the new value of the parameter v' is given by:

$$v' = v(a + 100.0)/100.0$$

Note that we have used 100.0 rather than 100. We must avoid integer division. Parameters must be held as real numbers whilst in use though they can often be stored as integers with, or without, some implicit scaling factor.

Much of the skill in designing a good simulation resides in the correct choice of attenuators. Of course, in the design stages, some guesswork may be necessary but experience with the game will usually suggest refinements. As a rule it is a good idea to start by underestimating the size of the various effects.

Where the degree of attenuation depends on some variable such as a unit's level of fatigue, another formula is used. Suppose that we require to calculate the speed corresponding to a fatigue level of $f\%$. The attenuator a might be chosen to represent the percentage speed reduction corresponding to a fatigue level of 10%. If we denote the initial and final speeds as v and v' respectively, the formula to be used is:

$$v' = v\left(1.0 - \frac{a}{100.0} \cdot \frac{f}{10.0}\right) \quad (a \geqslant 0)$$

FATIGUE

We give here the briefest description of one method of simulating the accumulation of fatigue. Fatigue is assumed to be an exponential phenomenon, increasing only slowly at first and then becoming increasingly important. Recovery – the reduction of the fatigue level – during rest is also slow at first as anyone who has been woken after a short period of sleep can testify.

The maximum fatigue level of 100% is assumed to correspond to total exhaustion, but should not be reached by any unit with a responsible commander – perhaps!

The fatigue level F after a period of time t during which a unit has been engaged in some activity is given by:

$$F = F_0 e^{k_1 t} + k_2(e^{k_1 t} - 1)$$

where F_0 is the fatigue level at the start of the activity, and k_1, k_2 are constants. In practice it is inconvenient to use the formula in this form because the type of activity may vary during the period t. What is required is some method of increasing the fatigue level in each fatigue update cycle to take account of the work done in that cycle only. By expanding F as a Taylor series we obtain the approximation:

$$F_n = F_{n-1} + k_1 (F_{n-1} + k_2)\Delta t + k_1^2(F_{n-1} + k_2)\Delta t^2/2$$

where F_n is the fatigue level after the update (in cycle n), F_{n-1} is the fatigue level before the update, and Δt is the activity period for fatigue updates. Constants k_1 and k_2 are the same constants as were used in the first formula. For this approximation to be satisfactory Δt must not be too large. The following values give a satisfactory fatigue curve reaching 100% from 0% in 24 hours:

$k_1 = 0.0014$
$k_2 = 15.365$
$\Delta t = 30$ (minutes)

For recovery after a unit has bivouaced we use a similar formula:

$$F = F_0 + k_4(e^{k_3 t} - 1)$$

where F_0 is the fatigue level at the start of the bivouac and k_3, k_4 are constants. The Taylor series approximation is:

$$F_n = F_{n-1} + k_3(F_{n-1} - F_0 + k_4)\Delta t + k_3^2(F_{n-1} - F_0 + k_4)\Delta t^2/2$$

where F_n, and F_{n-1} are interpreted as before. Note that f_0 must be retained during the bivouac. Recommended values for the constants are:

$k_3 = 0.00585$
$k_4 = -1.709$
$\Delta t = 30$ (minutes)

One might expect the values of k_1 and k_2 to be subject to attenuation according to the unit's activity in the current simulation cycle. In most cases it is sufficient to attenuate only k_1 according to the transport mode. If formulae of the types shown above are unfamiliar it is valuable to write a 'research' program to gain some experience of their behaviour.

OBSERVATION

The capability for hidden movement is perhaps the greatest advantage conferred by the computer in the field of war gaming. Observation is clearly a matter of probabilities. If we know the probability that one unit will detect another in some given interval of time we can simulate observation by sampling a uniform distribution. For example, if unit A has probability 0.3 (or 30%) that it will detect unit B during one minute's worth of observation, the program can sample a uniform distribution of integers in the inclusive range (1,100) using a function such as IRAND (Section 5.3), then, if the result is less than or equal to 30, it is recorded that A has spotted B. If the result is greater than 30 A has not spotted B.

How can we determine the probability that one unit will spot another? Obviously it will depend upon the visibility of the target unit, and on the 'ability to observe' of the observing unit. We call the latter the observer's *acuity*. An objective measure of both visibility and acuity is essential.

Acuity and visibility

Imagine for a moment that there are such things as 'standard' observers and 'standard' objects to be observed. At some range (under ideal conditions) the probability that a standard observer will detect a standard object in, say, one minute of observation time, is 0.5. Now let us substitute a real observer (a unit in the game) for the standard observer. At the currently fixed range the observation probability will be different from 0.5, but we could move the standard object to some other range at which the probability returns to 0.5. For the present we define this range to be the acuity of the real observer.

Similarly, we could retain the standard observer but substitute a real object (another unit in the game). The range at which the observation probability is 0.5 is defined, for the present, to be the visibility of the real object.

For any combination of real or standard observers and objects let us call the range at which the observation probability is 0.5 the *half-range*. If we denote the half-range for the standard observer standard object situation by S, and for the real observer real object situation by R, it can be shown that S and R are related to the acuity a and the visibility v of the real observer and real object by:

$$SR = av$$

Now we would like to dispense with our hypothetical standard observers and standard objects about which we know next to nothing! If it happened that S was equal to R we would have the half-range for the real observer real object situation given by:

$$R = \sqrt{(av)}$$

This suggests a more practical composite definition of the acuity and the visibility. We simply say that the acuity and visibility are ranges satisfying the above equation for the half-range. Thus, a real observer with acuity 500 metres would detect a real object of visibility 2000 metres with probability 0.5 if the distance separating them was 1000 metres which is the square root of 500 times 2000.

The observation probability function

In general, observers and target units will not be separated by a distance equal to the half-range. We need to be able to calculate the observation probability for any range. The true form of this function is not, and probably never will be, known. However, common sense tells us that if the range is very small the probability will be very close to 1.0 (certainty), and if the range is very large the probability will drop to a value close to 0.0. Furthermore there is no reason to suppose that the function is discontinuous. If a close object is slowly moved away from the observer the observation probability will fall quite slowly at first. It seems reasonable to suppose that it will fall most steeply around the half-range. These considerations suggest that the function relating observation probability to range is an S-shaped curve similar to that marked (1) in Figure 6.1. The most manageable function displaying this behaviour is given by:

$$P = \frac{1}{2} - \frac{1}{\pi} \arctan (k(r - R))$$

where P is the observation probability, k is a constant, r is the actual range, and R is the half-range defined as $\sqrt{(av)}$. The slope of this function at a range r equal to the half-range is given by $-k/\pi$. If k were strictly constant for all observations the probability would fall at a constant rate near the half-range which seems unrealistic.

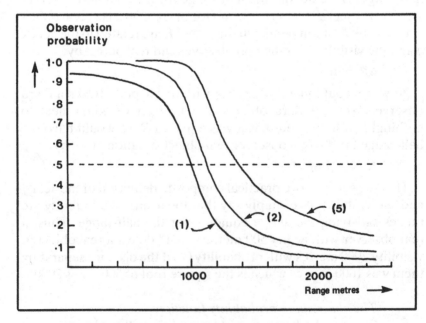

Fig. 6.1. Observation probability functions.

It would be better if the slope were made inversely proportional to the half-range, and a value of:

$$k = 2\pi/R$$

has been adopted with considerable success. Hence the following final form of P is recommended:

$$P = \frac{1}{2} - \frac{1}{\pi} \arctan \left(\frac{2\pi}{R} (r - R) \right) \quad (R = \sqrt{(av)})$$

Observation over extended periods

The observation probability P defined above is the probability that an observer of acuity a will spot an object of visibility v at a range of r (under ideal conditions) within a time interval of one minute. However, the activity period for observations will generally be longer than one minute. Supposing that it is n minutes – what is the observation probability over this longer period?

The probability that the object will not be observed in any one-minute period is just $1 - P$. The probability that it will not be observed in two one-minute periods is $(1 - P)^2$. In general the probability that it will not be observed in a period of n minutes is $(1 - P)^n$. Hence the probability that it will be observed, at some time, during the n minutes is given by:

$$P_n = 1 - (1 - P)^n$$

The behaviour of this function as it relates to P is illustrated in Figure 6.1. The curve marked (1) is the function P for observation over a unit time and the curves marked (2) and (5) are for two and five minutes of observation respectively. The acuity and the visibility are both assumed to be equal to 1000 metres, hence the half-range is also 1000 for P, but note how it increases as the period of observation increases.

Attenuation of observations

Attenuators for the observation phase should operate only on the acuity of the observing unit and the visibility of the target unit. Acuity will be affected by the state of motion of the observer and the type of terrain through which he is passing. Visibility will be affected by the time of day, the weather conditions, and the type of terrain in which the target unit is situated. Visibility may also be increased if the unit is on the move. Remember observation is not solely a visual activity. Motorised vehicles may be detected by their sound even in dense woodland.

A very important factor is the observation 'status' of the target unit. Once it has been spotted its visibility should be considerably increased. If contact is eventually lost its visibility reverts to normal.

Implementation notes
It is important to program the observation phase as efficiently as possible. Potentially there is a great deal of computation to be performed. The following approach is suggested.

In an outer loop the program selects the next target unit for observation. If this has status 'under observation' the known observing unit is tested first. If contact has been lost it becomes necessary to test the other units of the observing side either until one of the units spots the target unit, or until all observing units have failed to spot the target unit. Much time can be saved by rejecting all observations at a range greater than twice the half-range for the appropriate observation period. No great accuracy is required for this kind of test and the 4% distance approximation formula of Section 5.5 will suffice for calculating the range.

The observation probability function relates to 'ideal' conditions one prerequisite of which is, naturally, that there should be a line of sight from one unit to the other. The line of sight test should be left until last because it could entail considerable computation. As line of sight tests occur in other areas, in calculations relating to artillery for instance, the subject will now be presented in some detail.

LINE OF SIGHT CALCULATIONS
A common problem in games played over terrain is to determine if an observer at one point can see a 'target' object at another. Apart from considerations of observer acuity, target visibility, and observation probability (see above), it is necessary to establish if there is a clear line of sight (LOS) between the two points.

The condition that there is a clear LOS is simply that there is no point on the ground profile (long section) between the observer and target, whose *angle of elevation* exceeds the angle of elevation of the target. Figure 6.2 shows a ground profile (dashed) with an observer at the point marked 0 and a target object at the point marked n. As we are interested in all (or rather, many) points on the ground profile we invent a parameter i which takes integer

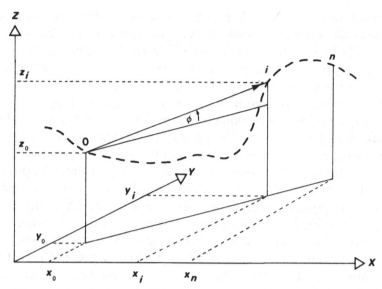

Fig. 6.2. A ground profile.

values from 0 to n along the profile. In the diagram, a typical intermediate point, marked i, is shown. Its angle of elevation ϕ_i is given by:

$$\phi_i = \arctan\{(z_i - z_0)/d_i\}$$

where d_i represents the horizontal separation of points 0 and i. A program could evaluate this expression for each point i in the range $(0, n)$ and perform the necessary comparisons with the angle of elevation ϕ_n. Fortunately, this is not necessary as many short cuts are possible.

First, we note that the computation can be stopped as soon as one point i for which $\phi_i > \phi_n$ is encountered. Second, we can avoid evaluating the arctangent because an angle in the range $(-90°, +90°)$ is *monotonically* related to its tangent. That is, there are no two angles in the range which have the same values for their tangents. As the angle increases so does the tangent. Thus, we perform the comparisons using the quantity in curly brackets, without calculating ϕ.

The third short cut involves substituting the absolute values of *projections* for the distances d_i and d_n. For example, we might substitute $|x_i - x_0|$ for d_i, and $|x_n - x_0|$ for d_n. Provided the projections are non-zero, the result of the comparison will be unaffected.

Whether to use X or Y projections is decided before any inter-mediate points are tested. We use the former if $|x_n - x_0|$ is larger than $|y_n - y_0|$, otherwise we use the latter. The quantity $(z_n - z_0)/|x_n - x_0|$ (or $(z_n - z_0)/|y_n - y_0|$) is evaluated once only, at the start of the sequence of tests. Let us denote it W_n. For each step along the profile, i is incremented, and $(z_i - z_0)$ is compared with $W_n|x_i - x_0|$ if we are working with X projections, or $W_n|y_i - y_0|$ if we are using Y projections. Note that this is faster than performing the division and comparing directly with W_n.

It remains to determine the number of steps n along the profile, and how the program is to advance to the next point. Assuming that the program is equipped with a movement algorithm of the type described in Section 5.6 this is a simple matter. We assume the existence of a special unit, a 'ghostly surveyor' perhaps, whose sole purpose is to travel between observers and targets and report his position and level after every step of each journey. Unlike other ghosts, he is permitted to cross water! If an elevation test shows that the remainder of his journey is unnecessary he moves instantly to the start of the next possible LOS profile. If he reaches a target a LOS has been established.

In general it will be necessary to allow for the operating height of an observer. For example, whilst his feet may be at ground level, a man observes at a height around six feet above them. Similarly, the size of the target may affect LOS calculations. There may be intervening woodland which effectively raises the ground level by some agreed amount. All such considerations may be treated by augmenting the levels z_0, z_i, and z_n.

MODELLING COMBAT

In 1916 F. W. Lanchester published an analysis of combat situations which is accepted as valid by all except, it seems, those who design recreational board war games! We outline the basis of his analysis here. A thorough presentation can be found in Braun [20].

The mistake which many designers make is to assume that the final outcome of an engagement is proportional to the numbers of combatants on each side, whereas in fact it is the *damage rate* which is proportional to these numbers. Consider an engagement in which unit A is fighting with unit B. Let us use A and B to denote the number of combatants on each side at any time t during the engagement. (Depending on the types of unit, A and/or B might equally well represent the number of tanks, the number of aircraft, etc.) If A and B are not too small, if all parts of each unit are active in the engagement, and if neither side gets reinforcements during combat, we have:

$$\frac{dA}{dt} = -b^2 B \quad \text{and} \quad \frac{dB}{dt} = -a^2 A$$

where a^2 and b^2 are the *combat effectiveness coefficients* of units A and B respectively. We use squared quantities only to ensure that they are positive, and to avoid the occurrence of square roots at a later stage.

For those unfamiliar with the calculus the first equation says simply that, over a short interval at time t the value of A decreases at a rate proportional to B, the constant of proportionality being b^2. The second equation says the same sort of thing about B.

Dividing the two sides of each equation, one into the other, the rules of calculus tell us that we obtain:

$$\frac{dA}{dB} = \frac{b^2 B}{a^2 A}$$

Integrating this from time $t = 0$ to time $t = T$ we have:

$$a^2 A_T^2 - b^2 B_T^2 = a^2 A_0^2 - b^2 B_0^2$$

where A_0, B_0 are the number of combatants at time $t = 0$ (the start of the engagement), and A_T, B_T are the (lower) values at time $t = T$. In a fight to a finish either A or B will fall to zero. As the right-hand side of the last equation is constant unit A wins if $a^2 A_0^2 > b^2 B_0^2$ and unit B wins if the opposite inequality holds. In reality a fight to a finish is very rare. Units should normally break off the engagement after they have sustained losses around 30%, or lower.

What the last equation tells us is that the total effectiveness of a unit is proportional to the *square of the number of combatants*. This is known as Lanchester's Square Law. Thus, if the player of a war game combines two units of the same type the net effectiveness is four times the effectiveness of one unit operating alone.

To simulate an engagement continuing over a number of combat cycles we must discover how A and B change with time. Returning to the first two equations we can differentiate the first with respect to time then substitute for dB/dt from the second equation to obtain:

$$\frac{d^2 A}{dt^2} = a^2 b^2 A$$

This may be solved to give:

$$A_T = A_0 \cosh(abT) - B_0\left(\frac{b}{a}\right)\sinh(abT)$$

where cosh and sinh denote the hyperbolic cosine and hyperbolic sine functions respectively. These are defined as:

$$\cosh(x) = (e^x + e^{-x})/2 \quad \text{and} \quad \sinh(x) = (e^x - e^{-x})/2$$

In a similar way we can obtain for B_T:

$$B_T = B_0 \cosh(abT) - A_0\left(\frac{a}{b}\right)\sinh(abT)$$

If the combat activity period is fairly long, so that A and/or B are liable to be substantially reduced in each cycle, it will be necessary for the program to evaluate the expressions for A_T and B_T above. Few languages are equipped with the hyperbolic functions SINH and COSH so it may be necessary to program them directly with the exponential function. If, on the other hand, the combat activity period is short, it may be sufficient to decrement A by an amount equal to $\Delta t b^2 B$, and B by an amount equal to $\Delta t a^2 A$ in each combat activity period of length Δt. Obviously the combat efficiency coefficients a^2 and b^2 must be set to represent the damage done in unit time. If Δt never varies they can be defined to be the specific damage done in one activity period, then Δt will not enter the calculations.

Determining combat efficiency coefficients

As is the case for many simulation parameters, the determination of combat efficiency coefficients is largely a matter of knowledge of the actual forces involved in the historical period represented, of trial and error, and of 'tuning' until acceptable results are obtained.

The combat efficiency coefficient, a^2 say, of a given type of unit depends equally on the engaging and the engaged unit types. We cannot expect 'tidy' precedence relationships. For example, in a medieval scenario, archers may be very effective against cavalry (horses provide large targets), cavalry may be effective against infantry because of its speed and weight, but it does not follow that archers are effective against infantry who may deploy behind shields. Hence the basic values of a^2 should be stored in two-dimensional arrays with indices corresponding to unit-type numbers.

a^2 is subject to attenuation from a variety of sources, the most important of which is 'range'. In general it will be necessary to find a function relating a^2 to distance. The arctangent function introduced to simulate observation is particularly applicable to artillery. We could use an attenuator defined by:

$$\alpha = \frac{1}{2} - \frac{1}{\pi}\arctan\left(k(r - R)\right)$$

where r is the range separating the engaging units, R the range at which α is equal to 0.5 (the half-range), and k determines the slope $(-k/\pi)$ of the function at the half-range. For the purposes of observation we were able to relate k to R, but this will not work for combat. Some weapons are effective up to the half-range and ineffective thereafter, others become steadily less effective with increasing range. The parameters k and R may be stored in two-dimensional arrays of the same size as that used for a^2.

Other factors which attenuate a^2 are the types of terrain occupied by the units, their state of motion and formations, their fatigue levels, the weather, in fact almost every parameter of the game. After all these have been applied to find the actual combat efficiency coefficients, the program can calculate the decrements to the respective unit strengths (usually stored as a percentage of the initial strengths). Most war gamers would agree that the quality of the simulation can be improved by introducing a random element. An acceptable way to implement such a random element is to sample a random normal distribution, using one of the RANORM function subprograms introduced in Section 5.3, and add the result to the corresponding strength decrement. The mean should, of course, be zero, and a suitable value for the standard deviation might be around 2% of the initially calculated decrement.

Small units

The foregoing method for simulating combat is applicable only when units are reasonably large in a statistical sense. If units comprise a single item of hardware, such as a single tank or a battleship, it becomes necessary to simulate the fall of shot.

The essential errors of gunnery are angular and it is convenient to differentiate between elevation errors and lateral errors. Each error can be sampled by a call to the RANORM function with a mean of zero in both cases but with possibly different standard deviations. The distance errors, E_x and E_y say, specify where the shot falls in relation to the target. To a first approximation, they are given by the products of the range and the angular errors. The combined error distribution is called an elliptical normal distribution. For a hand-held gun shooting at a fixed vertical target the distribution is effectively circular, but for long range gunnery the distribution may be highly elliptical. In practice it is the gun elevation which is related to range estimation that contributes the greater error. Actual values for the standard deviation (usually called the 'dispersion' in the context of gunnery) are hard to obtain, and some inspired guesswork is called for.

6.4   Management games

There are many shades of management game – business games with a manufacturing or retailing bias, investment games, farm management games, and so on. All have an uncompromisingly capitalist objective – maximise the 'profit' in some enterprise that provides the scenario for the game. However, we use the term loosely and some games are concerned not so much with maximising revenue as with attaining the optimal performance as measured in some other units. Thus, for example, the player of a hospital management game will seek not so much to extract the highest fees from the patients, as to maximise the throughput of patients. At least, one hopes so.

With the exception of sports, management games are perhaps the most institutionalised of all games. They lend themselves to team play with the various team members adopting distinct roles corresponding to counterparts in some real organisation. There have been a number of sponsored competitions with school teams figuring amongst the most successful participants. This is encouraging because for many years it has seemed that the regular educational syllabus fails to instruct school leavers in the everyday practicalities of commercial life.

Some management games are equally suitable for solitaire play. In these the opposition is provided by only partially predictable trends in supply and demand.

If they teach anything at all, management games clarify the nature of an optimum. They quickly reveal the stark truth that whilst you can obtain the 'best performance at a given price', or the 'best possible performance at any price', you cannot in general – despite what the politicians tell us – obtain 'the best possible performance at the lowest price'.

They also reveal the less obvious fact that, if one is to be objective about performance and cost, it is essential to value them in a common currency. The local council which must share limited funds between highway maintenance, waste disposal, staff salaries, social services, etc. wishes to achieve the optimal allocation. Whether they like it or not, or are aware of it or not, they have to find a trade off between the desirability of good roads, the health hazards of inadequate waste disposal, the social penalties of neglecting the aged and infirm, and so on. Sometimes such considerations are pushed into the fuzzier recesses of the municipal mind but the trade off is nevertheless there, for all to see, in the final allocation of funds. The concept of a trade off enters the design of a management game very directly. Every objective variable has to be measured in comparable units so that it can contribute to a single overall measure of the performance achieved by the player.

SIMULATION ACTIVITIES

The activities of a typical management game with a manufacturing scenario are suggested below.

A decisions input phase.

A query phase.

An open reports phase.

A trends computation phase.

A processing phase.

The activity periods for each will depend on the particular scenario. They might each be around one day if the model relates to a firm producing small consumer items. We shall briefly review each of these activities.

Decisions phase

Players' decisions are communicated to the program in a command input phase. The prompted graph-structured syntax presented in Chapter 4 is ideal for the purpose. Typical commands will relate to:

The ordering of raw materials.

Production volumes for each manufactured item.

Pricing policies.

Expansion or contraction in terms of staff and plant.

Advertising budgets.

Many of the commands should specify ongoing policies. Life is much easier if daily orders for materials and the production of stock are automatically continued until further notice. The problems of command transmission which are present in war games are generally insignificant in a management game with centralised operations.

Query phase

In the query phase each player may request information about material and stock levels, warehouse capacity, available capital, and forecasts of supply and demand. One possibility made feasible by the computer is the acquisition of information concerning a competitor's intentions. This will relate mainly to an opponent's pricing decisions which, though input, have not yet been put into effect. Such intelligence must, of course, be carefully rationed by the program!

Open reports phase

Information about recent sales volumes and current prices are available to all players, and are output in the open reports phase.

Trends computation phase

Materials supply and cost, market demand, staff availability, and the effectiveness of advertising will vary throughout the duration of the game. They may be subject to seasonal variation, and all will experience random fluctuations. It is important to facilitate some degree of player prediction – there is little fun in playing a management game in which the parameters fluctuate wildly. In a later subsection we suggest a simple method for generating trend functions.

Processing phase

This is the phase in which the program completes its calculations relating to manufacturing and sales achievement. These will differ somewhat from those specified in the decisions phase, again, as a result of random fluctuations.

A GENERAL VIEW

At a fundamental level all management games have the same structure. It is a cyclic structure with four components as follows:

(a) Determine an objective.

(b) Assemble and/or allocate resources for the achievement of the objective.

(c) Execute the resource-dependent steps to obtain achievement of the objective in some degree.

(d) Measure this achievement and return either to component (a) if a new objective is necessary, or to component (b) if the same objective will suffice.

This suggests that it would be feasible to construct a management game simulation language capable of generating a program for almost any desired scenario. The language would be equipped with a means for defining the syntax of players' commands (a 'metasyntax'), a dictionary to be completed with scenario-dependent terms (or jargon), and the capability of accepting functions to be incorporated in the resulting program for the computation of trend curves and measures of achievement. The complete specification and implementation is left as an exercise for the (very) advanced reader!

Most people are happy to write a new program for each scenario, though the substantial portion devoted to free-format input and command processing should be reuseable.

TIME SERIES

In order to make predictions about the future the player of a management game – or for that matter a real-life manager – needs to examine past data relating to supply, demand, stock levels, production volumes, and other factors. Such predictions will be the basis for his immediate policy decisions.

Any set of measurements of some process which varies with time is called a *time series*. Let us distinguish between time series for data which are unaffected by the decisions of the player, and time series for data which are so affected. We call the former *external* time series because they lie outside the player's influence. The latter are designated *internal* time series. Depending on the scenario and the extent of the simulation model, figures for the total supply of some raw material, the total demand for some product, the arrival rate of patients at a hospital, the grain yield per acre of farming land, might be regarded as external time series. Typical internal time series might comprise figures for price levels, production volumes, hospital discharge rates, and land allocation.

What the player–manager attempts to do is to extrapolate the currently available time series into the future. If this is difficult for an external time series, it is doubly difficult for an internal time series because he must estimate the effects of his own decisions, and those of his opponent(s). Where an external time series might exhibit some degree of regularity, an internal time series is likely to contain discontinuities. We shall therefore confine ourselves to describing external data from now on.

In real life, external time series are obtained by actual observation of the factors over some reasonable length of time. In a management game they must be 'invented'! That is, they must be derived in accordance with some acceptably 'realistic' formulae. It seems sensible to use the same sort of formulae to create time series as are used in their decomposition by analysts.

There are *additive* and *multiplicative models* for time series. For reasons similar to those given in the discussion of attenuators in Section 6.3, the multiplicative model is regarded as the best.

A time series is deemed to incorporate a *trend component T*, a *periodic component P*, and a *random component R*. In the multiplicative model each measurement *M* is assumed to satisfy the equation:

$$M(t) = T(t)P(t)R(t)$$

where (t) may be read as 'at time t', t being the time at which the measurement was made, or to which it relates.

As an example, let us invent a time series to represent the total demand for package holidays as measured by total sales within each of a number of defined periods. In Figure 6.3, the time t represented along the horizontal axis is taken to be the serial number of a bi-monthly accounting period. The half-month ending 31 December 1981 corresponds to t equal to 1, the first half-month of January 1982 corresponds to t equal to 2, and so on. The time series was constructed by specifying trend, periodic, and random functions as described below, and then evaluating the product defined above for each value of t.

(a) *The trend function*. A linear trend function:

$$T(t) = 20t + 1000$$

was used and is shown as the dotted *trend line* superimposed on the plot of the time series. It is customary to express trend in the same units as the time series – in this case 'demand per half-month'.

Management games 191

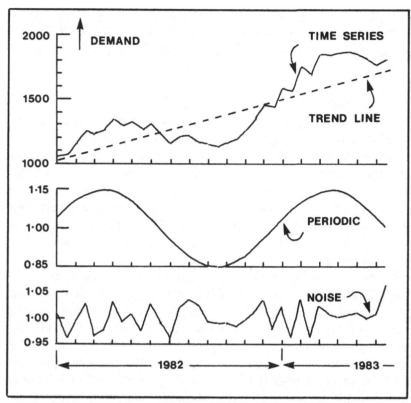

Fig. 6.3. A time series and its components.

(b) *The periodic function*. A seasonal factor was expressed by the equation:

$$P(t) = 1.0 + 0.15 \sin (2\pi t/24)$$

This is a sinusoidal function with a period of one year or 24 half-months. Note that P is a dimensionless number analogous to the attenuators used for modifying war game parameters (Section 6.3).

As our model is multiplicative $P(t)$ must oscillate about the value 1.0, hence the first term of the equation. The amplitude is 0.15. If we wished to shift the function with respect to the time axis we could add a phase-constant to t.

(c) *The random function*. The random effects, or *noise*, arise from a multitude of sources which suggests that we should sample a random normal distribution. In a multiplicative model the mean must be 1.0, but the standard deviation is open to guesswork. We have chosen a value of 0.03 which gives 'convincing' variability to the final time series obtained as the product of T, P, and R.

These components are shown in the diagram, but take note of the different vertical scale used for each plot.

Generation of time series

The example above shows how a time series may be generated by a management game moderator. Furthermore it could randomly select such parameters as the slope of the trend line, the amplitude and phase of the periodic component, and the standard deviation of the noise. The program might produce some initial data to enable each player to make a start in predicting future data. During play new values will be announced as, and when, they are generated. However, what we have described is really too simple.

There are standard mathematical procedures for the decomposition of time series, but it is generally recognised that in most practical cases the human eye can do just as well provided the data is presented in a graphical form. Given a time series cooked to the recipe given above, most players would quickly identify the periodic element and then the trend line. The residual noise can easily be checked to see if it follows a normal distribution. If it does, then the player has probably estimated the main components correctly. How can we make things more difficult and, perhaps, more realistic?

To increase the standard deviation of the noise component would certainly mask the other components, but this might not be realistic. Furthermore prediction would become rather pointless.

The trend function could be made non-linear. For instance, a quadratic polynominal:

$$T(t) = at^2 + bt + c$$

could be used. a, b, and c are coefficients chosen by the program which must take care to ensure that the sign of T cannot change during the time span of the game, unless such an occurrence has a meaningful physical interpretation.

The periodic component can be made more complicated by 'adding' two or more sinusoidal functions with different phase. If the period (one year in the example above) is different for the different components the player's analysis may become too difficult.

There is an echo of Eleusis (Section 2.6) in all this. What we want are computer generated time series which represent reality, and which are capable of analysis by the good player after a few rounds of play – his reward being seen in the increased profits resulting from better forward planning.

CONCLUSION

The ability to predict the behaviour of time series is not the only skill required of a player. He must try to assess the nature and mood of the opponent(s) – are they likely to be cautious or are they going to risk everything on the 'big kill'? Where games are played for training purposes within a business organisation the players may be equipped with powerful aids for determining their optimal responses. However, there is little point in designing recreational management games which require players to solve complex problems in operational research. The accent should be on human interaction.

6.5   **Sports simulations – a warning**

Amongst the fraternity of established games designers – those who have had games published and marketed by someone other than themselves – it has long been acknowledged that sports simulations are, by their nature, an unmitigated flop! If this seems a contentious assertion let me emphasise that I refer to 'true' simulations which attempt to reproduce the logical conditions under which decisions in the simulation will parallel those in the sport. I do not include arcade games in which the similarity is restricted to the title.

The evidence supports this view. At any time one may find board games for golf, soccer, cricket, and baseball on the shelves of the local game store. But are they the same games that were on sale last year? No, they are not – none seems to survive for any length of time before it is withdrawn.

In my view the reason is that those who believe that they would enjoy such games are, in the main, people who are active in the sport concerned. In comparison with the genuine article they find a simulation to be an anticlimax. However tactical the sport it seems that the real enjoyment derives from the exercise of physical skill – it is hitting the ball that counts!

There may appear to be a few exceptions, but on investigation it transpires that they are not sports simulations at all. They are, in fact, management games in which the player adopts the role of soccer manager, racehorse trainer, bookmaker, or whatever.

All this may come as a disappointment to the sportsman or woman who envisages projecting his happy days on the pitch, court, or course onto the home computer. The dedicated golfer might be inspired to implement a terrain model of the type described in Chapter 7 in order to realise his ideal course. Whilst this is entirely feasible, I would advise him that the resulting game will quickly drive him back to the golf course.

7
Terrain models

7.1 Introduction

There can be few home computer enthusiasts who have not encountered a 'lunar lander' program. The object of this game is to execute a soft landing of a lunar module with limited reserves of fuel. The more sophisticated versions model the rocky lunar terrain along a line vertically beneath the flight path. A soft landing in an unsuitable area then becomes as catastrophic as a hard landing anywhere else! These programs use a particularly simple one-dimensional ground model which makes them feasible for the slowest of machines with the slowest of BASIC interpreters. The model is one-dimensional because there is only one independent variable specifying the horizontal position of a given point. The ground level is regarded as dependent data and does not contribute to the dimensionality of the model.

More general ground models – those representing a surface – are two-dimensional and generally demand a fairly high computing speed. For these, compilers such as FORTRAN are commonly used.

Ground models have names which reflect the type of data stored and the field of application. A model which stores only the ground level is usually called a DTM (digital terrain model), though this acronym is often used for more comprehensive models as well. Programs associated with excavation sometimes use a DGM (digital geological model) to store data on soil and rock types obtained from borehole tests. Programs concerned with the distribution of plant species use a DFM (digital flora model), and so on. For the purposes of games played over simulated terrain it is generally sufficient to store data giving ground levels and terrain cover only. The latter term is understood to include man-made constructions such as roads, bridges, and towns, as well as natural features such as lakes and forests.

Whilst ground models are often associated with large scale applications on mainframe computers it should not be thought that microcomputers have insufficient power and capacity to venture into this field. Indeed, so important is the provision of a DTM for many simulation games, and so rich the variety and potential of such games, that it was felt advisable to devote a whole chapter to their form and construction. A specific model which has proved its worth in several microcomputer games is presented in some detail.

Use of a DTM

Before discussing the construction of a DTM let us be quite clear about how it will be used. The function is to provide data associated with any given point of the represented terrain, and to provide it rapidly. A point is located by its plan coordinates measured from some predetermined origin. In civil engineering literature these coordinates are often called *eastings* and *northings*. However, we shall usually refer simply to the X and Y coordinates of the point. Note that these are measured from the origin in a strictly horizontal plane, and not by measuring distance along the ground surface which might, of course, depart considerably from the horizontal.

We must distinguish carefully between points at which the program requires data and points for which data is stored in the DTM. The former might be any points within the area covered by the DTM, but the latter are discrete points arranged on a regular grid. Clearly, some form of interpolation will be required, and in Section 7.7 we extend the ideas of Section 5.8 to two dimensions.

We may summarise operations with a DTM as follows.

The DTM, which has been created in some previous computer run, resides on a backing store medium – tape or disc. The first action of the games program is to load all, or part, of the DTM into memory. When it is very large, or covers an irregular area of ground, it may be necessary to divide it into *blocks* with, perhaps, no more than one block in memory at any one time. In fact, the majority of games require only a single-block DTM loaded into memory once and for all. A few, such as the golf simulation hinted at in Section 6.5 will need to load additional blocks from time to time.

As the program moves its simulated objects about the simulated landscape it will interrogate the DTM to find the vertical level and terrain type at the point occupied by each object. This is normally done by calling function subprograms, one for the level and another for the terrain type, using the X, Y coordinates of the object as parameters. As this is likely to be a very frequent operation it is vital to ensure that the interrogation functions are efficient.

Sometimes it may be necessary to update the DTM to record changes in the terrain. In a war game, for example, existing bridges may be destroyed, or new ones built. Open ground may be churned up by vehicles, and have to be reclassified as broken ground. Such changes are generally made on an ad hoc basis. Nevertheless, they should be executed by subprograms so that the main program is, as far as possible, independent of the DTM methodology. Ideally, it should be possible to use different types of DTM without having to alter the main program.

7.2 Structure of a DTM

It is advisable to organise every DTM as a *block DTM*, even when it comprises only a single block. The adoption of a uniform approach will facilitate editing, and allow the model to be extended if it must cover more ground.

Consider the island shown in Figure 7.1. A DTM must model the entire island and a narrow strip of its coastal waters. Whichever direction were chosen as nominal 'north' it would be inefficient to enclose the whole within one DTM block. Inevitably many points would lie well out to sea where data is neither required nor available. The use of several blocks, as shown in the diagram, reduces the amount of data to be stored, and confers another advantage. Each block is equivalent to a self-contained single-block DTM which may have its own grid spacing and range (see below). Where terrain is hilly it is important to use a grid interval sufficiently fine to allow interpolation to be carried out with reasonable accuracy. In such terrain, a coarse grid would increase the chance that isolated hills and valleys might be missed completely. The northern part of the island is somewhat more hilly than the southern part, and block number 2 uses an appropriately fine grid interval.

The central part of the island is covered by both blocks. In this

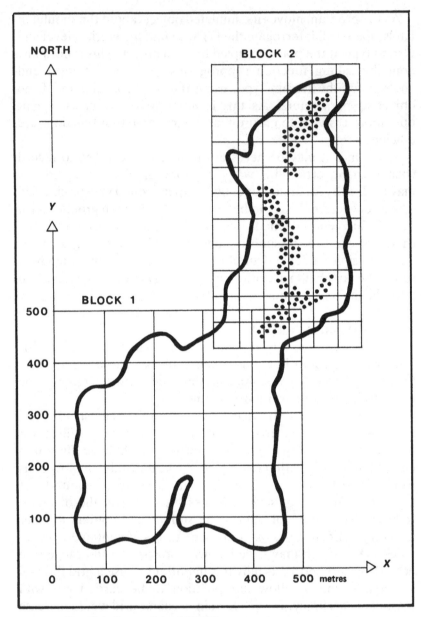

Fig. 7.1. A two-block DTM.

area either block may be used, but it is preferable to use block number 2 because it has the finer interval and would yield more accurate interpolated levels than block number 1.

A DTM must have a *block directory* which holds the following information for each block of the model:

(a) The *block address*. This will typically be a record number in a random access disc file. If no random access device is available the whole DTM must be held in main memory, and this item might then be replaced by an address in memory, or an index number for an array element at the start of the block.

(b) The *global coordinates* of the *local origin* for the block. Each block has its own local coordinate system with an origin situated at its south–west corner. The global coordinate system covers the whole area over which the simulation is conducted. Only the DTM access routines employ local coordinates.

(c) The *grid interval* for the block. It is perfectly feasible to have different grid intervals in the X and Y directions, and some DTM programs allow this. However, the facility is rarely used, and we shall assume that a simple square grid is adequate for simulation games.

(d) The *X and Y ranges* for the block. These are simply the block dimensions in each direction. Alternatively they may be the numbers of cells in each of the coordinate directions. The former allows faster block selection when there are a large number of blocks, but both possibilities should be considered when designing a DTM program.

(e) The *datum level* for the block. Negative ground levels, and levels which are large, are perfectly admissible. However, they are unpopular at the input stage, and can be avoided by employing a local datum level which is added to all levels stored in the block. The value of the datum is retained in the block directory to facilitate subsequent block editing. The datum level must not be confused with the level of the block origin. The latter has no special significance, and is treated in the same way as the levels at other points in the block.

As an example, the block directory for the DTM of Figure 7.1 is shown in Table 7.1. This is an array having seven rows (one for each numerical item of the directory), and two columns (one for each block). The block addresses, shown symbolically, are discussed after the table.

200   *Terrain models*

Table 7.1. *DTM block directory*

Data item	Block 1	Block 2
ADDRESS	A1	A2
X ORIGIN	0.0	325.0
Y ORIGIN	0.0	425.0
INTERVAL	100.0	50.0
X RANGE	500.0	300.0
Y RANGE	500.0	550.0
DATUM	0.0	0.0

The block addresses (A1 and A2 in the example) will depend on the block sizes and the particular file format used. The first few records of a DTM file are reserved for administrative data. Block number 1 will start in the first available record after this, block number 2 will start in the first available record after block number 1, and so on.

DTM DEFINITION DATA

The administrative data at the head of the DTM file will often occupy just one logical record, though if there is a large number of blocks, or if the record length is small, it could occupy several records. The information contained is as follows:

(a) The *DTM title*. A short character-string naming the area of ground modelled. It may be sufficient to rely on the file-name (the name by which the operating system recognises the file), in which case a stored title may be dispensed with.

(b) The *number of blocks* in the DTM.

(c) The *block directory*.

(d) A *global datum level*. This could be an optional item, possibly of value when modelling very high ground. For example, a program may be required to output levels as heights above sea level. Such levels can be quite large, and may be troublesome at the input stage. By using a global datum all the input levels, for every block of the model, are reduced by a constant amount prior to input. The global datum is then added to all levels during input, or at a later stage.

BLOCK FORMAT

The format of a DTM block must be kept very simple to facilitate speed of access. Each block consists of a rectangular array of *elements*. Each element corresponds to one grid point and contains whatever data is relevant to the model. If this data is extensive then the element could require several words of memory. However, we have assumed that simulation games will need only the ground level and terrain type. The level is generally stored as an integer value (height in feet or metres) and is converted to a real value at the interpolation stage. The terrain type number is a small integer and it is often possible to pack both items into a single word of one, or two, bytes. In Section 7.5 we describe a DTM suitable for many simulation games on a microcomputer, and for which the block elements comprise a single byte only.

What happens when no data is available for a grid point within a block? The usual procedure is to store a 'magic number' to indicate the absence of data. For example, if a DTM contains levels in the range from -250 metres to $+3200$ metres, the absence of the level at a grid point could be indicated by a pseudo-level of, say, -999 metres. The use of magic numbers is frowned upon by purist programmers, and indeed they can be dangerous. However, considerations of operational efficiency outweigh ideology in this case. Obviously, you must be careful that your chosen magic number cannot occur as a genuine item of data.

Block paging

Paging is the term applied to the operation of transferring blocks between memory and secondary storage such as discs. DTM blocks are paged in as they are needed, that is, they are read into memory from the DTM file. Paging out, the reverse operation, is performed only when blocks have been amended to represent altered terrain.

As far as possible, paging should be minimised. The program using the DTM should collect points at which ground data is needed so that maximum use is made of the currently resident block, before paging in a new block. Many simulation games are efficient in this respect because there is often a 'centre of activity', and a majority of operations will involve few blocks at any time. If the program is likely to be, or is shown to be, inefficient as regards paging, two solutions are possible. In the first, the DTM is extended to include a larger number of blocks with a more generous degree of overlap between neighbouring blocks. The second solution is to employ larger blocks, and consequently fewer of them.

7.3   DTM input and editing

The program which prepares a DTM is normally quite separate from the program which makes use of it. The output file of the first becomes an input file for the second. Where the DTM represents real terrain the levels are obtained either by transcription from a contour map or by direct field surveying. Unless you are both wealthy and patient, and possibly misguided as well, the latter is not a practical option. Levels can be read from a contour map with the aid of a transparent plastic overlay marked with a grid appropriate to the block interval. No great sophistication is necessary for a simple DTM input program. However, consideration should be given to the following features:

(a) *Mode of use.* The one program should be capable both of accepting new data, and of editing data already on the DTM file. The user indicates the mode of use at the start of a run and, as far as DTM blocks are concerned, the only difference is that for new data the block buffer in memory is initialised to the 'absent data' indicator, whilst for the editing function, the block is first loaded from the DTM file.

The volume of DTM data may be considerable, and the program should permit the input of data for different blocks in separate sessions.

(b) *Prompting.* The program should prompt the user with the local block coordinates of the next grid point due for input. When editing, the existing ground data for the grid point should also be displayed. The user should be able to indicate 'no change' in the editing mode, or 'no data' in the input mode, merely by hitting the RETURN key. In the days of batch-processing mainframe computers, and card decks, DTM data was particularly laborious to prepare. Each card had to contain the X and Y coordinates as well as the level and other terrain data, to guard against accidental droppages. The on-line terminal has made life much easier for the user of bulk data programs.

You may be tempted to include a facility for reading X and Y coordinates in order to locate a single grid point to be edited. This is not recommended. Unless blocks are very large indeed, it is far simpler to execute a block edit using the 'no change' facility until the required grid point is reached, and thereafter to the end of the block. Note that to implement a 'no change' facility using the RETURN key, as described above, you could incorporate an item-oriented input facility such as that described in Section 4.2.

(c) *Block output*. The input program must obviously be supported by a program able to print or display the DTM in a digestible
format. Such a program may produce merely a tabular listing of
levels and terrain type data for checking purposes, or it may
produce various types of map. We shall not discuss further details
here but certain forms of output are described in Section 7.6.

7.4   Generating a DTM

Of particular interest to games programmers is a method
for generating a fictional, though realistic, DTM. Such a DTM can
be the basis of many fascinating exploration games in which the
program reveals ground data only for the area which can be seen by
the expedition.

A DTM generator, like an input program, will normally be quite
distinct from the game program which uses the resulting DTM file.
However, it is unlikely to be as flexible, and in particular it is
difficult to generate multi-block DTMs. The difficulty lies in
matching up the data in areas of overlap and block adjacency. We
shall consider only a single-block generator here, which will be
adequate for most gaming applications.

At the start of a generator run the program must read the
following essential data:

(a) The *grid interval*.

(b) The *X and Y ranges* for the block to be generated. These
must be integer multiples of the grid interval.

(c) The *minimum and maximum permitted levels*.

(d) The *percentage (by area) of ground at the minimum level*, and
a similar value for ground at the maximum level. It is not easy to
produce intermediate levels in specified quantities without sacrific-
ing realism. The intermediate levels are produced by a 'smoothing'
process to be described later.

(e) The *terrain cover data*. This specifies such quantities as the
total length of all roads, the total length of rivers, the number and
size of towns, and the percentage areas assigned to the different
types of terrain.

(f) *Process control data*. This is data which specifies such
parameters as the degree of smoothing to be applied to the levels,
and the 'persistence' with which the program attempts to achieve
the specified percentages of terrain cover.

The program builds the DTM block in a block buffer within

memory. Essentially this is a two-dimensional array having, say, M rows and N columns. Each element, located by its indices i and j, corresponds to one grid point. Whether an element comprises one, two, or more bytes is immaterial at this stage. We simply assume that an element is capable of holding both the ground level and the terrain type number for a point.

BASIC OPERATIONS

Two mathematical processes are central to the operation of the generator. These are '*spotting*' and '*random walking*'.

Spotting

This is the selection, at random, of a grid point having specified characteristics. For example, the program may need to spot a point having the minimum level and a terrain type number implying 'open ground'.

One method of spotting might be to use a random number generator (Section 5.3) to produce two integers in ranges corresponding to the dimensions of the block buffer. The program would call the random number generator once for i and once for j, and would then test the resulting point to see if it satisfies the criteria. If the point fails to satisfy the criteria a new point is randomly selected and the test repeated. Obviously, when there are few suitable points in the block, this procedure will be inefficient. Furthermore, whilst the random number generator should produce equiprobable row selections and equiprobable column selections, there is no guarantee that every element (i, j) will be spotted with equal probability. Successive values in the cycle of a pseudo-random number generator are not truly independent and caution must be exercised when combining them.

A more sure-fire method of spotting is first to construct a list of all points satisfying the criteria, and then to sample the list at random. However, the list of points could be as large as the block buffer. A practical compromise is to use the first method while more than, say, 10% of the grid points satisfy the criteria, then to switch to the second method when there are fewer. Clearly, there must be a preliminary pass to count the suitable points, but no separate list of points is constructed until it is necessary.

A third method, which gives a biassed result, is to spot any point at random, and then to conduct a cyclic search of the block until a suitable point is reached. It is not difficult to see that this method will tend to select points lying close together in clumps. Such a bias is not necessarily a disadvantage here, though it would be a serious fault in many programs employing random selections of array elements.

Random walking

Random walking is the process of taking a succession of steps in random directions. In the context of a DTM block we are constrained to take unit steps in directions selected from the eight permitted directions. The topic was discussed in some detail in Section 5.4.

We are now ready to describe the process by which the DTM is generated. The levels are assigned first, and the terrain cover, which often depends upon the ground level, second.

GENERATING GROUND LEVELS

All grid points are initially given a level equal to the mean of the minimum and maximum levels. A grid point at the mean level is spotted for the start of a random walk. At each step of the walk the new grid point is reset to the minimum level. The random walk is constrained to remain within the block but is not prohibited from revisiting points which have already been assigned the minimum level. If it were so constrained the low ground would have an unsatisfactory spidery distribution, and the later smoothing process could be adversely affected. When a certain number of steps have been executed, a new start point is spotted for a new random walk. If all the low ground is to be connected then a very large number of steps should be allowed for the first random walk. If the low ground is to be fragmented each walk is terminated after a small number of steps. In either case, the assignment of minimum levels is terminated when the required percentage specified in (d) has been achieved.

The same procedure is now used to assign the maximum levels. However, the random walks are now constrained to avoid points which have the minimum level.

When the minimum and maximum levels have been assigned a smoothing operation is performed. A number of passes are made through the block buffer to raise points near high ground, and depress points near low ground. The number of such passes, or cycles, is one item of the control data in (f) above.

In each cycle every point is examined, and its neighbouring

points contribute to an amendment of its level. This amendment is recorded in the buffer only after a stage at which it cannot affect other amendments. Hence, a temporary buffer holding two rows of elements is required. In the temporary buffer, at any time, will be the row undergoing amendment and its preceding row which has already been processed. When the current row is finished its preceding row can be copied into the main DTM block buffer.

Smoothing

Suppose that the current smoothing cycle has reached element (i, j) in the block buffer. Let us denote its current level by $L(i, j)$. If this level is a minimum or maximum it is left unchanged, and the cycle continues with the next point which corresponds to element $(i, j + 1)$ if $j \neq N$, or $(i + 1, 1)$ if $j = N$ and $i \neq M$. If it is neither a minimum nor a maximum level it is amended according to the formula:

$$L(i, j) = (1 - \rho)L(i, j) + \rho A$$

where A denotes the average level of the neighbouring points, and ρ denotes a '*relaxation factor*' in the range $(0.0, 1.0)$.

In calculating the average level of the neighbouring points, account must be taken of the fact that corner points have only three neighbours, and edge points have only five neighbours. Note that if the relaxation factor ρ is zero there will be no smoothing, whilst if it is equal to 1.0 no account will be taken of the current level of the point to be amended.

The degree of smoothing will depend on the relaxation factor, and the number of cycles of the process. If both are small there will be little smoothing. If both are large, levels along any line between a minimum and a maximum will show nearly uniform changes. Experimentation will show what values are suitable for the type of terrain you wish to generate.

Levels equalisation

A more severe form of smoothing results from allowing the minimum and maximum levels to be amended by the process described above. As a result, the finished DTM will generally have less terrain at the extreme levels than was specified in (c) at the beginning of this section. A few cycles of levels equalisation are recommended for the production of rolling terrain with smooth contours around hills and valleys. However, equalisation does not

produce realistic terrain unless preceded by the standard smoothing process in which extreme levels are held constant.

GENERATING TERRAIN COVER

When all points have been assigned a level, the program
turns its attention to 'dressing' the ground. All points are initialised
to the most common type of cover specified in (e). Other types of
terrain are applied, in the specified amounts, to convert a proportion of these points. The *linear features* such as roads, railways,
rivers, and canals are assigned immediately after the initialisation
and before the other types of *area cover* with the exception of lakes
which are created in conjunction with rivers.

A DTM is a discrete representation of a continuous phenomenon, and some degree of 'jerkiness' has to be tolerated. If adjacent
grid points are associated with a particular type of linear feature,
that feature is assumed to run in a straight line from one point to the
other. Figure 7.2 shows the interpretation of linear features
adopted here, and in the program described in Section 7.5.

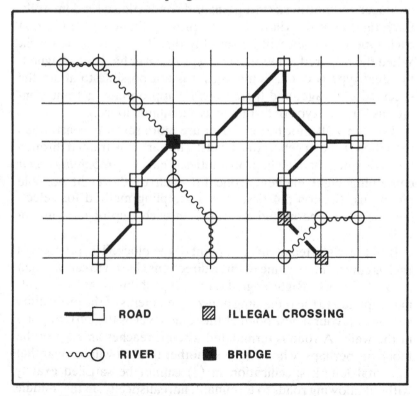

Fig. 7.2. Linear features.

Note the localised branching of linear features at junctions. This is a natural consequence of the assumption stated in the previous paragraph. In a game program using the DTM, the side branches could be removed by tests on all local grid points. However, this is not easy to program, and there is a severe penalty on processing speed. The side branches are not unduly unrealistic, and are best accepted without modification.

The width of a linear feature is small compared to the grid interval, so its assignment must not preclude the assignment of another type of cover to the point. A particular system of terrain type numbers which allows this is decribed in Section 7.5.

Where different kinds of linear feature cross, some sort of bridge is necessary. As data is recorded only at grid points, crossings such as that shown at the bottom right of the diagram cannot be allowed. A normal bridge is shown near the centre of the diagram. In such a situation a bridge 'code' is substituted for the road and river type numbers.

Apart from that used for initialisation, all terrain cover is produced by spotting a start point and conducting a random walk. Each random walk will be of appropriately limited length so that each type of terrain will be sensibly distributed over the block. When the required amount of any type of cover has been assigned, the next type is done. Sometimes it is not possible to attain the specified coverage, and there must be appropriate 'get out' conditions for each type of terrain to avoid infinite loops.

Random walks for terrain cover are more severely constrained than those used in generating levels. They are constrained through the action of a list of eight probabilities. That is, a *probability vector* containing eight elements, one for each of the eight possible directions. Section 5.4 describes a sampling method for selecting one of the permitted directions in each step of the random walk.

Roads are started at an edge point of the block. The progress of each is constrained to one of three directions chosen to carry it right across the block. Right-angled turns are prohibited, and a weighting is applied to the remaining non-zero elements of the probability vector to favour a new point at the same level as the current point in the walk. A road is terminated when it reaches an edge of the block or, perhaps, when it meets another road. It will be clear that the total length specification in (e) cannot be satisfied exactly without allowing roads to terminate, unrealistically, in the 'middle of nowhere'. The specifications in (e) must be treated as approximate guides, and the same consideration applies to all types of cover.

Rivers, as all know, run downhill. Hence the source of a river must be located in high ground. Each step of the random walk is constrained to avoid higher ground than that set for the current point. Thus, directions which lead to higher ground have their corresponding elements in the probability vector set to zero. To avoid river loops, each step is constrained from moving adjacent to an existing river point. Where rivers intersect roads, bridges are indicated.

Eventually, a river can proceed no further without violating a constraint. At this stage a lake may be formed. Starting at the last river point, the random walk is permitted to visit existing water points subject to the levels constraint.

Towns are spotted on road points, and the number of steps in each random walk is limited by the relationship between the town size and the grid interval.

Marsh may be produced by spotting a point at the edge of a lake, and constraining the random walk to the fringes of the lake.

The highest levels are often devoid of trees, and forest may be constrained to avoid such points. Broken ground might be the appropriate terrain for hilltops.

CONCLUSION

We conclude this section with some discussion of the programming aspects relevant to the implementation of a DTM generator.

It is evident that there are many similarities between the various stages of the assignment process, both for levels and for terrain cover. The question arises whether the whole could be unified by means of a 'driving list', or *driver*. This would take the form of a decision table to be read and acted upon by a single short piece of program. Such a driver would contain some sort of definition of the spotting conditions and random walk constraints for each type of data in the DTM.

The 'driver' approach is certainly feasible. However, many of the constraints are quite complex, and considerable programming skill would be required to derive a driver format with sufficient flexibility. There is no doubt that the 'easy' way to write a DTM generator is to have separate code for the levels and for each type of terrain. Of course, any program should perform the common operations such as spotting and random walking with suitable subprograms, but the constraints acting mainly through the probability vector are most easily specified in custom built code for each type of data.

It should be borne in mind that the volume of code needed is not large and can conveniently be split into two parts, one program to generate levels, and the other to assign the terrain cover. Indeed, it is helpful to separate the two main activities so that levels can be examined before terrain cover is produced.

7.5   A DTM for microcomputer games

The single-block DTM described here is in use with several successful, though unpublished, microcomputer games. It is generated by the methods presented in Section 7.4, and is stored in a DTM file. The games programs which make use of the DTM are quite separate from the generator. They start by reading the DTM to a block buffer, which resides in memory throughout the run. Each element of the block buffer consists of a single byte only. Hence, for example, 2K bytes of memory can easily accommodate a 40 by 40 block and its supporting data. For a grid interval of 500 metres this would represent an area of 400 km^2.

How this compact format is achieved is detailed below.

Levels

Eight distinct ground levels are recognised at grid points. Interpolation (Section 7.7) yields real-valued levels for any points within the block. The grid point levels are not stored explicitly within the block. Instead, integer pointers requiring just three bits are stored. These identify the actual levels in a separate list which forms part of the DTM definition record.

There is no requirement for the eight grid point levels to be equally spaced. This can be advantageous when much of the action of a game program is confined to an area which contains no extreme levels. Accuracy can be improved by decreasing the separation of levels in this area, and increasing it elsewhere. However, it must be pointed out that this expedient is more relevant to DTMs representing real terrain than it is to those produced by a generator.

Terrain cover

Seven types of area cover, two linear features, and one type of point feature (a bridge) are recognised. It would seem attractive to allocate one bit for each type of feature, but a number of combinations are impossible, and the method would be uneconomic as regards memory space. Four bits in each block element are used to hold the terrain type number minus one. These are allocated as follows:

```
 1  OPEN GROUND
 2  BROKEN GROUND
 3  SCRUB
 4  FOREST
 5  OPEN GROUND+RIVER
 6  BROKEN GROUND+RIVER
 7  SCRUB+RIVER
 8  FOREST+RIVER
 9  OPEN GROUND+ROAD
10  BROKEN GROUND+ROAD
11  SCRUB+ROAD
12  FOREST+ROAD
13  BRIDGE (RIVER+ROAD, OPEN GROUND ASSUMED)
14  TOWN
15  LAKE
16  MARSH
```

Note that when the generator creates a bridge, it is necessary to impose the 'open ground' terrain type on the area cover.

Any type of terrain may assume a 'damaged' status. A single bit in each block element is used to signify the status. Damaged ground is relevant for a DTM to be used in a war game. Other games may profitably use this bit to allow 16 grid point levels or, alternatively, to double the number of terrain types. The interpretation of damage is the responsibility of the program using the DTM. One war game adopts the following interpretation:

```
DAMAGED OPEN GROUND=BROKEN GROUND
DAMAGED ROAD=BROKEN GROUND
DAMAGED BRIDGE=RIVER+EXISTING AREA COVER
```
Other damaged terrain is unaltered.

Block elements

Each block element, corresponding to one grid point, is organised thus:

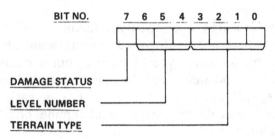

The programs which use the DTM are written in a micro-computer implementation of FORTRAN that includes facilities for logical operations on single-byte variables. The level-number and terrain type number can be extracted from an element, BUF(I,J) of the block buffer by means of the two statements:

```
LEVNO=1+(BUF(I,J).AND.112)/16
TERNO=1+(BUF(I,J).AND.15)
```

The actual level is obtained by using LEVNO as the index in a reference to the vector containing the eight recognised grid point levels. The terrain type number, TERNO, is used in many ways, but quite often as the index in references to arrays containing such data as vehicle speeds and visibility ranges. The damage status is obtained simply by testing the sign of BUF(I,J).

Those who write in an assembler language will have no difficulty in implementing the unpacking operations shown above. However, most versions of BASIC, PASCAL, etc. provide no logical functions. Furthermore, the majority of these lack the single-byte integer variable type. If such languages are used any unpacking must be carried out arithmetically as described in Section 4.6.

DTM definition data

Section 7.2 explained how a DTM file must start with various items of administrative data held in a DTM definition record. The specific DTM discussed here is of the single-block variety, and there are a number of simplifying assumptions. As a result the DTM definition record omits the item specifying the number of blocks, the block directory is shorter, and the global datum level is replaced by the vector of eight actual levels. The full DTM definition record is listed here.

(a) The *DTM title*. An eight character-string naming the ground represented by the DTM.

(b) The (single) *block directory*. This contains only:

The *grid interval*.

The *X and Y ranges* of the block. These are stored as the number of cells in each of the coordinate directions. Note that the corresponding dimensions of the block buffer will be one greater than these values.

(c) The *actual levels*. A vector of eight levels stored as real values.

Note that the coordinates of the block origin (south–west corner) are assumed to be (0.0, 0.0).

At the start of a run using the DTM the definition record is read directly into the relevant variables, the size of the block is calculated, and the corresponding number of records read into the block buffer.

7.6   DTM output

This section illustrates some useful DTM outputs, *or maps*, and discusses how these might be used in conjunction with a game program. All have been produced on a dot-matrix printer to a consistent format, and all relate to one particular DTM generated by the program described in Section 7.5. Your games may require maps prepared to a slightly different format, or displaying different information, but it is hoped that the samples shown here will suggest a starting point. If no printer is available the maps may be displayed on a VDU, but partitioning (see below) may be necessary.

The numbers surrounding each map (Figures 7.3–7.7) are the DTM grid coordinates used in constructing *map references*. Hyphens (minus signs) and vertical bar characters are used to indicate a boundary, but note that the true boundary of the DTM block coincides with the exterior grid lines, and that no terrain is defined between these and the indicated boundaries. All symbols, with the exception of those used in the contour maps, lie at the intersection of grid lines.

To illustrate the form of a map reference, the bridges marked % in map 3 lie at map references 0510 (easting 05, northing 10) and 1604 (easting 16, northing 04). Programs will usually need to output map references for points which are not coincident with DTM grid points. In Section 5.6 we introduced the concept of a *fine grid* which overlays the DTM grid. If this is assigned an interval equal to one tenth of the DTM grid interval, the Ordnance Survey system may be used. The easting and northing coordinates are extended by a further digit to specify 'tenths of a DTM grid interval'. For example, a point lying north–east of the bridge at 1604, and halfway across the DTM cell, would have map reference 165045.

The values in the body of the map (Figure 7.3) are 'pointers' to the actual levels stored in the DTM definition data (Section 7.5). Note that the columns are separated by one blank print position. On most printers and VDU screens this will yield acceptably 'square' DTM cells.

Symbols (Figure 7.4) have been substituted for the level indices. The higher the ground the greater the 'print density' of the symbol. When viewed from some distance the density map gives a general impression of the 'lie of the land'.

The terrain (Figure 7.5) at each grid point is indicated by a symbol as shown in Table 7.2.

Map 4 (Figure 7.6) is identical to map 3 (Figure 7.5) except that the river, road, and bridge symbols are replaced by the symbols denoting the area cover at the corresponding grid points.

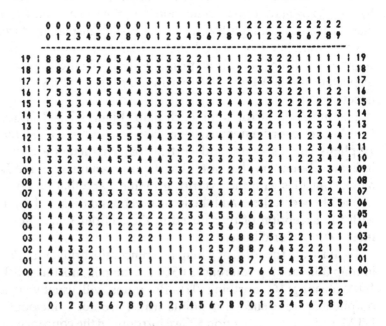

```
          0 0 0 0 0 0 0 0 0 0 1 1 1 1 1 1 1 1 1 1 2 2 2 2 2 2 2 2 2 2
          0 1 2 3 4 5 6 7 8 9 0 1 2 3 4 5 6 7 8 9 0 1 2 3 4 5 6 7 8 9
         ---------------------------------------------------------------
19 | 8 8 8 7 8 7 6 5 4 4 3 3 3 3 2 2 1 1 1 1 2 3 3 2 2 1 1 1 1 1 | 19
18 | 8 8 6 6 7 7 6 5 4 3 3 3 3 3 2 1 1 1 2 2 3 3 2 2 1 1 1 1 1 1 | 18
17 | 7 7 5 4 5 5 5 5 4 3 3 3 3 3 2 2 2 2 3 3 3 3 2 2 1 1 1 1 1 | 17
16 | 7 5 3 3 4 4 5 4 4 4 3 3 3 3 3 3 3 3 3 3 3 3 2 2 1 1 2 2 | 16
15 | 5 4 3 3 4 4 4 4 4 3 3 3 3 3 3 3 4 4 4 3 3 2 2 2 2 2 2 2 | 15
14 | 4 4 3 3 4 4 4 5 4 4 4 3 3 2 2 3 4 4 4 4 3 2 2 1 2 2 3 3 3 | 14
13 | 3 3 3 3 4 4 5 5 5 4 4 3 3 2 2 2 3 4 4 4 3 2 2 1 1 1 2 3 3 4 | 13
12 | 3 3 3 3 4 4 5 5 5 5 4 4 3 3 2 2 3 4 4 4 3 2 1 1 1 1 2 3 4 4 | 12
11 | 3 3 3 3 4 4 5 5 5 5 4 4 3 3 2 2 3 3 3 3 2 2 1 1 1 2 3 4 4 | 11
10 | 3 3 2 3 4 4 4 5 5 4 4 4 3 3 2 2 3 3 2 3 3 3 2 1 1 2 2 3 4 4 | 10
09 | 3 3 3 3 4 4 4 4 4 4 4 3 3 2 2 2 2 2 4 4 2 1 1 1 2 3 3 4 | 09
08 | 4 4 4 4 4 4 4 4 4 3 3 3 3 2 2 2 3 2 2 1 1 1 1 2 3 3 | 08
07 | 4 4 4 4 4 3 3 3 3 3 3 3 3 3 3 3 3 3 3 2 2 2 1 1 1 2 2 4 | 07
06 | 4 4 4 4 3 3 2 2 3 3 3 3 3 3 4 4 4 4 3 2 1 1 1 1 1 3 5 | 06
05 | 4 4 4 3 3 2 2 2 2 2 2 2 2 3 3 4 5 5 6 6 3 1 1 1 1 1 3 3 | 05
04 | 4 4 4 3 2 2 1 2 2 2 2 2 2 2 2 3 5 6 7 8 6 3 2 1 1 1 1 2 2 | 04
03 | 4 4 4 3 2 1 1 1 2 2 2 1 1 1 1 2 2 5 6 8 8 7 5 3 2 2 1 1 1 1 | 03
02 | 4 4 3 3 2 1 1 1 1 1 1 1 1 1 1 2 5 7 8 8 7 6 4 3 2 2 2 1 1 1 | 02
01 | 4 4 3 3 2 1 1 1 1 1 1 1 1 1 1 1 2 3 6 8 8 7 7 6 5 4 3 3 2 2 1 | 01
00 | 4 3 3 2 2 1 1 1 1 1 1 1 1 1 1 1 1 2 5 7 8 7 7 6 6 5 4 3 3 2 1 1 | 00
         ---------------------------------------------------------------
          0 0 0 0 0 0 0 0 0 0 1 1 1 1 1 1 1 1 1 1 2 2 2 2 2 2 2 2 2 2
          0 1 2 3 4 5 6 7 8 9 0 1 2 3 4 5 6 7 8 9 0 1 2 3 4 5 6 7 8 9
```

Fig. 7.3. Map 1 – levels (indices).

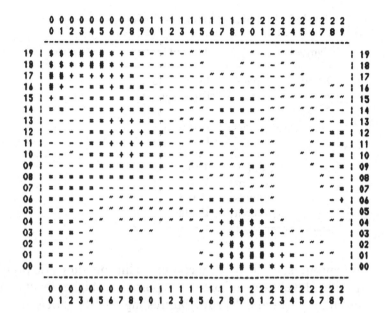

Fig. 7.4. Map 2 – levels (density map).

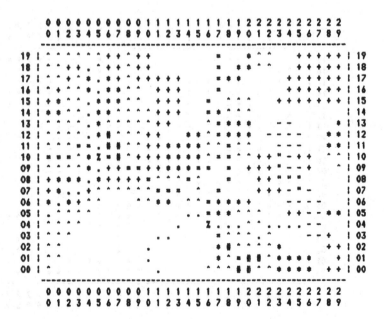

Fig. 7.5. Map 3 – terrain cover.

Table 7.2. *Terrain cover symbols*

Symbol		Type of terrain
Blank	(space)	– Open ground
∧	(up arrow)	– Broken ground
*	(asterisk)	– Scrub
+	(plus)	– Forest
–	(minus)	– Lake
"	(quote)	– Marsh
#	(X-hatch)	– Town
.	(point)	– River
=	(equals)	– Road
%	(percent)	– Bridge

A contour is, in the present context, a line dividing grid points at a specified level from adjacent grid points at a higher level. Whilst contour maps (Figure 7.7) are 'interesting' they are not as useful as might, at first sight, appear. If contours for more than a few levels are output on a single map, they can look confused.

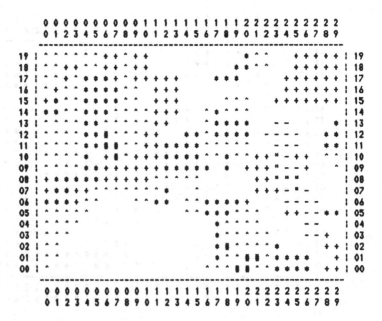

Fig. 7.6. Map 4 – terrain cover (linear features removed).

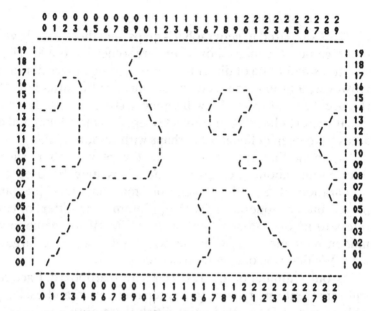

Fig. 7.7. Map 5 – contour map (level 3 only).

In the map shown in Figure 7.7 the underline character is used for portions of a contour running east–west. The characters vertical bar, left and right oblique, and left and right bracket, have been used in the spaces which horizontally separate the grid points in the other maps. The logic necessary to determine which character gives the best fit to the contour at each position is not discussed here.

Partitioned maps

If a map is too wide for the printer or, as is more likely, too large for the VDU screen, it must be output in separate parts. The format is unchanged but the rows and columns in each partition lie between specified limits. These limits should be accepted as normal parameters of the output subroutine.

In games where the players have limited knowledge of the terrain, partitioned maps will be the normal form of output. For example, consider a game in which an expedition progresses across uncharted territory. When the expedition reaches a new grid point the corresponding DTM block element can be flagged as 'visited'. The 'damage' bit (Section 7.5) might be used for this purpose. On a request for output, the program will produce maps showing only the visited points, or a small area around them.

Use of maps

Compared to geographer's maps, and those used in various board games, the maps shown here are somewhat crude. They are also too small to be of direct use for recording moves during play. However, a little manual effort can improve the situation. Map 3 (Figure 7.5), for example, will be more comprehensible after the linear features have been connected up, and after lakes and other areas have been delineated, perhaps with coloured inks.

Assuming that the game allows the players to receive full information about the terrain, the maps may be used to aid preparation of a single, large scale, map on which the game is played under moderation by the program. The latter, of course, refers to its own stored copy of the DTM. If the game involves hidden movement, each player will need a separate large scale map. We describe one method of preparation.

Cut out a number of squares of coloured cardboard. Each colour will represent one type of (area) terrrain cover, and each square will cover one DTM grid point. Stick these onto a large sheet of cardboard so that they correspond to map 4 (Fig. 7.6). Note that each grid point lies at the centre of a square, not at a corner. The outermost rows and columns of squares must now be divided by a heavy line to indicate the true boundaries of the map. Referring to map 3 (Figure 7.5), mark roads and rivers as a series of straight line segments between the centres of relevant squares. Mark the DTM grid coordinates around the large scale map as shown on the output maps. By reference to map 1 (Figure 7.3) write the level index (or the actual level) in each square. The result is a map over which playing pieces may be moved or, alternatively, details may be recorded on a transparent plastic overlay.

When the game is such that terrain details are withheld from players until they are discovered in some way, large scale maps are not appropriate. The program will then output a series of maps with increasing detail as the game progresses. Partitioned maps may be used to economise on the volume of output produced. Another approach is to produce full maps having a special 'null' symbol at grid points where there is a lack of information. Transparent plastic overlays might be a convenient means for players to record unit moves and plan future moves.

7.7   Interpolation for ground levels

With a sufficiently large memory, and sufficient labour to assemble the data, we could produce a DTM having such a fine interval that interpolation would be unnecessary. However, in practice a DTM block may have a grid interval some hundred times larger than that which would obviate the need for interpolation. We describe the simplest technique for determining the level of a point, P say, which is not coincident with a grid point. The method also works for points which do coincide with grid points, so one piece of code will suffice for all points.

We refer back to Figure 5.4 in Section 5.6 which shows the relation between a right-handed coordinate system and an array such as might hold a DTM block. Included in the diagram is a typical grid cell with corners labelled A, B, C, and D which encloses the point P.

First it is necessary to find the levels which have been stored for the grid points A, B, C, and D. This is a simple exercise in array access, but some clear thinking is required. Let us denote the block array by BUF dimensioned to have M rows and N columns.

Starting with the coordinates (x_P, y_P) of P, we require to find the coordinates (x_A, y_A), (x_B, y_B), (x_C, y_C), (x_D, y_D) of the cell corners, and the levels z_A, z_B, z_C, z_D. If we denote the block origin coordinates by (x_0, y_0) and the grid interval by G, the following formulae relate coordinates and array indices:

$$i_A = \text{MAX0}(\text{INT}(I),2) \qquad j_A = \text{MIN0}(\text{INT}(J),N-1)$$
$$i_B = i_A \qquad j_B = j_A + 1$$
$$i_C = i_A - 1 \qquad j_C = j_B$$
$$i_D = i_C \qquad j_D = j_A$$

where I and J are real-valued quantities given by:

$$I = M - (y_P - y_0)/G \qquad J = 1 + (x_P - x_0)/G$$

The functions MAX0 and MIN0 select, respectively, the greatest and least of the integer arguments in brackets. INT denotes the integer part of the quantity following it in brackets. MAX0, MIN0, and INT are provided as intrinsic functions of FORTRAN. In other languages they may have to be programmed explicitly.

Having found the cell corner indices i_A, j_A, i_B, etc., the corresponding coordinates are given by:

$$x_A = x_0 + G(j_A - 1) \qquad y_A = y_0 + G(M - i_A)$$
$$x_B = x_A + G \qquad y_B = y_A$$
$$x_C = x_B \qquad y_C = y_A + G$$
$$x_D = x_A \qquad y_D = y_C$$

The level-numbers for the cell corners are read directly from the array BUF using the indices (i_A, j_A) etc., and are used as indices to obtain the actual levels from the DTM definition data.

Interpolation for the level z_P of point P is carried out by fitting a smooth continuous surface over the cell. Before presenting the formula let us visualise the form of this surface.

Imagine the four cell corners suspended in space at their correct vertical levels. Suppose that we connect adjacent corners by rigid straight rods along the sides of the cell. Now choose a point at any known fraction of the distance along one of the rods, and connect it to the corresponding point on the opposite rod by means of a tightly stretched string. By proceeding to tie together many pairs of opposing points in this way, for both pairs of opposite rods, we produce a sort of unwoven 'patch'. Each string is perfectly straight, but the surface produced is curved. By indicating the diagonals AC and BD, which are parabolas in the surface, Figure 7.8 attempts to give a perspective impression of the surface generated by the strings.

The surface is a second order surface, a quadric, known as a hyperbolic paraboloid. Or rather, a part of one, since it is bounded by the cell edges. Since the publication of a well known paper by Coons [21], this interpolated surface has been widely dubbed a Coons' patch.

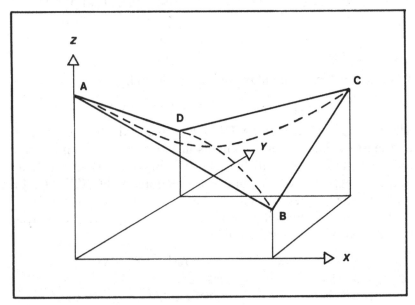

Fig. 7.8. A quadric patch.

We can find the level at any point of the patch by a linear 'blending' of the levels at the cell corners. For convenience we shall introduce *ratio coordinates* for point P. That is, we find two numbers s and t which express how far across the cell P lies with respect to corner A. The quantities s and t are ratios in the range $(0,1)$ relating to the X and Y directions respectively as follows:

$$s = (x_P - x_A)/(x_C - x_A) \qquad t = (y_P - y_A)/(y_C - y_A)$$

We can now express the level of point P as:

$$z_P = (1 - s)(1 - t)z_A + s(1 - t)z_B + stz_C + (1 - s)tz_D$$

Note how the formula yields the levels at the cell corners A, B, C, D when s and t are, respectively, $(0,0)$, $(1,0)$, $(1,1)$, and $(0,1)$. Note also that such patches have positional continuity over the whole DTM block. The slope of the surface is continuous in every direction within each cell, but is not continuous across cell boundaries. For DTM applications this is not normally a serious shortcoming.

We must now consider how to find z_P when one, or more, of the cell corner levels is not known. Recall that this situation may occur in a DTM representing real ground, though not in a generated DTM representing fictional ground. The absence of data is detected by the occurrence of a 'pseudo-level' indicator as described in Section 7.2.

Three points known

The three known cell corners lie in a plane, and we assume that this plane covers the whole cell so that the unknown corner also lies in the plane. Thus the sum of the levels on one pair of diagonally opposite corners is equal to the sum of the levels for the other pair of corners. Hence, we can calculate the unknown corner level as the sum of the levels at the two adjacent corners minus the level at the opposite corner. We may then use the four-point formula given above.

Two points known

Again, we assume that a plane gives the best surface fit over the cell. The line joining the two known cell corners is assumed to be the steepest occurring in the cell. There are two cases to consider. First, if we know the levels at two adjacent corners, we estimate the level at each unknown corner to be equal to that for the known corner adjacent to it. Second, if we know the levels at diagonally opposite corners, we estimate the level at both unknown corners to be equal to the average of the known levels. The four-point formula may then be used.

Note that this approach only works for square cells. If the cell is not square, the preliminary assumptions are made, but the mathematics is slightly more complicated.

One point known

Without using data from adjacent cells, the best fit is obtained by assuming that all points in the cell are at the same level as that of the known corner.

8
Abstract games

8.1   Introduction

Throughout the last two chapters the computer was cast in the role of moderator – as environmental medium, umpire and referee, or just plain dogsbody. With the possible exception of a few management games it is not feasible to program the machine to serve as opponent where simulation games are concerned, at least, not as a competent one. The reason is that, in every turn of a simulation game, the player is faced with a practically unlimited number of options. A war game commander, for example, may choose to move any subset of his many units, and each chosen unit may be instructed to move to any one of an astronomically large number of attainable positions. The program cannot possibly test every option, nor is there any clear cut method for reducing the options to be tested. It is the human player's knowledge of the reality simulated by the program that enables him to make sensible choices, rather than his logical or computational expertise.

In an abstract game the number of options is limited by the rules and the scenario. Of its nature, the game represents a highly idealised world of few dimensions populated by simple creatures which interact in very few ways. In such games the machine can, and often does, provide a worthy opponent. This by no means precludes its use as a moderator for abstract games, and we have already cited Kriegspiel (Section 2.5) in this context. Nevertheless, in this chapter we shall concentrate on the programming of a machine opponent because, where abstract games are concerned, this is where the main interest lies. We shall assume that there are two players, at least one of which is the machine.

Algorithms and heuristics

Anyone interested in computer methods will meet these terms repeatedly, and few terms are explained in so many different ways by so many writers. Rather than review the various nuances of meaning we shall simply define them as they are understood here.

An *algorithm* is a precisely formulated procedure for finding the solution to an unambiguously stated problem. If a method is not guaranteed to solve the problem in a finite number of operations, it is not an algorithm. A good algorithm is one which finds a solution quickly and, for certain classes of problem, it is possible to measure the quality of an algorithm in terms of its 'rate of convergence' to the solution. For games-related problems this is rarely possible and, although we shall be interested to find good algorithms rather than bad ones, we shall rely more on instinct than analysis in making comparisons.

A *heuristic method* is a precisely formulated procedure for searching for the solution to a problem. It will not necessarily find the solution, although sometimes it will. In the sense that one may be 'remote from' or 'near to' the solution, a heuristic method should move towards the solution and, in so doing, must be guided in some way. This guidance is usually provided by a number, called a *heuristic*, which might indicate how far away the solution lies. Alternatively, a heuristic might imply only that such and such a step is possibly better than any other feasible step.

Where some confusion arises is typified by the use of the title 'α–β algorithm'. This algorithm, which we shall discuss shortly, is not guaranteed to find the winning strategy in a game. Why, then, is it called an algorithm? Simply because 'find the winning strategy' is not the problem to be solved by the algorithm. Its aim is to solve a certain subproblem – which it does without fail – constituting one stage in a heuristic method whose aim is (hopefully) 'find the winning strategy'.

8.2   Merit values and game trees

MERIT FUNCTIONS AND VALUES

If a computer program is to make any sense of the position reached in a game or, more particularly, the position reached after it has selected its move, it must have some objective way of measuring the benefits and penalties which could accrue from the position. We too have our own, usually less objective, means of assessment. Where, in a game of Chess, we can say: 'I have seen a similar position before, and it sometimes leads to a weakness on the Queen's side of the board', the program has two options.

It can evaluate the position, as it stands, in terms of immediate captures, control of vacant squares, the degree of protection enjoyed by the Kings, and so on, and obtain a numerical measure assumed to be related to the 'quality' of the position – from its own point of view. Alternatively, it can execute trial moves on behalf of both players, and try to predict the likely outcome of the position. In that case, its assessment of the current position will depend upon its assessment of future positions.

In either case a point is reached at which a 'static' assessment is necessary. That is, an assessment based only on a single game position. Of course, when the program looks ahead, it will have to make many static assessments in deriving a 'dynamic' assessment for the actual position reached.

The numerical measure of 'position quality' is known as a *merit value* and is obtained from the evaluation of a *merit function*. Here, again, different writers diverge in their terminology. Games theorists (Section 2.2) use the terms *pay-off* and *pay-off function*, whilst others speak of *values* and *evaluation functions*. The 'merit' terminology seems to enjoy the widest circulation.

A simple heuristic method

Suppose, for a moment, that someone (or some computer program) discovered a merit function for Chess that measured the quality of every possible position with absolute reliability and accuracy. After a move by its human adversary the program would evaluate the merit function for each position which could be reached after one legal move. There are, on average, between 30 and 40 possible moves from a Chess position, so it might be supposed that little computation would be involved. However, for all we know such an omnicogniscent merit function might require years of computer time. After the necessary pause the program would announce its move as that which led to the maximal merit value, with confidence that it could not do better!

As far as Chess is concerned this is pure speculation. But there are some games for which this simple technique is very effective. Three-dimensional noughts and crosses is one such game. It is played in the 64 cells of a $4 \times 4 \times 4$ cube and the winner is the first player to get four of his symbols in a straight line. The merit function attaches a weight to each vacant cell of the cube to reflect the number of potentially winning lines which pass through the cell. Thus the central cells of the cube attract a larger weighting than other cells. An additional weight is attached to cells of value to the opponent, particularly to those in which he could place a final winning symbol. The author can attest that such a program is very hard to beat.

In general it is not possible to find a merit function as reliable as that used for three-dimensional noughts and crosses. It then becomes necessary to write a program capable of looking ahead.

GAME TREES

A *game tree* is a graphical representation of a game, and is intended to help systematise a look-ahead process. Suppose we identify every game position with a node in a directed graph (Section 4.4), and every legal move with a branch of the directed graph. The direction of a branch connecting two nodes indicates which represents the earlier position and which the later.

If every distinct game position is represented by one, and only one, node of the graph it should be evident that the graph could contain *cycles* (closed successions of branches) representing the fact that certain positions can be repeated after some number of moves, *loops* (single-branch cycles) representing a 'passed' turn in which a player leaves a position unchanged, and *parallel paths* (distinct successions of branches which originate and end on common nodes) representing the attainment of a position by distinct series of moves. Cycles, loops, etc. do not aid the analysis of the look-ahead process to be described here, and we eliminate them as follows.

Every game position which can be derived by a single move from any other position is assigned its own unique node in the graph. Hence no node has more than one in-branch. A particular position may therefore be represented many times throughout the graph. Such a structure is a tree – in our case a *directed tree*.

An example – the game of Kono

It is always difficult to find examples which illustrate ideas with acceptable brevity and generality. The game of noughts and crosses (two-dimensional) has been used by some writers, but the game tree is too large to be reproduced in its complete form. The game of Kono is used here.

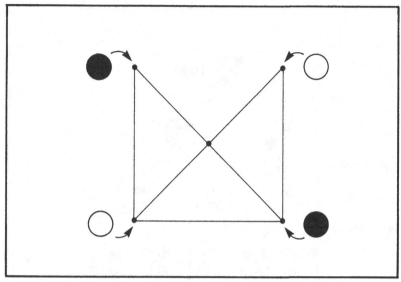

Fig. 8.1. Kono board and starting position.

Kono is played throughout the far east with minor variations, and is listed in Murray [22] whose classic study of abstract games is, incidentally, still the best source for games-hunters. It is played on a board containing only five playing points linked as shown in Figure 8.1. Each player has two pieces which remain in play throughout the game. The diagram shows the starting position. By alternately moving one piece to any adjacent vacant point the players endeavour to trap both the opponent's pieces, so that he is unable to move.

Kono is really a somewhat trivial game played mainly by children, but it serves to illustrate a game tree and the basic operations of look-ahead processes.

It can be seen from Figure 8.1 that it does not matter who takes the first move – we assume that it is White.

The game tree for Kono is illustrated in Figure 8.2. Note that, in most cases, a player's move is forced – a situation represented by a node having only a single out-branch. There are, in any case, never more than two legal moves from a position. Where a position has complete lateral symmetry it is immaterial which of a players' pieces is moved to the central point, so we do not illustrate both options. Technically, the game is a draw because, by correct play, a player can always avoid defeat. Thus the tree is actually infinite in extent but, as the starting position is repeated, we can truncate the diagram.

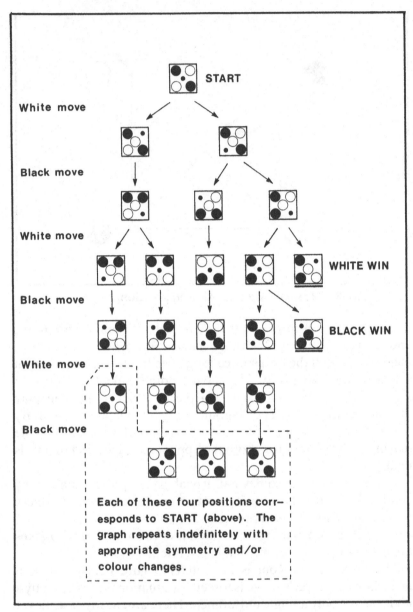

Fig. 8.2. Game tree for Kono.

The top node of the tree shown in the diagram corresponds to the starting position, and is the *root* node for this particular tree. If we drew any subtree, it too would have a root node and, in general, we are interested in the tree rooted at the node corresponding to the current position in the game. Note that it is conventional to draw trees with their roots at the top of the diagram – 'in the air'.

Storage of tree data

As you may know, or will have guessed, it is completely unnecessary to expand the full game tree in computer memory. A complete description of the current position, the root, is certainly needed but, as the program looks ahead down the tree, it stores only the minimal data necessary to define moves.

As the method used for storing this data is intimately related to the manner in which the look-ahead is conducted we continue the discussion under the next subheading.

Tree search and backtrack

The process of looking ahead to future nodes of a tree is known as a *tree search*, abbreviated to *search* if the context is obvious. There are several ways of conducting a search. We describe these with reference to Figure 8.3 which is a multi-purpose redraft of the tree in Figure 8.2. Each node is labelled with a letter and branches will be identified by quoting the ordered pair of node-letters in brackets.

To the left of the diagram are indicated *ply-numbers* relative to the root node. This term, borrowed from the timber trade, seems

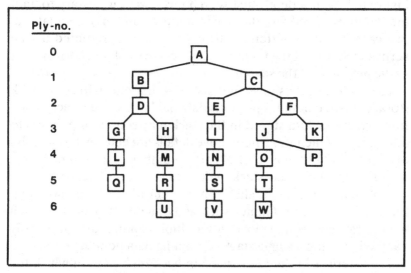

Fig. 8.3. Labelled game tree for Kono.

Table 8.1. *Depth-first search table*

Ply-no.																								
0	A	A	A	A	A	A	A	A	A	A	A	A	A	A	A	A	A	A	A	A	A	A	A	A
1	B	B	B	B	B	B	B	B	B	B	C	C	C	C	C	C	C	C	C	C	C	C	C	*
2	D	D	D	D	D	D	D	D	*		E	E	E	E	E	F	F	F	F	F	F	F	*	
3	G	G	G	H	H	H	*				I	I	I	*		J	J	J	J	K	*			
4	L	*		M	*						N	*				O	P	*						

appropriate to a discussion of trees! However, some writers refer to *level-numbers* instead. Whatever position has been reached in a game, the set of all positions which can be reached after one move has ply-number 1, those reached after two moves have ply-number 2, and so on.

In a *breadth-first search* the program examines all nodes at ply 1 before moving on to examine all nodes at ply 2, and so on. A search of this type is sometimes used in the solution of shortest-route problems on a graph, but it is rarely used for progressing through a game tree.

A *depth-first search* is simpler to program, more economical with memory space, and lends itself to some quite sophisticated methods for reducing the amount of work to be done. We therefore confine the discussion to this type of search.

Table 8.1 details an exhaustive search to ply 4 of the tree in Figure 8.3. (For a depth-first search it is always necessary to limit the depth by specifying the maximum ply-number.) The data, in this case just node-letters, is held in a *stack* represented by the vertical columns of the table. Each successive column corresponds to the next step of the search.

The table clearly shows the 'last in – first out' nature of stack storage. Each column represents data held in a simple stack array. In practice the data stored in the stack may consist of pointers to other areas of memory where move details are held. Alternatively, the move details may be held in a number of different arrays accessed by the same stack index. Such arrays are sometimes described as being 'in parallel'. The system adopted depends upon the particular game. Games such as Draughts (Checkers) which incorporate compound moves for multiple captures are most easily handled by using a single stack containing data pointers.

The asterisks in the table indicate *backtrack* steps in which the search returns to the previous node but can find no further out-branches leading to a node at the next ply. In fact, the entire process of depth-first search is often called 'backtrack'.

A very important part of the game program is a procedure for efficiently generating the next legal move or, equivalently, finding the next node of the tree. The programmer must be careful not to regenerate positions which have already been examined at some earlier stage of the search. This requires the imposition of some type of order on matters such as the selection of the next piece to be moved, the selection of the next direction for the move, and the selection of the distance moved. As we shall see in the following section, the order in which trial moves are generated can greatly influence the speed and efficiency of the program.

Conclusion

We have discussed the sequence in which nodes are generated and examined during an exhaustive search, but we have said nothing about how we assess which is the best (announced) move from the current position represented by the root node. Clearly, as the search reaches new nodes of the tree something must be done with the merit values. What this is, is the subject of the next section.

8.3   The α–β algorithm

The purpose of the α–β algorithm is efficiently to derive merit values for the immediate successor nodes of the root node, and so indicate what move is best from the point of view of the program. The algorithm also assigns a merit value to the root, though this has no particular significance except in relation to the internal workings of the algorithm itself. First, though, it is necessary to describe a simpler algorithm based upon an exhaustive search of the tree down to some predetermined ply-number.

MINIMAX SEARCH

Suppose that you are playing a two-person game and it is your opponent's turn to move. He is presented with a set of merit values, measured from 'his point of view', and corresponding one-to-one with his possible moves – which does he choose? Of course, he chooses the move with the maximum merit value. Now, suppose you were able to make the choice for him. You would obviously choose the move having the minimum merit value in order to damage his position as much as possible.

As far as the machine is concerned it must be programmed to allow for his behaviour so that, in looking ahead, it selects maximal merit values from amongst those associated with nodes having an odd ply-number, and minimal merit values when nodes have an even ply-number.

The minimax search algorithm proceeds as follows:

(1) Initialise the 'current' node to the root node, for the start of a depth-first search.

(2) Attempt to execute one move (down the tree) from the current node to a hitherto unvisited successor node.

(a) If the move is successful update the current node and repeat the operation.

(b) If no move can be made because the current node is at the ply limit of the search, or because the current node has no out-branches, go to operation (3).

(c) If no move can be made because all successor nodes have already been visited go to operation (4) unless the current node is the root node in which case the algorithm is terminated.

(3) Evaluate the (static) merit function for the current (terminal) node. Let M denote the merit value.

(4) Backtrack to the preceding node, and let P denote its ply-number.

(a) If no merit value has yet been assigned to this node then assign a (dynamic) merit value of M to it.

(b) If the node already has a merit value, V say, then replace it with M if:

> either $M < V$ and P is odd
> or $M > V$ and P is even

Whatever action is taken above reset M to the merit value for this node.

Go to operation (2).

The result of applying a minimax search is represented in Figure 8.4 which shows part of a game tree with associated merit values. The search is terminated at ply 3. Groups of nodes sharing a common predecessor are enclosed in a sausage labelled S_1, S_2, etc.

In the diagram M_1, M_2, etc. denote static merit values derived for terminal nodes. The subscripts indicate the order in which they are calculated as the search proceeds. The dynamic merit values associated with non-terminal nodes are indicated as maxima, and minima, of the merit values occurring in the sets S_1, S_2, etc. Thus,

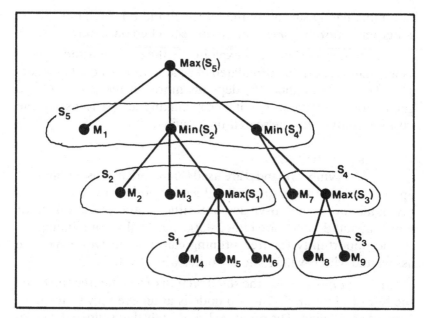

Fig. 8.4. Result of a minimax search.

for example, $\text{Max}(S_3)$ denotes the largest of the merit values associated with nodes in set S_3. The subscripts of the set-names S_1, S_2, etc., indicate the order in which the sets are completed.

Search economisation

The number of nodes to be searched increases very rapidly as the limiting ply-number is increased. In Chess, for example, a 1-ply minimax search might typically involve the generation and examination of 30 nodes. A 2-ply search might involve about $30 + 30^2$ nodes, a 3-ply search $30 + 30^2 + 30^3$ nodes, and so on. For the majority of games it is essential to find some way of reducing the amount of work if the program is to look ahead to a depth sufficient to ensure a reasonable standard of play.

Two main methods are employed for game trees.

(a) *Preclusion or pruning.* This depends upon the program recognising parts of the tree which will have no effect on the merit values assigned to the nodes at ply 1. When such parts are found they are 'pruned' away and discarded.

(b) *Fusion or merging.* If the program can recognise the game position represented by a node as identical to the position represented by some node reached at an earlier stage of the search, it can immediately substitute the results found for the latter. Thus, congruent or *isomorphic* subtrees are searched once only.

The pruning method (a) is exploited in the α–β algorithm which, as we shall see, can be formulated in a game-independent manner. The success of method (b) depends more on the nature of the game. For some, the work entailed in making comparisons of game positions outweighs the search-time saving.

α–β PRUNING

The symbols α and β are used for historical reasons, and are applied, respectively, to merit values for nodes at even and odd ply-numbers. Hence α-values are either static merit values or maxima, and β-values are either static merit values or minima.

The opportunity for tree pruning can arise in two ways, one associated with α-values and the other with β-values.

(a) *α-cutoff*. Consider the small section of a game tree shown on the left of Figure 8.5. The top node is at an even ply so its merit value is an α-value. The program has already determined the merit values shown, the underlined value 11 being the most recent. It is immaterial whether the values on the bottom line are static merit values for terminal nodes, or are maxima of sets of values from a lower level. The value 34 has already been 'backed up' to the node at the odd ply which, in a minimax search, would receive a

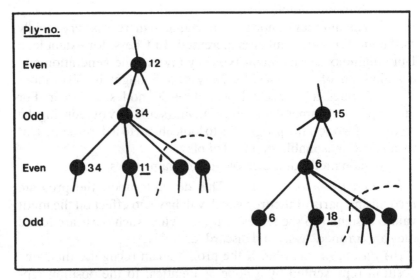

Fig. 8.5. Alpha-cutoff (left) and beta-cutoff (right).

'minimum' value. The 11 which has just been produced is less than 34 so would certainly replace the value 34 at the odd ply node. However, the 11 is less than the 12 at the even ply node above so would not replace the latter because even ply nodes collect a 'maximum' value. Whatever values occur in the part of the tree below the dotted line they cannot 'increase' the value at the odd ply node and so cannot affect the 12 at the top node. This part of the tree can therefore be ignored completely. The dotted line represents an α-cutoff.

The rule for an α-cutoff is that the occurrence of an α-value that is less than or equal to an α-value two levels (plies) higher up the tree allows the program to prune away all remaining branches and nodes originating from the intervening odd ply node.

(b) *β-cutoff*. The section of tree shown on the right of Figure 8.5 illustrates a β-cutoff. The argument proceeds in the same way as before except that 'maximum' becomes 'minimum' and vice-versa. Likewise 'less than' becomes 'greater than' and vice-versa.

We summarise the example very briefly. The 6 on the lower line has already been 'backed up' to the even ply node above which collects a 'maximum' value. Hence the newly produced 18, under-lined, will replace the 6 at the even ply node. However, it is greater than the 15 already assigned to the top node which, being at odd ply, collects a 'minimum' value. It cannot, therefore, affect the latter value. The part of the tree below the dotted cutoff line cannot decrease the value at the even ply node, so may be ignored.

The rule for β-cutoff is that the occurrence of a β-value that is greater than or equal to a β-value two levels (plies) higher up the tree allows the program to prune away all remaining branches and nodes originating from the intervening even ply node.

Cutoff implementation

The idea of pruning away part of a tree which, as we have said, is not explicitly stored in memory, may be somewhat mystifying. It is, however, a very simple process.

A cutoff affects only the sequence of nodes to be searched. It enables the program to skip to a node which would otherwise be reached at a later point in the search. One of the parameters of the search is the ply-number of the node from which the next step is to be made. All that is necessary to implement a cutoff is to reduce this parameter. The operation is incorporated in the flowchart introduced in a later subsection.

Improving performance

We describe three ways in which the performance of the
α–β algorithm may be enhanced. All are to some extent game
dependent. That is, they depend on the programmer – and hence
the program – having some knowledge of the distribution and
range of merit values likely to occur in the particular game concerned. All three methods aim to detect cutoffs at the earliest
possible stage.

(a) *Node ordering*. Consider the α-cutoff shown at the left of
Figure 8.5. If the merit value of 11 had been determined before the
34 at the same ply, the latter would have been included in the
cutoff, and some computer time would have been saved. Similarly,
in the β-cutoff shown at the right of the diagram, it would have
been better to determine the merit value of 18 before the 6 at the
same ply. Ideally, we would like to order the nodes in each S-set
(Figure 8.4) so that the node most likely to cause a cutoff is
examined first. Without evaluating merit values for all the nodes of
a set, which would defeat the object, we must rely on knowledge of
the game applied at the 'next node' level of the program.

Because all merit functions are measured from 'the point of
view' of the player (machine) moving from even numbered plies,
this means simply that within each S-set the nodes should be
ordered so that the node examined first is that corresponding to the
'strongest move from the point of view of the player on whose
behalf it is made'. In practice, we can rarely achieve this ideal
ordering, but some attempt should be made because the savings
can be very considerable – even 'dramatic'.

(b) *'Killer' cutoffs*. On the assumption that cutoffs are caused by
strong moves, the program can keep a record of which nodes
caused cutoffs. In subsequent machine moves the program can
then reorder the nodes in an S-set to increase the chance of an early
cutoff.

For many games this is not as easy as it sounds. The identification
of the same node in different machine turns is often difficult.
Nevertheless, it should always be considered at the design stage.

(c) *α–β 'windows'*. An obvious programming technique related
to the nodes which have not so far received a merit value, is to
assign pseudo-merit values of minus infinity to nodes at even ply,
and plus infinity to nodes at odd ply. Knowing something about the
range of actual merit values enables us to substitute tighter values
and so hasten the detection of cutoffs. The pseudo-merit values

chosen define a window within which actual values are expected to lie. If, in a particular case, a value lies outside the window the assigned value will not change, and detection of this fact allows the program to widen the window and repeat the calculations for the node concerned. Thus, bad windows can actually increase the amount of work to be done. In the author's experience windowing is relatively ineffective. However, he may have applied it to the wrong games! In any case, the technique is incorporated in the flowchart below.

There is great scope for the invention of game-dependent accelerators for the α–β algorithm. One might, for example, envisage a modification to permit a contribution from the static merit values of non-terminal nodes. These might, in some cases, contain high class information not utilised in the standard algorithm presented here.

In view of the commercial value of Chess playing machines and the like, one suspects that many of the recent advances remain unpublished.

8.4   Programming the α–β algorithm

This section is intended to give you a flying start in programming the game-independent part of the algorithm represented by the subprogram ALPHAB. The section is divided into three parts presenting a short descriptive list of game-dependent subprograms called from ALPHAB, a list of variables used by ALPHAB, and a program flowchart for ALPHAB itself. To understand fully the ideas presented it is essential to set up a sample game tree with fictional static merit values at the terminal nodes, and 'play through' the flowchart in the manner suggested in Section 3.6.

You are urged to collect together all game-independent parts, including ALPHAB, in the form of a library – or 'skeleton' program – which may be linked to the game-dependent parts of an actual game program in the simplest possible way. This will free you to concentrate on the merit function which will embody all the facets of skill, inspiration, and intellectual adventure!

GAME-DEPENDENT SUBPROGRAMS
The following subprograms are called from ALPHAB:

NOBEST – Indicate that, as yet, no best move from the position represented by the root node has been determined.

BEST   – Record details of the best move from the root node, so far determined.

NEXNOD – Attempt to execute a forward step to the next unvisited node. If the step is successful set the indicator STEP (see below) to 1, else set it to 0. The step is performed from that node, on the current path from the root, which lies at 'level' L (see below). Note that all backtracking is performed in ALPHAB through the control of L.

EVAL   – Evaluate the static merit function for the current (terminal) node. EVAL is a function subprogram, so needs at least one actual parameter. We use the variable PLAYER (see below). Remember that merit values are always calculated from 'the point of view' of the player moving from the root node.

VARIABLES

The following variables provide the interface between ALPHAB and the game-dependent subprograms. Execution speed is very important for the α–β algorithm and it is suggested that the variables are stored in a globally accessible part of memory, such as FORTRAN common store. This will enable the game-dependent subprograms, with the exception of EVAL, to dispense with formal parameters.

PLAYER – Identification (1 or 2) of the player moving from the root node. This variable is particularly necessary when the program is to play against itself for the purposes of research or self-improvement (learning).

L   – The 'level' of the current node in the search. This is defined here as equal to the ply-number plus 1.

LMAX   – The maximum level of the search. E.g. 5 for a 4-ply search.

S   – The parity of the current level defined as $+1$ for odd levels (even plies) and -1 for even levels (odd plies).

STEP — An indicator set by NEXNOD to 1 when it moves to a successor node, and 0 when it is unable to move either because there is no such node, or all such nodes have already been visited earlier in the search.

LASTEP — An indicator set in ALPHAB to show whether the last call to NEXNOD produced a new node, or not.

V(LMAX) — An array of dimension LMAX holding merit values for each node of the current path from the root node. Note that, in a tree, such a path is unique. V(L) holds the merit value for the node at level L.

W — A window value initialised in some game-dependent part of the program. Merit values outside the range $(-W, +W)$ are regarded as unlikely to affect the move finally chosen as the best. If, however, they do, then ALPHAB re-enters itself with a doubled value for W.

T0, T1, T2 — Temporary working variables.

The variables W, T0, T1, T2, the array V, and the function EVAL are all of type REAL.

ALPHAB FLOWCHART

A program flowchart for subroutine ALPHAB, using the variables introduced above, is shown in Figure 8.6. To achieve the necessary compactness the flowchart has been broken into two parts connected via the remote connectors labelled 2 and 3. Note that the connector labelled 5 is used only to identify the point at which a cutoff is handled.

8.5 A simple merit function

The strength of a computer opponent depends critically on the quality of the merit function. It is in devising this that the programmer must exercise his knowledge of the game in question.

To illustrate a typical merit function let us consider the game of Billabong. This is a simple race game popular with a few devotees, but unpublished because – as a board game – it suffers from an

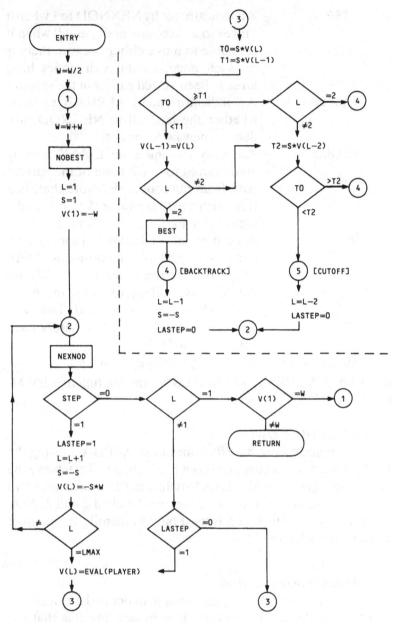

Fig. 8.6. Subroutine ALPHAB.

ergonomic deficiency. The player must, unfortunately, develop a facility for redirecting his eye quickly and accurately over a considerable expanse of the board. As a computer game, this difficulty disappears because the player can be warned, even corrected, if he makes a mistake.

THE GAME OF BILLABONG

Billabong is a race between teams of kangaroos which strive to be the first to complete a circular course around a billabong (a small pond). There are five kangaroos in each team, and each kangaroo has the ability to walk one square or to perform a succession of jumps over other kangaroos of either team. In a walk-move a kangaroo moves orthogonally or diagonally to any vacant square adjacent to that which he currently occupies. In a jump-move the kangaroo may execute any number of leaps in orthogonal or diagonal directions provided that:

(a) He leaps over one, and only one, kangaroo at a time.

(b) He lands on a vacant square symmetrically disposed on the other side of the 'pivot' kangaroo. That is, the launch and landing squares must be the same distance from the pivot kangaroo, and on the same row, column, or diagonal.

(c) He neither leaves the board, nor jumps across any part of the billabong.

A kangaroo may, often usefully, jump the same pivot kangaroo at different stages of the same jump-move. This ability to combine many jumps in a single turn sometimes allows a kangaroo to complete more than half the course in a single game-turn. Hence, a player must be careful not to present his opponent with too many pivot kangaroos.

At his turn, a player may select any one of his kangaroos for a walk-move or a jump-move. Passing is not permitted. The winner is the player who first completes the course with all of his kangaroos. Each kangaroo must cross the start–finish line twice or, more precisely, he must cross this line twice more in the east–west direction than in the west–east direction. Kangaroos start the game on any vacant squares alternately selected by their owners. The board is shown in Figure 8.7.

Included in the diagram are some angles measured clockwise from the start–finish line. Each square has such an angle stored in an integer array initialised at the start of a run. By using the square

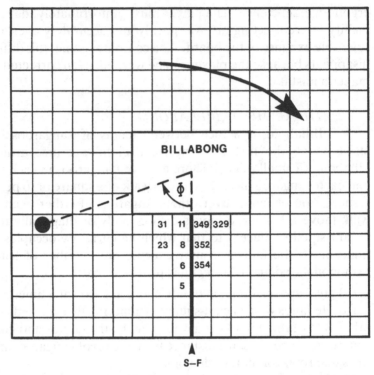

Fig. 8.7. Board for Billabong.

coordinates as array indices the program can rapidly find the angle (denoted Φ in the diagram).

To distinguish between the angles for squares occupied by kangaroos which have crossed the start–finish line a different number of times we invent a parameter called the *crossing number*. Before a kangaroo has passed the start line his crossing number is −1, after crossing the line from east to west his crossing number is increased by 1, and it is decreased by 1 if he crosses from west to east. Therefore, a kangaroo with a crossing number of 1 has completed the course.

The angle A of the kangaroo number K, owned by player number P, and having a crossing number X, may be evaluated by a program statement such as:

```
A(K,P)=ANGLE(I,J)+360*X(K,P)
```

where ANGLE is the name of the basic array of angles, I and J are the coordinates of the square occupied by the kangaroo, and A and X are two-dimensional arrays for angles and crossing numbers.

Merit function for Billabong

How is the program to assess the value of a position in Billabong? It might simply add together the angles for all the kangaroos in its team to obtain a 'total' angle. However, there may be times at which it is more important to impede the opponent (the human player) than to make good progress with its own team. This suggests that the total angle for the opposing team should be subtracted from the merit value. Perhaps the total angles for the two teams should be given different weightings to reduce the possibility of a slow game.

When a kangaroo finishes the course during a trial turn its angle must continue to make a contribution to the merit function otherwise comparisons will be distorted.

Kangaroos near the finishing line are prime candidates for the position of pivot. It may be necessary to provide some additional incentive for kangaroos to finish the course so that they are no longer part of the game – they jump into the billabong to cool off! One way to do this is to replace the crossing number X by some non-linear function of X when calculating kangaroo angles. The quantity $X^2 + 2X$ leaves the phase contribution unchanged when X is -1 or 0, but increases it by a factor of 3 when X is $+1$.

Another consideration is that back markers (the least advanced kangaroos) run the risk of finding no pivot kangaroos, and having to walk all the way home. Their angles should, perhaps, be given an additional weighting.

All this may be summarised as a merit function having the form:

$$M = w_1 T_1 - w_2 T_2 + w_3 B_1 - w_4 B_2$$

where T_1 and T_2 are the total angles for the computer team and our team respectively, B_1 and B_2 are the angles for the back markers in the two teams, and w_1, w_2, w_3, w_4 are weighting coefficients. As we can divide throughout by w_1 without affecting the comparison of merit values, there are really just three weightings to be determined by the program trials.

8.6   Learning programs

Given that the merit value for any game position depends upon a small number of numerical coefficients, such as the weightings used above, the program may be able to optimise, or at least improve, its own performance. To this end it must be able to modify the coefficients according to the results obtained. Such a program is said to 'learn'.

The most celebrated example of this kind of program is Arthur Samuel's Checkers (Draughts) program. This achieved a reputation for playing a very strong game. For interested readers the most accessible description is given by David Levy [26] in his excellent series of articles in *Personal Computer World*.

For a learning program to work it must have some way of assessing the result of a game or series of games. This might be some continuous measure of its margin of victory, or loss. Alternatively, it may have to play a series of games with fixed coefficients and count the number of wins.

It is very nice if the machine is programmed to play against itself, so that we can return in a week's time to discover how it has improved! However, there is a difficulty. One side must play to constant coefficients if the other is to discover how to modify its own coefficients in any reliable way. How do we know that the 'constant' player adequately represents a human player? We don't, of course. We could allow both sides to play with varying coefficients, but then we might return to find two idiots – one slightly better than the other – playing together. We cannot guarantee that any trial modification of the coefficients will improve the performance against a human player. Thus, regular intervention by a human player seems essential.

Let us assume that the constant player, human or machine, plays a reasonable game and may be accepted as a standard for a while. What strategy should be adopted for varying the coefficients in the merit function used by the learning player? Two approaches are briefly discussed below.

Univariate search

Imagine that each of the coefficients is associated with a coordinate axis in a space. For the three weightings suggested for Billabong it is easy to visualise w_1, w_2, and w_3 being identified with the X, Y, and Z axes of our ordinary three-dimensional space. However, there is no mathematical difficulty in extending the idea to a space having any number of dimensions.

The learning program starts by assessing its performance at one point of the space. It then selects one coefficient for variation. After incrementing this by some predetermined amount it plays trial games and again assesses its performance. If it is worse, it tries decrementing the coefficient from its starting value. If it obtains better results it again moves the 'point' in space along the chosen coefficient axis. This time, however, it doubles the increment. When the performance cannot be improved either by an increment or a decrement, the step size is halved and the program continues its trials. The program eventually reaches a point where neither a decrease or an increase by some predetermined minimum step size will produce an improvement. The whole process is now repeated for the next coefficient. The coefficients are treated cyclically in this way.

The binary search process sketched above is somewhat more tricky than the description implies. For instance, to ensure that the same point is not tested more than once it will be necessary to store results obtained earlier in the search. To avoid the possibility of oscillation about an optimal point no step size doubling is permitted once the step size has been halved.

The trial point in the coefficient space traces a zigzag path having a series of right-angled bends. The next method produces short cuts across the space.

The Spendley simplex search method
We describe only the basic version of this method due to W. Spendley [27]. Many enhancements have been published, notably those of Nelder & Mead [28]. The simplex search method (not to be confused with the simplex method of linear optimisation) is widely recognised as a very effective method for finding the maximum (or minimum) of a function such as that arising in the assessment of play performance where nothing is known about the form of the function beyond its values at isolated points of the coefficient space.

Again, let the coefficients of the merit function be identified with the axes of a Cartesian coordinate system. The program starts by assessing the performance at one starting point, (w_1, w_2, w_3) say. It then does the same for three other points $(w_1 + d_1, w_2, w_3)$, $(w_1, w_2 + d_2, w_3)$, $(w_1, w_2, w_3 + d_3)$. The quantities d_1, d_2, and d_3 are small increments. As a rough guide they should be chosen to be about one-tenth of the maximum conceivable range for their associated coefficients. To simplify the discussion we shall assume that all the ds are equal.

The four points, shown as A, B, C, and D in Figure 8.8, lie at the vertices of an irregular tetrahedron. In general, if there are N

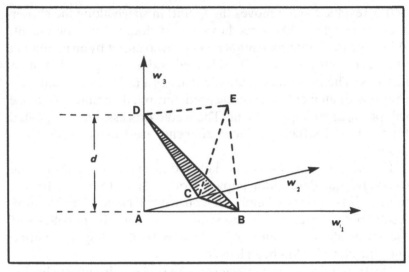

Fig. 8.8. Simplex search reflection step.

coefficients, the space has N dimensions, and the program generates $N + 1$ points at the vertices of an *N-dimensional simplex*.
However, we confine discussion to the three-dimensional case.

At every stage of the learning process the program holds information about the performance at each vertex of the current
simplex – initially ABCD. Let the performance at a vertex be
denoted by f subscripted by the vertex letter. Typically, f might be
measured as 'wins out of ten games'. In the case of Billabong
(above) f might measure the size of the win in a single game.

Depending on the relative size of the f values the program
transforms the simplex. The full Nelder & Mead method allows for
expansion, contraction, and reflection of the simplex. The basic
Spendley method, however, allows only reflection. Provided the
simplex size as measured by d is not too large, this will be sufficiently
good for a game learning program.

A reflection step consists of reflecting the 'worst' vertex – that
having the lowest value of f, say f_{min} – across the *centroid*, G say, of
the remaining vertices to obtain a new vertex. In Figure 8.8 A is
assumed to be the worst vertex and has been reflected across the
centroid of B, C, and D, to obtain vertex E.

If the new vertex is worse than the original worst vertex ($f_E < f_A$
in the diagram) we try reflecting the second worst vertex across the

centroid of the other three points. If this too gives no improvement over f_{min} we take the best vertex of the current simplex to represent the optimum – the best set of coefficients for the merit function. When a reflection produces a new vertex, or *image*, I for which $f_1 >$ f_{min} the reflected point is rejected and the image is included in the new simplex.

It remains to explain the derivation of the centroid, and the mathematics of reflection.

In the diagram we wish to find the centroid of the three vertices B, C, and D. This will be some point lying in the shaded triangle. It is a simple matter – the first coordinate of the centroid is just the average of the first coordinates of B, C, and D. Likewise, the nth coordinate of the centroid is the average of the nth coordinates of B, C, and D. Hence the centroid of B, C, and D lies at ($w_1 + d/3$, $w_2 + d/3$, $w_3 + d/3$).

Reflection is an equally simple matter. Suppose we wish to reflect a point (x_1, x_2, x_3) across a centroid (g_1, g_2, g_3) to an image point (y_1, y_2, y_3). As the centroid is equidistant from the reflected point and its image, and as all three points lie on a straight line, we have:

$$y_1 = 2g_1 - x_1, \quad y_2 = 2g_2 - x_2, \quad \text{and} \quad y_3 = 2g_3 - x_3$$

Thus, the simplex 'flips' around the coefficient space seeking the point which will give the best performance. If greater accuracy is required the whole process can be repeated with a smaller value of d, basing the initial simplex at the best point so far discovered.

It should be emphasised that this process is analogous to a blind man seeking the highest peak of a range of hills. He might well stumble to the top of one hill, but has no way of knowing if one of the other hills is higher still. Mathematically we say that the method locates a *local optimum* (in this case a local maximum). Except for certain problems with a special structure, there is no way – short of exhaustive evaluation – for finding the *global optimum*. Or rather, we may find the global optimum we seek, but cannot recognise it as such. We can, however, increase the probability that it will be found by repeating the search from a number of different starting points in the coefficient space.

8.7   Games of imperfect information

As described in Chapter 2 a game of imperfect information is one in which the players do not always know the current game state. In this section we discuss, in very general terms, how a computer opponent might play such a game.

We have assumed, up to the present, that it is possible to calculate the merit value at any node of the game tree. If the corresponding game state is completely unknown any play is as good, or as bad, as any other. In practice, however, this is never the case. It is always possible – in theory at least – to determine a set of feasible game states. If we can attach a probability to the existence of each feasible state we can program a probabilistic merit function.

Probabilistic merit functions

Suppose that the program is somehow able to deduce, at a given node of the game tree, that there are three feasible game states A, B, and C say. It may evaluate the merit function for each of these to obtain merit values M_A, M_B, and M_C – but which does it use?

If there was no information about which state was the most likely to exist it would seem reasonable to set the actual merit value E to the average of the three calculated values, thus:

$$E = (M_A + M_B + M_C)/3$$

Now suppose that the program has some means of calculating the probability for the existence of each game state. Denote these probabilities by P_A, P_B, and P_C. As the game states are mutually exclusive and cover all possible situations at the node in question we have:

$$P_A + P_B + P_C = 1$$

The idea of an average may be extended to define a quantity called the *expectation*, thus:

$$E = P_A M_A + P_B M_B + P_C M_C$$

By considering the extreme cases where one of the Ps is equal to 1 (certainty), and the others are zero, we have grounds for believing that the expectation merit value should be the one to use.

The applicability of this idea depends on two factors.

First, the program must have the capacity to evaluate all the merit functions. We have postulated just three above, but for many games there will be far more. The time taken to evaluate merit functions may preclude a search to any depth greater than 1-ply.

Second, the program must be able to calculate, or estimate, the probability for the existence of each feasible game state. It can base this only on experience of the play to date, and this might require a great deal of computer memory. Nevertheless, there is a technique based on a famous theorem of probability theory which can help in some circumstances.

Bayes' theorem
The players have some knowledge of the current game state. Part of this is shared knowledge, and other parts are known only to one player. A typical example is afforded by almost any card game. We know what cards we hold, and to complete our knowledge of the game state we want to find out what cards are held by the opponent(s).

Place yourself in the position of the program. It knows what game states 'might' exist at some node of the tree and aims to find out which are feasible by assigning probabilities to the existence of each. Suppose we make some move from this node. Provided that it is possible to calculate the probability, for each possible state, that this particular move would be made, then it becomes possible to calculate the probability that any state actually exists.

Let us carefully specify a notation for these various probabilities. Suppose there are N possible game states denoted $S_1, S_2, S_3, \ldots, S_N$. The probability that a particular move, T say, would result from the existence of state S_i is denoted by $P(T, S_i)$. We, or rather the program, wish to calculate the probability that state S_i exists. Denote this by $P(S_i)$. Bayes' theorem states:

$$P(S_i) = \frac{P(T, S_i)}{P(T, S_1) + P(T, S_2) + \ldots P(T, S_N)}$$

The quantities $P(S_i)$ for $i = 1, 2, 3, \ldots, N$ correspond to the probabilities P_A, P_B, etc. which are needed for the evaluation of the expectation merit value.

The future

It seems certain that computer games will play an expanding role in general education and training for specific skills. But in these days of increasing, often enforced, leisure time, recreational game playing may be equally important. In this short chapter we speculate about future trends and developments.

As we have remarked, Chess programs have already attained a high level of excellence, to say nothing of certain Draughts, Reversi, and Backgammon programs which are almost unbeatable. There may be academic interest in improving such programs further, but from the point of view of the ordinary games player it makes little difference whether he is beaten by a grandmaster level program, or merely by an international master level program! For this reason, I see little further development in the published versions of this type of program – the machine opponent in an abstract game. This is not to say that research will not continue in games playing areas related to artificial intelligence studies.

The really exciting future for games programs lies in the use of the machine as a moderator in simulation games of ever-increasing reality. The players will, in the main, comprise people who would otherwise have no access to the environment modelled by the program. To this end, it seems probable that a games development language will arise. We might even hazard a guess at the name!

GLAD (Games Language and Development system) is unlikely to be specified or implemented by a home computer buff. It will be an advanced system calling for great professionalism and many man-years of work. However, the resulting language will be accessible to the home computer programmer, and will enable him to design, write, and test complex simulation games very quickly.

Certainly GLAD will be equipped with the usual language

facilities for declaring variables, naming modules, performing ordinary calculations, and controlling the sequence of computation. In addition it will offer advanced features in a number of areas. These might include:

(a) Time control of the simulation will be taken over by a part of the system always resident with the final object code. All the programmer will have to do is specify suitable activity periods.

(b) Play-command syntax will be definable through the medium of an inbuilt meta-language – a language for defining a language. All syntax checking during play will be automatic and error reports will be output in a player-friendly and standardised way. Each command specification will be associated with programmer-selected modules for command interpretation.

(c) A game database will be definable by the programmer in very general terms – all the detail being looked after by GLAD.

(d) Graphical output will be programmable in a powerful and uniform way. At the present time, the graphics facilities of the various home computers are very far from standard. For gaming purposes the author has developed an experimental system of modular graphics along the following lines.

Graphical 'objects' may be defined and named. These are convex polygons identified by the coordinates of their vertices (corners). To allow concave polygons at the definition level appears to require too much computer time. Straight lines are defined as two-point objects, and a single pixel is a one-point object.

Objects may be combined, and named, to define more complex shapes such as concave and hollow figures. These are recognised as objects in their own right and are capable of being transformed in the same way as fundamental objects.

Objects may be displayed in outline or 'filled in', moved, rotated, and scaled. Of course, objects may be 'un-displayed' as well. Overlapping is allowed, and any object may be copied in situ to produce a congruent named object which can subsequently be moved away to a new position.

Such a system of 'geometrical macros' seems ideal for displaying the state of a game, and it is likely that GLAD will adopt a similar approach.

Much of the technology for the development of GLAD already exists in the fields of simulation languages and database systems.

Advanced communications systems, perhaps associated with the cabling of private homes, will enable games hobbyists to subscribe to societies devoted to playing large multi-person simulations. For these, it will be necessary to employ a central mainframe machine and the home computer will be relegated to the position of intelligent terminal.

It has been said that the electronics revolution is producing a nation of recluses. Perhaps, through the mediation of games, the trend can be reversed and we will all make friends again.

References

[1] Bowen K. C. *Research Games* (Taylor and Francis in association with the Operational Research Society, London 1978).

[2] Berlekamp E. R., Conway J. H. & Guy R. K. *Winning Ways*, Vol. 2 (Academic Press Inc., London 1982).

[3] von Neumann J. & Morgenstern O. *Theory of Games and Economic Behaviour* (Princeton, New Jersey, 1944, 1947).

[4] Wetherell C. S., Buckholtz T. J. & Booth K. S. 'A director for Kriegspiel, a variant of Chess' (*The Computer Journal*, 15, 66–70, 1972).

[5] Prichard D. *Brain Games* pp. 30–7 (Penguin Books Ltd., Harmondsworth, 1982).

[6] Gardner M. 'Mathematical games' (*Scientific American*, 223, No. 4, Oct. 1970).

[7] Abbot R. *Abbott's New Card Games* (Funk and Wagnall, New York 1968).

[8] Gardner M. 'Mathematical games' (*Scientific American*, 237, No. 4, Oct. 1977).

[9] Romesburg H. C. *Simulating Scientific Inquiry with the Card Game Eleusis* (John Wiley & Sons, Inc. – Science Education 63 (5), pp. 599–608, 1979).

[10] Hofstadter D. R. 'Metamagical themas' (*Scientific American*, 247, No. 3, Sept. 1982).

[11] Hofstadter D. R. *Godel, Escher, Bach: An Eternal Golden Braid* (The Harvester Press, Hassocks, Sussex 1979).

[12] Back D. R. 'The Back pages' (*Journal of the CP/M User's Group* (U.K.), 1, No. 7, pp. 74–82, Sept. 1982).

[13] Day A. C. 'The use of symbol-state tables' (*The Computer Journal*, 13, No. 4, pp. 332–9, 1970).

[14] Busacker R. G. & Saaty T. L. *Finite Graphs and Networks* (McGraw Hill Inc., New York 1965).

[15] Pfaltz J. L. *Computer Data Structures* (McGraw Hill Kogakusha Ltd., Tokyo 1977).

[16] Day A. C. 'Full table quadratic searching for scatter storage' (*Communications of the ACM*, 13, pp. 481–2, 1970).

[17] Tocher K. D. *The Art of Simulation* (Hodder and Stoughton, London 1975).

[18] Dreyfus S. E. 'An appraisal of some shortest-path algorithms' (Chapter 8 of *Perspectives on Optimization*, ed. Geoffrion A. M. Addison-Wesley Publishing Company, Massachusetts, 1972).

[19]   Franta W. R. *The Process View of Simulation* (Elsevier North-Holland Inc., New York, 1977).

[20]   Braun M. *Differential Equations and their Applications* (Springer-Verlag, New York, 1979).

[21]   Coons S. A. *Surfaces for Computer-aided Design of Space Forms* (MIT Project MAC-TR-41, 1967).

[22]   Murray H. J. R. *A History of Board-games Other Than Chess* (Oxford University Press 1952: reprinted by Hacker Art Books, New York 1978).

[23]   Broyden C. G. 'A mark-scaling algorithm' (*The Computer Journal*, **26**, No. 2 pp. 109–12, 1983).

[24]   Downey J. *Winning Badminton Singles* (ED Publishing Ltd., Wakefield 1982).

[25]   Elo A. E. *The Rating of Chessplayers, Past and Present* (B. T. Batsford Ltd., London 1978).

[26]   Levy D. 'Computer games' (series) (*Personal Computer World*, Sportscene Publishers Ltd., London, Vol. 3, No. 8, August 1980).

[27]   Spendley W., Hext G. R. & Himsworth F. R. 'Sequential application of simplex designs in evolutionary operation and optimization' (*Technometrics*, **4**, pp. 441, 1962).

[28]   Nelder, J. A. & Mead R. 'A simplex method for function minimization' (*The Computer Journal*, **7**, pp. 308–13, 1965).

Index

abstract games, 10, 223–49
activity period: 138, 167; vector, 167
acuity of observer, 177
adventure games, 19, 107
algorithm: alpha–beta, 15, 224, 231–40;
 definition of, 224; minimax search,
 231–3; grid movement, 146–8
ALPHAB (subroutine), 237–40
arcade games, 4
arrays, 52
ASCII, 77
assembly languages: review, 61–3
assignments: on a graph, 102
asymptotic curve, 127
attenuation of parameters, 174–5
automata, 25–6

backtrack, 229–31
BASIC (review), 58–9
batch-processing, 3
Bayes' theorem, 249
Billabong (game), 239–43
binary relation, 103
bit-mask, 116–17
Black Box (game), 24–5
bottom–up design, 39–40
branches of a graph, 102
breadth-first search, 230
bubble sort, 151
buffer: DTM Block, 203–4; I–O, 77–80

calendar variables, 164–7
calls in program, 50
cells: node and branch, 103–7
centroid of simplex, 246
character string; see text
Chess, 2, 16, 18, 23, 42, 159, 225
classification of games, 10
CLOCK (subroutine), 165
closed range, 122
coaching aid: computer as, 32
coarse grid, 137

coding, 56, 63
collision, 111–13
combat: model of, 182–6
commands: from players, 74, 76, 90–101
compass bearing, 140
compiler, 33, 67–71
complementary event, 119
context number, 98–9, 114–16
CONVRT (subroutine), 140
Coons' patch, 220
cumulative probability, 131
cutoff: alpha and beta, 234–5

damage rate, 182
Dalton's Weekly, 49
data: condensation, 16; structured, 97,
 101–7
database, 93
DAYSET (subroutine), 166
debuggers, 72
decision process, 2, 9
declaration of variables, 53
density of random walk, 131
depth-first search, 230
diameter of random walk, 130
digital terrain model (DTM), 136, 195–222
digraph, 102–7
direction: cosines, 141, 146; numbers,
 129–30
dispersion, 126
distance: approximations, 131–5;
 Euclidean, 132; Manhattan, 132
distribution of random variable: 123–9;
 normal, 126–7; rectangular, 120;
 uniform, 120
Draughts (Checkers), 244
dry run, 72
DTM: block, 196; block directory,
 199–200; definition data, 200;
 generation of, 203–10; input and
 editing, 202; output, 213–18
dump: of game state, 43

eastings, 136, 196
echo: of a character, 77
elapsed time vector, 167
elliptical normal distribution, 186
ERNIE (machine), 121
error: numerical, 133; program, 71–3
exchange sort, 151
expectation, 248
extensive form of rules, 26
external references, 69
extrapolation, 156

fatigue of military units, 175–6
fine grid, 138
flags, 116–17
floating point representation, 65
flowchart; 41–7; program, 44–7; system, 41–3
flow of control, 40
folding: of texts, 112
FORTRAN (review), 60–1
frequency distribution, 123
function: formal symbolic, 155; monotonic, 181; procedural, 155; subprogram, 50; tabular, 155

game: attempts to define, 9; -independence, 75; objective, 12; of imperfect information, 12; of perfect information, 11; scenario, 12; state, 12, 43; theory, 11; tree, 226–31
GLAD (language), 250–1
global variable, 53
Go (game), 159
graph, 102–7
graphical objects, 251
grid: coarse, 137; fine, 138; movement algorithm, 146–8

half-range, 177
handshaking, 77
hashing; 109–14; by division, 111
hash-number, 111
heuristic, 224
histogram, 123
hyperbolic: functions, 184; paraboloid surface, 220

identifier, 48–9
independent events, 120
information: imperfect, 12, 247–9; perfect, 11
inside–out design, 40
interactive computing, 3, 33
interpolation: 154–7; for ground levels, 218–22; Lagrange, 157; linear, 156; polynomial, 157, quadratic, 156
interpreter, 33, 66–7
IRAND (function subprogram), 122
item-oriented input, 76, 80–90

key: in hashing, 111–12; in sorting, 149
killer cutoff, 236
knowledge diagrams, 12–15
Kono (game), 226–30
Kriegspiel (game), 23

Lagrange interpolation, 157
Lanchester's square law, 183
language: processing, 66–71; reviews, 57–63
lawgiver: computer as, 26–9
learning program, 243–7
levels; ground, 182, 195; interpolation for, 218–22; program, 36; search, 230, 238
Life (game), 11, 25
linear: interpolation, 156; text storage, 107–9
line of sight (LOS), 180–2
link editing, 67–71
local variable, 53
logical operations, 116, 212
loop: in a graph, 226; in program, 47
Lunar Lander (game), 195

machine: code, 35, 62; infinity, 151; opponent, 15–18, 223–49
macro, 62
magic numbers, 201
management games, 23, 186–93
map: DTM, 213–18; partitioned, 217; reference, 213–14
mapping function, 110–13
mean: arithmetic, 124–5; square deviation, 125
memory image, 71
merit: functions and values, 224–5; probabilistic, 248
meta-language, 251
minimax search algorithm, 231–3
missing value problem, 31
moderator; computer as, 19
module, 36
motion: simulation of, 135–49
multi-person games, 17
mutually exclusive events, 119

names: in program, 48–9
Nelder and Mead simplex search, 245–6
nodes of a graph, 102
Nomic (game), 28
normal distribution: 126–7; frequency function, 126
northings, 136, 196
notation: adopted in book, 6, 75
Noughts and Crosses, 225–6

object program, 68
observation: 176–80; probability function, 177–9

op-code, 62
open coding, 85
operating system, 58
opponent: computer as, 15–18, 223–49
optimum: local and global, 247; nature of, 186

packing constant, 84
parallel processing, 16
parameter: actual, 54; formal, 54; list, 54
PASCAL (review), 59
passwords: use of, 42, 95
pay off, 225
P-code, 71
percentage probability, 119
piracy, 4
ply number, 229
polynomial interpolation, 157
port status, 77
probability: 118–20; vector, 131, 208
procedural function, 155
program: design, 33–56; errors, 71–3; flowchart, 44–7; names and identifiers, 48–9; puns, 35; testing, 71–2
programmer, 7
projections 144–6; 181–2
pseudo-: destination, 142; level, 201; random numbers, 121
puzzle, 11

quadratic interpolation, 156
quadric, 220

random numbers, 120–4
random variable: continuous and discrete, 124; distribution of, 120, 123–9
random walk, 129–31, 205
ranking competitors, 30
RANORM (function subprogram), 128–9
READIT (subroutine), 82–90
recursive calls, 50
referee: computer as, 20
relaxation factor, 206
relocatable code, 68
repeat–until loop, 47
representation: 34; chain of, 103
research simulation, 158
residual time, 143–4, 169–70

sampling normal distribution, 127–9
scalar variable, 64
scenario, 12
scheduling of simulation activities, 170
scope of a variable, 53

search: of game tree, 229–37; economisation, 233–4
SEASET (subroutine), 166–7
second: computer as, 18
self-modifying games, 28–9
shortest route algorithms, 148–9
simplex search, 245–7
simulation: activity, 162; continuous and discrete, 160; cycle, 162; event driven, 162–3; games, 158–94; languages, 161; real time, 162; research, 158; unit time increment, 162–3
smoothing, 156, 206
sort: exchange, 151; bubble, 151; tournament, 152–4
SORT (subroutine), 153–4
sorting, 149–54
sports, 10, 31–2
stack storage, 230
standard deviation, 126
stepwise refinement, 55–6
subprogram, 50
symbol-state tables, 83–8, 97
symbol tables, 68
syntax; diagrams, 90–5; of commands, 76, 90–101
system flowcharts, 41–3
systems analysis, 40

tabular function, 155
terminator: for data item, 80
text: storage and retrieval, 107–16
text-number, 98–9, 107–16
time: advance methods, 162–3; control 162–70; real, 162
time series, 189–93
top–down design, 36–9
tournament sort, 152–4
trade off, 187
tree: for game, 226–31; search, 229–37
trend: 188; function, 190

umpire; computer as, 20
uniformly distributed random variable, 120
univariate search, 244–5

variable types, 51–2
variance, 124–5
vector of probabilities, 131, 208
visibility, 177

war games, 21, 171–86
while loop, 47
whole circle bearing, 140
windows: in alpha–beta algorithm, 236–40